P9-DIW-426

How the Other Half Works

How the Other Half Works

Immigration and the Social Organization of Labor

Roger Waldinger
and
Michael I. Lichter

UNIVERSITY OF CALIFORNIA PRESS
Berkeley · Los Angeles · London

University of California Press
Berkeley and Los Angeles, California

University of California Press, Ltd.
London, England

© 2003 by
The Regents of the University of California

Library of Congress Cataloging-in-Publication Data

Waldinger, Roger David.
  How the other half works: immigration and the social
organization of labor/Roger David Waldinger, Michael
Ira Lichter.
       p. cm.
  Includes bibliographical references and index.
  ISBN 0-520-22980-0 (Cloth : alk. paper)—ISBN
0-520-23162-7 (Paper: alk. paper)
  1. Alien labor—California—Los Angeles County.
2. Unskilled labor—California—Los Angeles County.
3. Immigrants—Social networks—California—Los Angeles County. 4. Employer attitude surveys—California—Los Angeles County. 7. I. Lichter, Michael Ira,
1960– II. Title.
  HD8083.C2 W35 2003
  331.6'2'097949409049—dc21
2002007571

Manufactured in the United States of America

10 09 08 07 06 05 04
10 9 8 7 6 5 4 3 2

The paper used in this publication meets the minimum
requirements of ANSI/NISO Z39.48-1992 (R 1997)
(*Permanence of Paper*). ♾

For Joey—R. W.
For my grandparents—M. L.

Contents

Illustrations

FIGURE

Acknowledgments

Those of us who have pursued a career in academia presumably chose to do so in search of the contemplative life. But the sad reality is that most of us have succumbed to the over-programmed cycle of excess production and activity that seems to characterize much of American life. Thus, we begin with a confession: that other commitments got in the way of completion of this book, which is why it took much longer to finish than we anticipated. But this is also reason for us to commence with heartfelt thanks to those who helped start the project and kindly waited until it was done.

Responsibility for the project's inception truly belongs to the distinguished geographer Allen Scott, in his former incarnation as Director of the Lewis Center for Regional Policy Studies at the University of California, Los Angeles (UCLA). Thinking that immigration would be a fruitful point of focus for the Lewis Center, Allen enlisted Roger Waldinger to write a grant proposal that Allen then submitted to the John Randolph Haynes and Dora Haynes foundation. Fortunately, the Haynes foundation, long an important source of support for research on Los Angeles, saw merit in the proposal. We are deeply grateful to the foundation and especially to Diane Cornwell, its executive director, for support of this project and for so patiently awaiting its completion. Many thanks also to Allen, without whom we would never have begun; his assistance and support has meant a great deal to Roger Waldinger throughout his career at UCLA.

Even the most generously supported project usually requires some additional financial help, and this one is no exception. Small grants from the UCLA Academic Senate, the UCLA Institute of Industrial Relations, and the UC-MEXUS program made all the difference to us, and we are glad to have this opportunity to express our appreciation.

Roger Waldinger enjoyed the luxury of a sabbatical during 1998–99, during which he devoted much attention to this book. He is deeply grateful to his home institution, UCLA—and indirectly, the taxpayers of California—for such generous support.

For most of its existence, this project was housed at the Lewis Center, a unit within UCLA's School of Public Policy and Social Research. Vanessa Dingley, then the center's assistant director, oversaw the complicated logistics with the good-humored efficiency for which she is widely and justly admired. It was a pleasure working with her and we are delighted to thank her publicly for all her help.

Collecting and processing the data on which this book is based involved a small army of helpers, and we are grateful to everyone who assisted us. Special thanks go to the past and present graduate students who helped develop the study's questionnaire and did many of the interviews: Daniel Malpica, Richard Massaro, Julie Press, Elizabeth Roach, and Margaret Zamudio. An additional word of gratitude for Johanna Shih, who contributed interpretations of several parts of the data. A number of gifted UCLA undergraduates, including Deborah Ho, Divya Gupta, and Folosade Windokun helped manage and code the interview data, working under the direction of Elizabeth Roach and Marian Katz; we are grateful to them as well. Judy Iriye, a Los Angeles native then completing her B.A. at Harvard University, spent a summer on the project, in search of exposure to the research process. That she ended up going to law school says something about what she found, but we certainly enjoyed her presence and are happy to acknowledge her help. Roger Waldinger is also delighted to have yet another chance to thank Deborah Ho, then a UCLA undergraduate, for research assistance of the most extraordinary kind.

Given the book's extended gestation, portions made their way to numerous readers, though some of the earlier incarnations we sent around are only vaguely perceptible here. The names of those who read and commented on our papers show how fortunate we are to belong to the intellectual community interested in the questions posed by this book. A special word of gratitude to Mehdi Bozorgmehr, Rogers Brubaker, Claudia Der-Martirosian, Katherine Edin, Herbert Gans, Robert Gottlieb,

Jacqueline Hagan, Nelson Lim, Douglas Massey, Ruth Milkman, Daniel J. B. Mitchell, Ruben Rumbaut, Julie Silverstein, and John Skrentny. Earlier versions of some chapters were presented to colleagues at Middlebury College, University of Pennsylvania, University of Chicago, University of Wisconsin, Harvard University, and Yale University, as well as to gatherings on the University of California—Berkeley and UCLA campuses. We learned much from those encounters and wish to thank everyone who took our ideas seriously and tried to help. Roger Waldinger also thanks his colleagues in UCLA's Department of Sociology for providing a uniquely supportive and stimulating intellectual environment, without which this book could not have been written.

We consider it a piece of signal good luck to have engaged the interest of our editor, Naomi Schneider. A wonderful reader, whose sharp eye caught problems we had hoped to keep hidden, Naomi, by her enthusiasm for this project, ensured that it saw the light of day. She also found us two wonderful reviewers in Steve Gold and Mary Waters. We tried hard to respond to their probing criticisms; while probably not successful, we ask their continuing indulgence and thank them for their great help. Thanks, also, to Suzanne Knott, the project editor at the University of California Press, who made sure that this manuscript actually got into print, and to the copyeditor, Paula Friedman, for her meticulous efforts to improve our prose.

This book draws on lengthy interviews conducted with over two hundred business owners and managers; their cooperation and interest was essential. We suspect that our interviewees may not like the interpretations we offer of what they told us, but we can assure them that we have made every effort to be faithful to the record. We remain deeply grateful for the time and information they provided us.

Last but not least, we want to mention those whose support mattered the most—our families and close friends.

Roger Waldinger notes that a preoccupation like this does get in the way of family life. As usual, the members of Roger's family reminded him of other matters of importance in the world; as usual, they were right. Good times were had in writing this book; the best times were spent with Hilary, Max, Mimi, and Joey. Special thanks are due to Silvia Reyes, without whose help the Waldinger household would have come to a halt. After the penultimate draft had been written, Roger's mother, Renée, turned her critical eye to the manuscript, preventing many a gaffe. Of course, thanking her for this help is only the beginning.

For Michael Lichter, this project stretched over a period in which he lost three grandparents: Lillian Harrison, Esther Ungerleider, and Irving Ungerleider. He is grateful for the love and inspiration they gave to him and others during their lives. He is also grateful to Roger for his (mostly) patient mentoring, for the assistance he has provided over the years, and for the suggestion that Michael participate in this project and work with him on this book. Finally, Michael owes a debt of more than gratitude to his friends and colleagues who have been associated with the UCLA Center for the Study of Urban Poverty and made it such a vibrant intellectual environment, especially Elizabeth Gonzalez, David Grant, Melvin Oliver, Julie Press, and Abel Valenzuela.

PART ONE

How the Other Half Works

CHAPTER I

Introduction

Across the threshold of the twenty-first century, America again finds itself transformed by immigration. Stretching back nearly four decades, the immigrant tide has yielded newcomers in unprecedented numbers. Evidence of a changed nation shows up wherever one goes. Venture deep into the heartland, and one runs into foreign accents; dig a little deeper, and one encounters the networks that link the immigrants and the institutions that sustain them.

But the most impressive signs appear in the country's chief urban concentrations. Travel to New York or Los Angeles or Miami or San Francisco, and the sounds are those of the tower of Babel, the faces those of a cross-section of humanity. In these capitals of immigrant America, we seem to have returned to the turn of the past century. Amid the dawn of a technologically different (we hesitate to say *new*) age, the numbers tell us that immigrant America has returned.

But have we just come full circle? Native Americans included, we all arrived from somewhere else. True, not all came in eager search of a better life—those transported to the new world as slave ship cargo, for example, were anything but hopeful fortune-seekers. Nevertheless, a nation of immigrants is how we think of ourselves; after all, our country bears the peculiarly abstract name of the United States of America; it is a place that no one claims as a motherland or fatherland.[1] As unsettled as the newcomers' advent often makes us, we realize that there is something here of which to be proud: immigration is proof of the power of the American dream.

Although the new immigrants quickly find out that the streets are not paved with gold, this too is part of our shared historical experience. Conditions may be tough in the cities of immigrant America, but the opportunities have to be better than the prospects "back home." Ours is a world of instantaneous global telecommunication, where "my hometown" is only a click of the internet-connected mouse or, at worst, a telephone call away; if opportunities in the United States did not beckon, why would the immigrants come? Why would they stay?

There is something deeply familiar about America's re-emergence as an immigrant magnet. There is also something bewildering. Last time around, there seemed a fit between the evolving economy and the types of immigrants we received. The American economy on the brink of the twentieth century was growing at a rapid clip. In a tight labor market, employers wanted no more than brawn and a willingness to work hard—just what the newcomers provided. Arriving with no capital, few useful skills, and—the Jews excepted—limited literacy, the southern and eastern European predecessors of the 1880–1920 period moved easily into the new urban economy's bottom rungs: servants, laborers, longshoremen, *schleppers* all. Gradually, their descendants moved toward the top, making the best of the old factory-based economy, which allowed for a multigenerational climb up the totem pole. Immigrant children did well just by hanging on through the high school years, with well-paid manufacturing jobs awaiting them upon graduation. The third generation continued through college and beyond, completing the move from peddler to plumber to professor (the dirty secret being that the wages of brainwork did not always exceed the earnings enjoyed by workers in the skilled crafts).

In some ways, contemporary immigration has turned the process around.[2] The hidden story of today's immigration involves the many newcomers who arrive here with considerable advantages and quickly accumulate more. Well-educated, entrepreneurial, entering the professions in growing numbers, these newcomers fit right into the new economy, eschewing the bottom and entering at or near the top.

The story of highly educated immigrants who bring the skills required by the New World Order is, however, but half the tale. Contemporary immigration to the United States has a split personality, its legions of scantily schooled laborers and service workers uncannily recalling the immigrant proletarians of yore. But now, unlike then, the least-skilled workers are overwhelmingly foreign-born, with the schooling gap separating them from natives extraordinarily large.[3]

Somehow, America is making room for large numbers of immigrants who are not simply recently arrived, unfamiliar with American ways, and unable to make do in English but also lacking the rudiments of formal schooling that nearly all U.S.-born adults, regardless of ethnic background, take for granted. Our postindustrial, high-tech economy would seem to have no place for "foreigners" with little more sophistication than their European predecessors of a century ago. Yet these immigrants appear to enjoy other traits that employers sorely want. The predictions of economic experts notwithstanding, the newcomers are working, often holding jobs at enviable rates. And although the hard-working immigrant fits the iconography of American life, the public is more than a little ambivalent, concerned that new immigrants are taking jobs that would otherwise be held by less-skilled domestic workers with few other resorts.

WHAT ARE THEY DOING HERE?

Immigration scholars have no problem in plausibly explaining why less-skilled immigrants might *want* to come. Economic incentives provide the pull. For most immigrants, wages at the very bottom of the U.S. labor market tower over the alternatives available back home. True, one needs to take into account the cost of migration, a considerable factor for migrants traveling long distances. Those who attempt to enter surreptitiously, whether by land, sea, or air, pay an additional freight, first in the fees handed over to smugglers and *coyotes,* second in the potential costs of apprehension and return. There also is no guarantee that newly arrived immigrants will find a job. After all, theirs tend to be labor markets in which joblessness, if only of the frictional sort, is usually high. Many others, moreover, have come upon the same idea of bettering their lives by heading for the United States, which means that arrival puts one at the end of a long queue of newcomers vying for the same jobs. For the individual migrant, therefore, competition with other newcomers adds an additional item to the cost of moving to the Promised Land. Still, the balance sheet is likely to favor coming; those who forecast that the benefits of migration will outweigh the associated costs have good grounds for wagering on life in this particular piece of the New World.

This narrative of migration—related mainly, but not exclusively, by economists—illuminates the considerations that motivate potential immigrants.[4] But one could also say that it simply elaborates on common sense: it stands to reason that people are not going to migrate unless they have good reason. If one is looking for an understanding of why migrations begin or intensify, the conventional narrative does not provide a convincing explanation. Unless the comparative advantage of moving to the United States, taking account of the associated costs, increases, migration rates would, one might expect, remain where they were—as opposed to the dramatic uptick experienced by the United States in the three past decades.

Consider Mexican migration to California, the best case in point. Although Mexicans might have done well in crossing the border at almost any time over the past century, their migration to the United States has ebbed and flowed. The most recent inflection point (upward) dates to the mid-1960s. Between the 1860s and the 1960s, most who moved to California—and who presumably undertook the type of crude cost/benefit analysis imagined by the economists—came from elsewhere in the United States. Something changed in the 1960s, however, that in turn loosened the flow to *el Norte,* in a stream that has since expanded at an ever-increasing pace. What confounds the economists' story is that the California/Mexico wage gap was a yawning divide before as well as after the sudden increase in migration from Mexico. The underlying impetus to the migration inevitably lies somewhere else.

If migrants move in response to perceived opportunity, one has to wonder about the relationship between this perception and the reality to be encountered, given the economies of the destinations on which today's less-educated arrivals converge. As in the past, newcomers today are flocking to cities, heading for the very largest—Los Angeles, New York, San Francisco, Chicago—where their compatriots have already put down roots. There is nothing surprising about this predilection; it is simply that our understanding of the evolution of urban America suggests that the metropolitan economies should have little place for the low-skilled. In an era when the marketability of America's less-educated urbanites has plummeted, how can immigrants find even minimal success?

After all, America spent the last half of the twentieth century struggling with an "urban problem" derived from the barriers faced by ghetto-dwelling African Americans striving to get ahead. While academics, journalists, and politicians produced a plethora of explanations for the sluggishness of black progress, the most influential emphasized the mismatch between the requirements of urban employers and the skills of black ghetto residents, providing an account that took the following form:[5] African Americans entered the American metropolis as the least skilled of all workers, and apathetic reception in urban schools kept their offspring at the low end of the education spectrum. Consequently, they found themselves vulnerable as a steady accretion in skill requirements increasingly put less-schooled workers at risk, no matter where they lived. Moreover, the drift of jobs from the cities toward the urban fringe proved an additional disaster: disproportionately concentrated in cities, African Americans experienced the deindustrialization of urban America with particular severity. Suffering from residential segregation, they rarely had the option of following less-skilled jobs to the suburban and, later, exurban hinterlands. While America's major urban places generally recovered from the loss of their industrial base, over the past two decades, new sources of urban economic growth provided few viable alternatives for less-skilled men and women struggling to support families. And thus episodes of urban prosperity in the 1960s, 1980s, and late 1990s did little to help African-American fortunes.

This story enjoys the ring of plausibility, mainly because it links the fate of black city dwellers to the extraordinary and visible economic changes in American cities. The conventional wisdom, however, focusing on skill deficiencies of blacks, fails to give adequate weight to the considerable educational upgrading that African Americans have undergone since the bad old days—when they were employed at much higher rates; if the problem hinges on a diminishing demand for less-skilled workers, then the distance that African Americans have traversed over the past several decades should have greatly reduced their vulnerability. Persons with a high school degree or less may still be in trouble, but as of the late 1990s, this comprises a declining proportion of the black population, reflecting substantial improvement over earlier decades.

But the accounts emphasizing the mismatch between urban populations and economic boom have even more trouble explaining the immigrant tide that has transformed metropolitan America in recent decades. The limited education of the immigrants with whom we are concerned ought to put them at the bottom of employers' lists, but it does not. Unskilled immigrants, far less schooled than the least-schooled American blacks, have found jobs that, if the received wisdom of the last forty years is correct, should not exist. And the newcomers have not just discovered a handful of overlooked jobs, they have secured niches that allow them to work at remarkably high rates even during recessionary times. There is good reason to wonder at the paradox of high employment among less-educated immigrants when the American metropolis has long been said to suffer a shortage of jobs suited to the unskilled.

True, no one argued that the urban economy had dispensed with dish-washers and floor sweepers, but the new immigrant phenomenon is of a far greater magnitude. The massive infusion of less-skilled immigrants into urban America is convincing evidence that they have found a role well beyond such a small cluster of indelibly manual jobs.[6]

SEGMENTATION AND LABOR MARKET STRUCTURE

The answer lies in the social processes that structure America's economy, encouraging new groups to enter the U.S. labor market, there to consolidate their own space. Immigrants to the U.S. make their way to a labor market far from uniform in structure, consisting, instead, of several segments, where jobs of a particular type are linked with categorically distinctive workers.[7] The role played by gender in structuring access to jobs and occupations provides the best illustration. In spite of the massive entry of women into jobs from which they had previously been excluded, men and women continue to experience high levels of occupational segregation. The barriers that make it difficult for women to move into male-dominated occupations—and unlikely, if not quite so difficult, for men to move into fields dominated by women—tell us that when employers are looking for the most "appropriate" worker, suitability is largely determined *categorically*, heavily influenced by the sex of the person who *typically* fills the job. Much the same holds for ethnicity.

To each category of person, that is, a type of job. In our market economy, employers allocate jobs to the "best" workers, but "best" is not only defined in terms of the qualities—aptitude, skill, experience, productivity—that directly impinge on ability to get the job done. Any national or local economy bears the imprint of the social structure in which it is embedded. In a racialized society like the United States, entire ethnic groups are ranked according to sets of socially meaningful but arbitrary traits; these rankings determine fitness for broad categories of jobs. All other qualifications equal, members of the top-ranked group are picked first when employers decide whom to hire; the rest follow in order of rank. We refer to this ordering of job candidates by ethnic or racial groups as a *hiring queue*.[8]

The ordering of an employer's hiring queue is always subject to change. Growth pulls the topmost group up the totem pole, leaving vacancies that lower-ranking groups may seize, thus producing openings at the bottom, which employers can fill by recruiting workers from outside the economy—migrants. For awhile—the period often coincides with the working life of the migrants' generation—the newcomers work in the jobs for which they were recruited; however, their children are almost always oriented toward better prospects, thus creating new demand for migrants.[9]

Not only do workers get ranked. Jobs also stand in a hierarchy, with the characteristics that workers value (pay, stability, benefits, and autonomy) typically going together. So there are "good jobs" and "bad jobs," and the size of the potential pool of candidates varies with the quality of a given position. At the top of the labor market, there is often an ample labor supply; even if employers experience spot shortages, the job-seeker correctly perceives that the number of good jobs is almost never sufficient.

At the bottom of the labor market, by contrast, the labor supply is inherently unstable. "Bad jobs" are a defining trait of our unequal (indeed, increasingly unequal) capitalist society. Insiders—members of the society by birth or socialization—have plenty of reasons to look for alternatives to jobs of the least desirable sort, starting with the fact that working at the bottom of the pecking order is inherently stigmatizing. But natives do not respond solely to a job's low standing, or to the inherently unpleasant, sometimes demeaning conditions associated with its performance. They also note that jobs at the bottom repeatedly attract stigmatized outsider groups, whose disrepute becomes an aspect of the work. So when economic expansion makes mobility possible, the established native workforce opts for the alternative—in quest of better coin, but also of greater esteem.

Replacements might be found at home, but the force of competition, often from countries where wages are lower, deters employers from the changes—higher wages, improved working conditions—needed to attract those natives not yet involved in paid labor. Hence, openings arise to be filled by workers from abroad. The stigmatized status of bottom-level work impinges differently on the immigrants, who operate with a dual frame of reference, judging conditions "here" by the standards "back home." As long as the comparison remains relevant, low-status—indeed, disreputable—work in an advanced capitalist society like the United States does not rate too badly.

These preferences, however, only tell us why immigrants might accept work that natives disdain, not why the newcomers can fill today's "bad jobs" with success. Recall that many immigrants arrive with scant levels of formal schooling, and that most portraits of the economy suggest that its skill demands are becoming increasingly severe. Yet immigrants somehow fit in.

One influential explanation emphasizes those forces in the broader economy that produce changes at *both ends* of the job structure. The economy requires an increasing complement of workers with higher levels of skill, but the "up-skilling" has been uneven, uncertain, and not as far-reaching as often thought. In fact, change works both ways: capitalism's destructive impulse *downgrades* many previously moderate-skilled jobs, even as technological innovations drive the proliferation of high-skilled positions. A case in point is the "dumbing-down" of cashier work by using "smart" cash registers, the demand for which simultaneously generates employment for a class of computer-savvy information technology workers.[10] Thus, the growth in the number of low-skilled jobs inevitably yields expansion in the number of high-skilled positions, producing a dynamic of skills polarization.[11]

The available data do not demonstrate that jobs in the middle of the skill spectrum have been rendered obsolete, as expected by those who focus on the *polarization* of skills, but instead show that there remain many jobs requiring relatively low levels of formal education or training. For our purposes, however, it is as important to ask whether low levels of schooling equate to low levels of skill. While there may well be some jobs for which the label of "unskilled" means what it says,[12] this number is small. In the real world of work, contingency, uncertainty, and unpredictability cannot be fully eliminated; moreover, getting things done in *any* line of work requires know-how of more than trivial degree. Workers usually cannot get this practical knowledge in school, but pick it up on the spot, through interaction with co-workers knowledgeable through hands-on experience.[13]

Put somewhat differently, work is a fundamentally social phenomenon; one both acquires the necessary skills and gets things done by working successfully with others. While one need not be exactly like one's co-workers, it usually helps—especially in a work world where jobs are scarce and where jealousies at the workplace may be fed by competition in the neighborhood or conflict on the street. Even if the established workforce will accept outsiders, one cannot learn if one cannot communicate: persons unable to participate in the linguistic community of the workplace may find it hard to get started. Therefore, who you are has much to do with what you do; social ties become the crucial factors lubricating movement through the labor market and across the threshold of the employer's door. Thus, at the bottom of the labor market, formal education counts much less than the ability to acquire job-specific skills through cooperation with specific others—which explains why newcomers with so little schooling have seen their economic role burgeon in recent years.

NETWORKS AND MIGRATION

We used to think about migrants as "the uprooted," to quote Oscar Handlin's famous immigration history of five decades ago; we might just as well describe them as "the transplanted," to cite a less celebrated but no less influential history produced twenty-five years later.[14] The shifting metaphors of our scholarly discourse convey the essence of the new approach; we now understand that migrants move not as solo adventurers but as actors linked to associates here and there, their social ties lubricating and structuring their transition from one society to the next.

These ties form *social networks*. Social networks provide the mechanism for connecting an initial, highly selective group of seedbed immigrants with a gradually growing base of followers from back home. The linkages work effectively because they involve social relationships that developed organically, having grown up before anyone left town. The key ties are those that connect kith and kin—who can act with the confidence that one will reliably and regularly help the other. Consequently, migrant networks provide durable, efficient conduits for the flow of resources needed to give newcomers the information and social support for moving to a new home and getting started.

Over time, migration networks evolve in such a way as to produce qualitative changes on both ends, making further migration easier. In the *host society*, veteran immigrants, as they consolidate their place, find it easier and less costly to help out, which widens the pool of hometown candidates to whom they can lend a hand. In the *home society*, a growing proportion of the community finds itself linked to expatriates in a position to provide assistance. In turn, these changes lower the costs and risks of movement, increasing migration's net expected returns. Very quickly, these processes of network consolidation and expansion make migration a self-feeding phenomenon, with ties to settlers diffusing so broadly that almost everyone in the home community enjoys access to a contact abroad.[15]

Network theory, our label for the account summarized above, has proven deeply influential for reasons not difficult to understand. It shows how the actions of individual migrants are rooted in social structure; it overturns the older "individualistic" view of migration, which cast the migrant as a solitary cost/benefit calculator. It also helps to explain how migrants, once established, get ahead. The connections that span immigrant communities constitute a source of *social capital*, providing social structures that facilitate action—in this case, the search for jobs and the drive to acquire skills and other resources to move up the economic ladder.[16] Networks tying veterans to newcomers allow for rapid transmission of information about workplace openings or opportunities for new business start-ups. The networks send information the other way, as well, telling bosses about applicants, thus reducing the risks associated with hiring.[17] Once in place, the networks reproduce themselves: once arrived, incumbents recruit friends or relatives, while entrepreneurs gravitate to the cluster of business opportunities already identified by their associates in the community. Moreover, relationships among co-ethnics are likely to be many-sided rather than specialized, leading community effects to go beyond informational value and engendering both codes of conduct and the mechanisms for sanctioning those who violate norms.[18] As this description makes clear, sociological attempts to theorize the economic sociology of immigration—whether under the label of *ethnic economy, ethnic enclave, ethnic niche*, or of the latest neologism of the day—involve applications of the basic social-network approach.[19]

So far so good—but network theory suffers from a built-in contradiction. It does a nice job of explaining why tomorrow's workforce looks a good deal like today's; it does not tell us how today's labor force configuration came to be. The relationship between today and tomorrow is not difficult to understand: the established immigrant workers learn about job openings before anyone else, and, once in the know, tell their friends and relatives the good news. They also reassure the boss that their referrals are the right candidates to fill the vacancies, a pledge that sounds all the more meaningful when the boss thinks that birds of a feather flock together, and likes the birds he currently has.

But not every new day is like the preceding day; at some point, today's immigrant veterans were outsiders, knocking on doors, with few if any contacts inside. How did the tables turn? To some extent, we have already provided the answer. On the one hand, conditions at the very bottom of the labor market keep workers engaged in extensive churning; a high turnover rate produces constant vacancies. On the other hand, immigrants line up for entry-level jobs at a more rapid rate than anyone else, precisely since, as mentioned above, the conditions and stigma associated with the economy's "bad jobs" motivates natives to seek other options. So, even if once excluded from bottom-level portals, immigrants quickly, through succession, build up concentrations at the economy's lowest points of entry. In the process, the number of immigrants with the ability to help a friend or family member obtain and keep a job quickly increases. Given bosses' usual preference for recruiting from inside, the immigrant presence automatically grows.

This type of explanation tells us why there are many immigrant sweepers and kitchen helpers. If these were the only possibilities, opportunities would be very limited and low-skill migration streams, a good deal smaller than they are. Network theory, however, contends that migration quickly becomes a self-feeding process; once the first crop of migrants take hold, the theory predicts that the networks will normally continue to grow.[20] For this to happen, some immigrant job-holders must come to possess more than inside dope about the next dishwasher or janitorial opening; they need to be in the position to grant access to better and more varied jobs to their needy friends and kin. In other words, they have to either rise to positions of authority or compel the authorities to comply with their wishes. But how do stigmatized outsiders manage to gain such leverage?

The answer lies in the power that immigrant social networks acquire, once imported into the workplace. As noted above, informal ties help because they meet the ends of workers and managers alike; social, rather than market processes, yield the most efficient result.[21] But matters can change, if and when the balance of power between workers and employer shifts. After all, veterans enjoy the benefits of insider knowledge, often having a better clue than bosses as to the likely comings and goings of their colleagues on the shop or selling floor. While they can filter that knowledge in ways that suit management's objectives, they also feel impelled to respond to the needs of their kin and associates chasing after jobs always in too short supply. From the workers' standpoint, therefore, nepotism is rarely too much of a good thing; not so for management, which discovers that bossing a department filled with cousins, friends, and neighbors involves no small constraint. In taking care of their own, moreover, veterans *implicitly* exclude those ethnic others who do not possess the right connection. Sometimes the numerically dominant group *explicitly* seeks to secure its place at the expense of anyone different—no surprise given the brutal competition among workers with the fewest options, and the related tensions played out on street corners and in workplaces. Of course, networks rarely place hiring mechanisms under watertight controls; outsiders almost always leak in. Still, the need to accomplish tasks through cooperation puts numerical minorities at a disadvantage—forcing management to attend to the preferences of those groups it counts on to get the work done. In the end, the ties that bind the workforce comprise a resource that group members can use to maintain and expand their share of employment, even *against* management's wishes.

Of course, the properties described above aren't unique to *immigrant* networks. The old-boy network of private boarding schools and country clubs need take lessons from no one when it comes to using connections to exclude. Craft unions in the construction trades know how to use informal ties among their (skilled) workers to play the same game, stomping on the employer's ability to run the firm as he or she would like. African Americans have also successfully implanted networks in particular sectors of the economy, especially government, and these have expanded in much the way described above.[22]

BUREAUCRACY AND BOSSES

As any student of sociology will recall, the development of bureaucracy involves the increasing separation of *person* from *position:* bureaucratization makes the job the property of the organization, taking it out of the hands of the individual who occupies it while also removing it from the grasp of his or her clique. The contemporary appreciation of the networked nature of organizational life leads today's student to respond by saying that practice and theory diverge. Nonetheless, the persistence and the continued usefulness of familial and ethnic ties within modern organizations signal only that universalism has yet to fully supplant particularism, *not* that particularism is again triumphant. The two tendencies co-exist in tension, defining alternative organizational strategies, each with its own costs and benefits.

Consequently, the everyday social structures of the low-wage labor market can provide fertile ground for ethnic networks to take root and grow, without yielding a situation in which network hiring is all-pervasive. For the reasons noted above, employers are sensitive to the perils of filling slots with the friends and relatives of incumbent workers. Extensive social ties among workers may be desirable, but only to the right degree. At bottom, *employers want workers whose first loyalty is to the organization, not to each other.*

Not in the business of building labor solidarity, employers have other reasons to ensure that the "birds of a feather" principle only gets applied when the occasion merits. Organizations have to be mindful of the face they present, since in some cases, having too many "of one kind" creates the wrong appearance. The problem does not arise when the work is demeaning and the consumers come from the dominant group; Anglo hotel guests in Los Angeles would have no objections to a housekeeping force that is foreign-born. But diversity does matter when the clientele takes a multi-ethnic form and both provider and recipient see the interaction as a source of respect. Under these conditions, evidence of exclusion leaves customers rankled; they certainly don't like to see people of their own kind left out, and often they prefer to encounter service providers who look or sound like themselves. Reputational considerations can work toward the same end, especially today, when organizations concerned about public image want to avoid the appearance of bias.

But trouble may loom whenever network hiring produces a mono-ethnic workforce, since homogeneity of this sort can both threaten the organization's legitimacy and leave it exposed to legal sanctions. Consequently, considerations of customer satisfaction or public legitimacy may put adequate, if not equal, representation of specific groups high on the personnel agenda. When confronted with these circumstances, organizations are likely to control the hiring process in ways that meet their goals; the key tool involves the time-tested method of formalization, applied to the recruitment of labor, the screening of candidates, and the final selection. Using bureaucracy in these ways limits the ability of a group *as such*, immigrant or otherwise, to colonize the workplace with its networks. It also introduces a set of screening and selection criteria applied, in theory, to all comers. To the extent that universalism implies fairness, this is good news for those excluded from the most powerful ethnic networks—an unfortunate crowd that, in the largest U.S. urban areas, includes most African Americans.

WHOM DO EMPLOYERS WANT?

In this context, we should take careful note of the skills and qualities that employers seek. Scholarly research tells us that literacy, numeracy, and familiarity with computers comprise the competencies that today's workers must possess. While cognitive skills, at some baseline level, are surely needed to do most jobs, this hardly exhausts the list. Simply put, bosses want *willing* subordinates. After all, employers are looking for workers who will do the job as told, with the minimum amount of "lip." In the postindustrial service economy, the quality of the service interaction matters more and more, so it is no surprise that employers are also searching for workers with a "friendly" feel, or approach.[23] But employers want not simply "friendly"—which to a large extent means the ability to keep a smile regardless of how unpleasant the customers or working conditions. They also prefer "cooperative" to "combative," and deferential over rebellious—in other words, a worker who knows her or his place.

But how to select those with the "right attitude" and reject those likely to cause trouble? Sifting and straining is one answer, but no test or check ever provides enough information to dispense with person-to-person assessment. And few organizations can devote the resources needed to examine with such care, especially when the jobs in question are not of great importance. Consequently, final decisions rarely involve a faceless bureaucrat choosing according to a set of inflexible criteria set in advance. Instead, particular people hire idiosyncratically, in ways that correspond to the specifics of their situation. In other words, the influence of stereotypes and prejudiced views can always creep through the organizational back door—big or small business notwithstanding.

Thus, stereotypes and prejudices are likely to matter, perhaps at the beginning of the hiring process in the small family-run firm, perhaps at the end of the day in the large, professionally managed organization. Job-related proficiencies also count, but the issue at hand involves the *personal* attributes that employers prefer.

We could turn to the abundant literature on prejudice and discrimination, much of it insightful, but most of it missing a crucial point.[24] The literature's central question—whom do I want as my neighbor, friend, colleague, or spouse?—betrays its understandable, indeed laudatory, concern with the conditions of equality. But this literature assumes that motivations in the personal realm operate in like fashion in public settings, a presumption that takes too much for granted. While one is the same person at home and at work, one's role certainly differs—the more so when the position at work yields authority over the activities of others. It may be that employers prefer to hire the very same type of people with whom they party and play, staying away from those whose company they would never entertain. But maybe not, since *personal* preferences—for *and* against—are not directly relevant to the relationship between the bosses and the bossed.

The employer is not looking for friends, just hired hands. All the more so, at the bottom of the labor market, where the work is typically disreputable and the social distance between the boss and the bossed is considerable, regardless of whether the two share an ethnic origin. On the look-out for persons ready to accept commands, the practical manager has little interest in workers whose social eligibility for friendship makes their subaltern status difficult. Considerations of social esteem also rule out closeness with the type of person willing to do jobs that otherwise qualify one for contempt. Put somewhat differently, the qualities that make for good underlings may well preclude the potential for relationships of a more intimate sort—and all for the better, since who wants intimacy with those assigned to tasks that one disdains? Thus it may be possible, perhaps even likely, that employers will *prefer* workers towards whom they feel a personal distaste.[25]

Any such preference will carry more weight if employers perceive what we earlier suggested, that immigrants comprise a class of worker that evaluates conditions "here" in light of how bad they are "there." Viewing the labor market through this lens, employers may choose immigrants over Euro- and African-American competitors whose sights have been set on rewards higher than those available at the bottom of the totem pole. If so, the choice takes a form for which the scholarly literature has not left us prepared: employers value immigrants precisely because they are not like "us." In this light, African Americans can be seen to be at a double disadvantage in the labor market, sharing the liabilities of the native-born American worker—that is, a sense of entitlement greater than the employer thinks appropriate—but few of the advantages that accrue to native whites. Thus, when the employer selects from a mix of candidates, African Americans may stand at the end of the queue.

It is not to exculpate the boss to note that other actors, as well as considerations beyond his or her personal preferences, normally come into play. To some extent, as already suggested, the employer may have little leeway. Personal preferences are unlikely to make much difference if a group, through its networks, has seized control of the hiring process; nor will these preferences matter much if some formal procedure provides the essential decision criterion or if no alternatives can be found to the person who shows up on the spot. Further, the wishes of customers—whose preferences for interacting with workers of the same background may be a force toward diversity or homogeneity—cannot be ignored. Therefore, discriminatory outcomes do not *necessarily* stem from employers' preferences, although management remains responsible for its decisions. And we note that the boss does not always have the last word, as actors both inside and external to the workplace may have their own points of view, which they advance whenever they have a chance.

ON THE BACKS OF BLACKS?

Scholars and policymakers worry that poorly educated native-born Americans stand vulnerable to competition with less-educated immigrants. If so, then less-skilled African Americans, already overrepresented in the labor market's lower ranks, are likely to comprise the most vulnerable group. History certainly provides reasons for anxiety. In the mid-nineteenth century, native-born Protestants had little fondness for the members of the Irish Catholic "race," whom they regularly characterized as "savage," "simian," "low-browed," and "bestial." But it did not take long for the Irish immigrants to realize that accepting the then-regnant racism toward African Americans would prove a convenient tool for moving up the totem pole and enhancing their ethnic esteem—though it took longer for the Irish to gain full membership in the "white" club.

The same holds true for the southern and eastern European immigrants who arrived at the turn of the twentieth century and were seen as, at best, "not quite white" in the eyes of their WASP predecessors. They were gradually let into the fold after establishing their legitimacy, in part by adopting the racist practices perfected by their "betters," namely, restriction of African Americans from their neighborhoods and from the jobs or unions they dominated.[26]

Can it happen again? While today's immigrants surely bring their own particularized hatreds and dislikes, history does point to the advantages of adopting the Euro-American disdain for African Americans. Moreover, joining the white bandwagon may be even easier now than in the early twentieth century, given the internationalization of the U.S. economy and its greater openness to workers from all parts of the world. In any event, our concern involves a narrower, more tractable question: are immigrants replacing or displacing black workers?

After at least two decades of study, immigration scholars have yet to produce a definitive answer.[27] One would think that the case for competition is compelling. Immigration increases the supply of labor, especially at the labor market's lower rungs. Under these conditions, expanding the pool of labor should make it more difficult for less-educated Americans to find work, and depress wages for those lucky enough to have jobs.

The argument sounds plausible, but convincing evidence has been scarce. Social scientists have looked for differences in unemployment and wage rates among cities and metropolitan areas that vary in the size of their immigrant populations, assuming that adverse effects will be found in those areas where immigrants have concentrated. Although results varied, most experts concluded that competitive effects were small. Immigration seemed to have no effects on the wages or employment of white natives, whether males or females, and very slight, if any, negative effects on the wages and employment of native blacks. Indeed, if anyone seemed to suffer from the immigrant influx, it was earlier immigrants of similar origins.

What accounts for these results? Economists remind us that immigrants can both replace natives *and* work alongside natives in supporting functions. For example, instead of succumbing to foreign competition as has the rest of America's clothing industry, Los Angeles's garment manufacturing has thrived, thanks to a steady flow of newcomers seeking work in the region's sewing shops. Immigrants may have displaced some native-born workers, but the industry's strength may have meant more work for local clothing designers, who are more likely than production workers to be U.S.-born; in this case, the adverse and positive effects of immigration may have canceled each other out. A city experiencing an influx of immigrants may find itself with more buying power than before they arrived (assuming that the immigrant inflow does not produce an even greater outflow of natives, who depart with their significantly greater buying power). Since many of the additional goods and services that immigrants consume are provided by Americans—consider the teachers who instruct immigrant children—immigration can have a further beneficial effect on jobs for the native-born.

Of course, immigration could have a positive or neutral effect on the native population as a whole, yet exercise an adverse impact on some particular native-born segment. In this respect, a crucial consideration is simply that the collective characteristics of African Americans may reduce their exposure to immigrant competition. Compared to the least-skilled immigrants, African Americans possess relatively high levels of education. Moreover, African Americans have moved into employment concentrations where the barriers to immigrant entry are high; the chief African-American niche involves the public sector, and government jobs prove difficult for low-skilled immigrants to obtain.

Measuring the impact of immigrants on natives is an endeavor fraught with dilemmas, including the best way to identify competing skill groups, and the appropriate areal unit in which competition might take place. For instance, it may be that standard research methods cause us to overlook the people most adversely affected by immigration. Until recently, researchers neglected to consider the possibility that internal migration acts as a safety valve, with the victims of immigrant competition seeking out other areas of the country where immigrants are rarer and their impact less evident. Low-income African Americans and others with few resources may not, however, have this option, leaving them tied to the inner city.

The debate over competition cannot be settled within the framework of this book. But we can make progress. At the minimum, we can try to illuminate the mechanisms through which immigrant and native groups contend over the division of labor—an adequate dividend when, as the well-known economist George Borjas will concede, "we still do not fully understand how immigrants affect the employment opportunities of natives in local labor markets."[28] We note that, for there to be widespread competition, both groups of workers would have to be actively looking for the same jobs. We suggest that relatively few African-American workers are even *trying* to compete with immigrants in the latter's industrial and occupational concentrations. At the same time, we find considerable evidence of conflict between immigrants and African Americans, and conflict is prima facie evidence of competition. For the most part, the instances of tension also involve situations in which the foreign-born workers hold the upper hand. Given the exclusionary effects of immigrant networks, the general preference among employers for immigrant workers, and the long-standing aversion of white managers towards African Americans, the latter appear to face some formidable barriers to employment.

One can imagine two scenarios. In the first, today's stigmatized immigrants replace African Americans as the least desired workers, hired only in the last resort. In the second, the newcomers, for whom there seems plenty of dislike, nonetheless push ahead of African Americans, shoving the latter to the very end of the queue.[29] Unfortunately, our material does not allow us to adjudicate between these two, leading us to a more modest, though not trivial, conclusion: the large-scale immigrant arrival is not doing anything good for less-skilled African-American workers. Moreover, the availability of the immigrants facilitates the activation of employers' preferences, which lead them to seek out workers from the group they perceive least likely to give trouble.[30]

STUDYING HOW THE OTHER HALF WORKS

This book documents immigration's transformation of the social organization of work. Our prism is the low-skilled labor market in Los Angeles, a somewhat singular region but still a microcosm of twenty-first-century America. Los Angeles, after all, is not an old, decaying inner city. Instead, it is America's quintessential suburb, the dynamic product of postwar U.S. capitalism. What better place than the City of the Angels and its environs—here defined as the County of Los Angeles—to study how immigrants fit into the new American order?[31]

Of course, our story encompasses more than just the immigrants themselves, who join what was already an ethnic mosaic of extraordinary complexity. Today's newcomers have moved into a region with a long and complicated history of migration. In moving to Southern California, today's immigrants have entered an area where the historic succession of migrant streams from diverse origins produced an elaborate ethnic division of labor, which the newest arrivals have rearranged without diminishing the strength of the boundaries. Moreover, the newcomers are hardly of a piece; differences in national origin, ethnic background, and language are at least as great among foreign-born Angelenos as among their native-born counterparts. Los Angeles's economy is where these groupings get thrown into the mix, an encounter not without feeling, often not of the most favorable kind. Workers jostle one another for a better job, often for any job; these conflicts reinforce a sense of in-group attachment and a complementary dislike for outsiders.[32]

This book is firmly planted in the broad sociological literatures on immigration and ethnicity. We engage the central concepts used by our co-workers in the field to build an argument directed at the main intellectual issues in play. Though informed by contemporary controversies, this is also a book of ideas developed in the effort to understand the material we collected in the field—it is *not* a book driven by the ideas with which we began.

Indeed, this book is very different from the one we imagined when we started. At the time, we undertook a project to see whether low-skilled immigrants were displacing low-skilled African Americans; as already noted, we found some indicators of competition, and plenty of evidence that the encounter between immigrant and African-American workers has not been frictionless. However, as we realized in the course of studying our notes and the transcripts of our interviews, the focus on competition obscured a more interesting development. That story involved the interlocking of ethnicity with the organization of a modern economy, an issue that broadened the scope of investigation and engaged us with issues we had not taken note of before.

From the standpoint of a positivistic social science, working in deductive fashion from a highly abstract set of general principles, ours is

opportunism of the worst kind. Perhaps. But we are happy to align ourselves with those intellectual traditions that validate and value a more in-
ductive approach to social analysis; we offer this book as an example of
grounded theory, our central arguments emerging from the intellectual
encounter with the raw material we collected. We have written the work
in such a way as to retain as much flavor and context as possible, while
also striving to give the reader enough data to take an independent, skeptical view of our arguments.

What We Did

From the outset, we opted for a comparative case study approach, focusing on a theoretically relevant selective portion of the low-wage labor
market. The argument for the comparative case study is straightforward:
it yields far more variation than found in a single case study, and much
greater depth than produced by a representative sample survey. In particular, it allows us to illuminate those institutional features that affect
the outcomes and processes of interest to us, but that would be lost in a
survey sampling the entire economy.

The Six Industries   Consequently, we selected six industries for close examination—printing, furniture manufacturing, hospitals, department
stores, hotels, and restaurants (see Table 1.1). Several criteria influenced
our selection. First, we sought to focus on industries that could reasonably be classified as low-skilled; as of 1990, the median level of education for workers in each of these industries stood at twelve years or less
of schooling. Second, we wanted to compare industries that varied in degree of immigrant penetration; hotels and restaurants, for example,
recorded very high levels of immigrant representation, with a quite different situation in department stores or printing. Finally, we wanted to
include industries that also varied in degree of African-American representation; hospitals, for example, include a disproportionately large
African-American component, whereas African-American workers were
conspicuously underrepresented in hotels.

Restaurants and hotels are prototypical service industries, featuring a
large proportion of menial, poorly compensated jobs. The health care industry also provides services, but hospitals have a much more elaborate
division of labor, employing significant numbers of workers with both
far more and somewhat less education than the average American. Although department stores employ clerical workers and also maintain

TABLE I.I. INDUSTRIES INCLUDED IN
THE STUDY

		African Americans	
		Low	*Moderate/High*
Latino Immigrants	*Low*	Printing	Department Stores, Hospitals
	Moderate/High	Furniture Manufacturing, Restaurants	Hotels

SOURCE: 1990 U.S. Census of Population.
NOTE: For African Americans, "low" indicates that fewer than 5 percent of employees in the industry were African American, according to the 1990 Census. For Latino immigrants, "low" indicates that fewer than 25 percent of employees in the industry were Latino immigrants, according to the 1990 Census.

shipping rooms and warehouse-type facilities, the bulk of the work involves direct contact with customers. Furniture manufacturing and printing represent the "small batch" end of manufacturing industries, requiring more skills than old-style "Fordist" mass production industries but not as much as older craft industries. Additional details on these industries and how their ethnic composition has changed over past decades can be found in the appendix.

The Survey   A team of faculty members and graduate students carried out the field research in 1992, 1993, and 1994. We conducted a series of in-person, in-depth interviews with managers and owners in 228 establishments throughout Los Angeles County (see Table 1.2 for a breakdown by industry).[33] In each instance, we spoke with the highest-ranking person we could meet who was involved in the hiring process. We structured our interviews with a series of closed- and open-ended questions. We began talking with respondents by asking them to identify the largest category of "entry-level" positions; the remainder of our discussion focused on these jobs and the workers who filled them. The interviews averaged roughly ninety minutes, ranging from under thirty minutes to more than three hours.[34]

The open-ended nature of the interview produced both a conversational tone and lengthy, often highly detailed discussions of matters perceived as important by respondents. In turn, the level of detail in the data that we collected allowed for a quasi-ethnographic investigation, in

TABLE I.2. SKILLS STUDY INTERVIEWS

Industry	Interviews Completed	Percent of Total
Department Stores	25	11
Furniture Manufacturers	39	17
Hospitals	36	16
Hotels	40	18
Printers	44	19
Restaurants	44	19
Total	228	100

SOURCE: Skills Study

which the transcripts and lengthy field notes provided clues to patterns that we had not anticipated at the start.

While we were interested in what employers had to *say* about immigrants, African Americans, and other ethnic groups in the workforce, we wanted to be able to evaluate these attitudes contextually, informed by an understanding of what employers *did*. Consequently, we started with relatively anodyne but highly pertinent questions, pertaining to skill requirements, recruitment practices, and selection procedures. Respondents' answers to these questions provided the basis for chapter 3. Our queries about these matters made no mention of immigration or ethnic differences in the workforce. But more often than not, our respondents spontaneously moved the discussion toward our underlying interests, talking about skills in light of the problems entailed in employing a workforce that did not speak English (the focus of chapter 4) or explaining the use of network hiring as a consequence of relying on immigrant workers characterized by tight connections (the substance of chapters 5–7).

Thus, the interviews gradually and almost naturally gravitated toward the potentially controversial questions having to do with perceptions about immigration or views of particular ethnic groups. That these were also practical questions, in the sense that employment strategies were informed by the respondents' understandings of ethnic differences in the labor market, and of their implications, facilitated the progression toward more sensitive topics having to do with ethnicity as such (discussed in chapters 8–9). Even so, we trod gingerly. To probe employers' attitudes and, through discussions of intergroup relations, the attitudes of employees, we began indirectly, asking employers how "managing diversity" was a challenge (the source for chapter 10); we then asked employers to supply accounts of how any particular group came to comprise the majority in their labor force. Finally, we inquired into views of the work ethic of the labor force generally, and only then, to gauge employers' perceptions and beliefs, asked their views of the "work ethic" of particular groups.

Thus, many respondents began telling their views of specific ethnic groups long before we asked; others, like the manager who answered, "I'll leave that to you sociologists," proved more guarded. A number of respondents expressed an "aversion to innate generalizations—generalizations about groups are prejudiced"; others objected to our efforts to elicit generalizations and contended that they could not "think of negative traits among workers employed here"; others sought to avoid an impolitic comment:

> *Employer:* Some of them [immigrants] seem to be more technical. A lot of it has to do with attitude. Some groups are hard to deal with.
> *Interviewer:* Any group in particular?
> *Employer:* I have my own feelings, let's skip that.

Some respondents were also suspicious about the direction in which our questions seemed headed, as with one manager who rebuffed our effort to ask about work ethic, conceding that "we no longer have an employee base who values walking uphill in the snow," but contending, "I'm always bothered by questions like this because of cultural biases." Overall, however, we found limited hesitancy to take on our questions. Managers gave responses that highlighted clearly defined, invidious distinctions among groups, while registering sensitivity to a range of differences within groups.

Still, there were systematic differences in self-censorship across organizations, with establishment size and conversational circumspection rising together. In smaller establishments, we were more likely to speak with an owner or general manager responsible for personnel and operations. By contrast, we usually talked with a human resource (HR) manager when visiting a larger organization, and almost always did, in department stores and hospitals. The owners and general managers evinced little discomfort in discussing ethnic matters, answering our questions with a frankness that often surprised us. Not so the human resource managers, who by dint of education, professional socialization, and sensitivity to the visible nature of the institution for which they worked, were more likely to be both more careful about their responses and more attentive to filtering out prejudices. "We learn to be color blind in human relations," noted one interviewee. "I feel that when I'm doing my job, no person has color, no person has a disability. We train ourselves not to notice a person's limp, or whatever." It is also the case that human resources has been a favored route of upward mobility for both women and minorities, making HR managers somewhat more likely to see ethnic diversity as a good in and of itself.

Nonetheless, tongues loosened in the course of conversations that lasted an hour or more. For example, a hospital manager who insisted, "I hate talking about groups like this because it's so general," went on to a later discussion of group traits in a detailed, highly specific way. Close inspection of the transcripts and field notes reveals that initial disclaimers rarely lasted for long. We should also note that self-censoring should reduce variation in the views of managers toward the ethnic groups with whom they interact and yield relatively favorable views toward more stigmatized groups. That we found relatively little flattening, with the human resource managers describing and ranking the workforce in light of the preferences already described, makes our evidence all the more credible.

A NOTE ON LOCAL GEOGRAPHY

In this book, we will often refer to the specific community in which a firm is located. We know this can be confusing to readers not intimately familiar to the area; we hope this brief note will help.

Los Angeles County boasts innumerable distinct communities, of which roughly 120 take the form of incorporated cities (see Figure 1.1). The City of Los Angeles has about one-third of the population of the county but a much smaller proportion of its area. The county is divided into several well-recognized if somewhat fuzzily defined areas. The Antelope Valley, in the northern part of Los Angeles County, is undergoing rapid real estate development, but is still sparsely populated. An area of hills and desert, it is home to such cities as Palmdale, Lancaster, and Santa Clarita. To the south and west of the Antelope Valley lies the San Fernando Valley, the suburban heartland of the 1950s and 1960s, physically separated from the central city by ranges of hills, though largely belonging to the City of Los Angeles.

The San Gabriel Valley, occupying a large area north and east of downtown, is probably most famous for Pasadena, home of the Rose Bowl, and Monterey Park, the nation's "first suburban Chinatown."

Figure 1.1. The Los Angeles Region

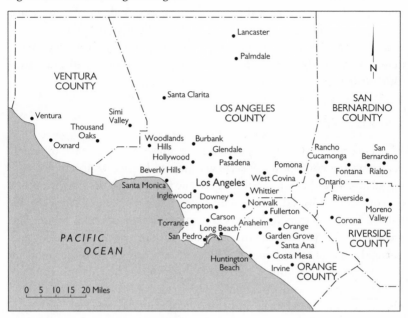

SOURCE: Adapted from *Ethnic Los Angeles*, edited by Roger Waldinger and Mehdi Borzorgmehr (New York: Russell Sage Foundation, 1996), p.6.

Glendale, the third largest city in the county (after Los Angeles and Long Beach), is also considered part of the San Gabriel Valley. The central city includes downtown Los Angeles and such nearby districts as Chinatown and Koreatown. As in most southwestern cities, much of the city center is not densely populated. East of downtown lies a sprawling, heavily Latino area, much of it consisting of unincorporated county territory.

Our headquarters at the University of California, Los Angeles, is firmly ensconced in the affluent "West" area of the county, which is located west of downtown and encompasses such well-known communities as Beverly Hills, Santa Monica, and Hollywood.

The area south of downtown encompasses most of what is popularly known as South Central Los Angeles. Underscoring the social nature of most geographical boundaries, the area is defined as much by the skin color of its residents as by physical landmarks or political boundaries. The South Central ghetto first came to national attention with the Watts Riots of 1965, and entered the national stage again in the early 1990s through films like "Boyz 'n the Hood" and "South Central" as well as the riots that broke out hours after the acquittal of the police officers who beat Rodney King. Watts, Compton, Inglewood, and Florence are among the communities in this area. The southern area of the county is known as the South Bay, dominated by the city of Long Beach and populated with mostly white suburbs like Torrance and more diverse cities like Gardena.

A ROAD MAP

We have organized our story into three primary sections, each of which begins with a conceptual overview, followed by two chapters presenting an analysis of our interview data. The first section details the nature of work in the low-skilled segment of the labor market, with special attention to how ethnicity affects the social organization of labor. The second section focuses on the interface between social networks and formal hiring practices, and the ways in which these two mechanisms for allocating labor affect who gets which jobs. The third section examines prejudice and discrimination, focusing on the nature of employers' ethnic preferences and the role of ethnic conflict at the workplace. In a concluding section, we revisit the question of competition between immigrant and African-American workers and then peer into the future, asking what our story portends about the role of the new Angelenos in years to come.

PART TWO

The Social Organization of Labor

CHAPTER 2

What Employers Want

As we enter the twenty-first century, Americans sense that we are moving toward a new world of work. As symbol of the emergent workplace reigns the computer, pervasive if not ubiquitous, with the revolution engendered by the microchip likely to entail both promise and peril. Total liberation from the drudgework of the industrial era may not be at hand, but automation is freeing human labor from the difficult, dangerous, and tedious tasks associated with the factory. Production is increasingly the domain of highly educated workers equipped with the technical skills needed to master and control the new technology; blue collars are passé. Manufacturing no longer occupies the economic centrality it once possessed—weakening the broader influence of its cultural patterns and skill needs. Because the service economy depends on the creation, transmission, and consumption of information and images, the demand for educated labor grows. As the skills of the labor force deepen, so grows the likelihood that work will involve a fuller use of human potential.

Thus, farewell to the factory, but not without regrets. With demand for less-skilled labor declining, academic commentators and vulnerable factory workers wonder where the millions of less educated workers will go. All may be well in the long run, as the economists assure us, but it is a long road from now to then. In the short run, workers are generally stuck with the skills they have: the forty-year-old worker who dropped out of high school at age eighteen enjoys little prospect of making up for his or her educational deficiencies. Moreover, the proficiencies learned

over many years, that once garnered a decent wage, are likely to prove
of little use when the factory downsizes or closes. Younger workers may
be hearing the message that extensive formal schooling is a must, but the
signal seems not to be coming across too clearly; there has been no sudden leap in college enrollment corresponding to the increased demand
for college-educated labor. Thus, the low-skilled worker has crossed the
threshold into the twenty-first century in big trouble, with wages down
and employment uncertainty up.[1] By the time we moved past the turn of
the century, the longest peacetime boom in U.S. history had finally
pushed real hourly wages up at all levels of the labor market—but the
increase came late, proved slight, and produced no increase in job
security.

The emergent labor market increasingly has room only for the highly
skilled, and nowhere more so than in the great metropolitan areas of the
United States. The city of information and services has largely replaced
the city of production, leading our most prominent analysts of urban
trends to worry about a mismatch between the skills of urban residents
and the requirements of urban employers. Minority city dwellers, in particular, simply do not seem to possess what employers want.

But something strange is going on in these very places that are apparently hurtling toward the computerized, skill-intensive work world of tomorrow; they are hosting a massive infusion of workers from outside the
country, workers whose education is even more deficient than that of
vulnerable U.S. -born workers who never continued beyond high school.
Even more peculiar is the immigrants' experience; poorly schooled, unfamiliar with American ways, and lacking in English fluency, they are
nonetheless finding work and maintaining remarkably high employment
rates.[2] Granted, the advent of the newcomers is not totally mysterious;
no one has yet figured out how to dispense with dishwashers and sweepers. But the immigrant presence in America's urban economies has
spilled far beyond this small cluster of manual positions, as more and
more employers have discovered the virtues of hiring the foreign-born,
employing them over a steadily widening spectrum of jobs.

So the continuing immigrant arrival provides good reason to re-
examine our assumptions about today's "new" world of work. There is
something painfully familiar about today's image of the emerging flexible, high-skilled workplace and its polyvalent worker—we have heard it
all before. In the 1950s and 1960s, the optimists in the social science fra-
ternity (as it truly was, then) offered much the same view. They contended that the "logic of industrialization" would inevitably transform

all societies, with capital-intensive production eventually replacing the hard, dirty, undesirable jobs that industry then had to offer.[3] In sociology, Robert Blauner chimed in with the view that technological shifts were pushing job skills along a U-shaped trajectory. In the not-so-distant past, highly skilled, highly satisfying jobs associated with craft production prevailed; job requirements then tumbled, under the reign of the mind- and spirit-numbing jobs of the Taylorized assembly line. In the second half of the twentieth century, Blauner forecast, the advent of continuous-process work, requiring teams of workers to act creatively when the automated system inevitably crashed, would begin to push skill levels and related job satisfactions back up the curve,[4] Slightly later, Daniel Bell, having previously announced the end of ideology, proclaimed "the coming of post-industrial society," a shift signaled by the growing importance of knowledge for economic growth, which in turn reflected a basic change in the nature of work. "The fact that individuals now talk to other individuals, rather than interact with a machine," intoned Bell, "is the fundamental fact about work in the post-industrial society."[5] Thus, contemporary arguments that the computer will deliver us from the routine, mundane activities of production and service represent the latest variation on an old theme.

Unfortunately, this perspective suffers from a recurrent inability to make sense of a salient aspect of the reality it purports to interpret: the arrival of successive waves of low-skilled migrant labor—often directly recruited—to fill jobs that, from this perspective, should not even exist. The 1950s, the intellectual heyday for the proponents of "industrial society" and the moment when America underwent its first "automation scare," came towards the tail end of the Great Migration,[6] with millions of displaced African-American sharecroppers still trekking to Northern industrial cities in search of work; with little in the way of education or marketable skills, African American migrants were still able to readily find jobs (even if those jobs were barely worth writing home about). Europe witnessed the same trend in the 1960s, with the massive recruitment of "guest workers" from increasingly distant locales. Like African Americans, these workers had the intolerable effrontery of not returning home when, in the mid-1970s, the great European industrial machine no longer hungered for their labor power. In the United States, where the economy has undergone wrenching transformations over the past three decades, immigrant flows have been simultaneously, and steadily, on the rise. Barring major changes in immigration policy, we can expect that roughly 800,000 legal immigrants will continue arriving each year for the foreseeable future. Evidently, the ever-advancing capitalist societies of the turn of the twenty-first century cannot do without immigrant labor. Setting aside for the moment the question of *why* late capitalism requires an immigrant labor fix, we must ask a more basic question: How is it that less-skilled immigrants find *any* place in the new world of work?

SKILLS: UPGRADED, DOWNGRADED, PERSISTENT

We begin by noting that the conventional view goes wrong, in part, because it ignores a more complex reality. Optimistic portrayals of the upgrading workplace have the character of "future schlock" because they ignore an opposing counter-tendency; capitalism's dynamism has a deeply destructive component, one day breaking down skills it created just the day before. Indeed, the application of computerized technology creates new niches, often initially filled with jobs that require highly skilled, semi-autonomous workers. Yet, if the pace of technological changes slows down, the jobs become standardized and the skills degraded; one only need glance at the cash register in a MacDonald's fast food restaurant to see the power of computers to "dumb down" work.

The argument that capitalism progresses by deskilling derives from Marx, and has been transported to the contemporary social sciences by a particularly successful modern exponent, Harry Braverman. According to Braverman, deskilling has derived from the fundamental opposition of labor and capital. The search for profits led the latter to unceasing efforts to gain command over the former. Capitalists pursued control through mechanization, through the transference of knowledge from labor to capital and its agents, and through ever more successful efforts at surveillance and monitoring—all with the aim of greater control over the exercise of labor power. As a corrective to the one-dimensional, excessively optimistic portrayals of technological progress, Braverman packed considerable punch; by its very nature, capitalism has continued reproducing the working class, on whose elimination the hopes of the prophets of "industrial" and "post-industrial" society rested. Put bluntly, Braverman observed that the normal functioning of capitalism produced plenty of crummy jobs, a statement no less true today than a generation ago, when he first wrote.[7]

Unlike mainstream analysts, Braverman was not willing to equate educational credentials and official certifications with "real" skills. In his view, credentials serve other important purposes: sending employers signals about a job candidate's personal qualities (as economists are wont to note),[8] and raising artificially high barriers to entry (as sociologists are more likely to point out).[9] More generally, it is one thing to observe that today's workers are better educated than yesterday's, quite another to show that today's workers are more highly skilled. The skills required by the job were, for Braverman, an empirical question, one likely to be influenced, if not decided, by the incessant pressures to reduce labor costs by reducing skills and by transferring control from labor to management. Clearly, the relationship between a worker's formal education and the skills required by the job was not, in his view, to be taken at face value; skepticism was particularly warranted when regarding the lower end of the labor market, where the undeniable upgrading in the educational attainment of workers hardly precluded the possibility that the actual proficiencies demanded by the employer remained unaltered or had even decreased.

Braverman's writings swept the field, at least among sociologists of work. As they pursued his leads, however, they realized he had gone too far.[10] On one hand, Braverman simply misread the underlying direction of change; right as he was about capitalism's destructive impulses, he failed to appreciate its creative tendency, all the more marked in a time of stepped-up technological change. As we now know from a large literature of strategic case studies and from analyses of larger-scale data sets, job requirements are, *on average,* heading upward.[11] In contrast to the futuristic scenarios periodically embraced by social scientists, most experts now acknowledge that there is nothing inevitable or unidirectional about skill enhancement. There are changes in both directions—*up*-grading *and de*-skilling.[12] Moreover, technology has no determinate impact on skill; an innovation that at one stage increases job proficiencies may be later altered so as to greatly reduce skill demands. The advent of the computer, its widespread application, and its effect on the acceleration of the product cycle have made cognitive skills increasingly important and salient for many classes of workers. But the effect is more modest than most think: skill deepening takes place, but its effects so far are relatively limited.[13] In other words, the revolution has been postponed; capitalism still needs its *proles*.

Braverman's other mistake involved accepting management's own propaganda at face value, especially as regards its success in deskilling. What management says and what workers do, Braverman forgot, are two different things. Because the fundamental ethnomethodological insight applies—the most basic forms of human interaction are subject to breakdown, misinterpretation, conflict—almost all jobs contain an ineradicable component of skill.[14] Following Marx, as forgotten by Braverman, moreover, workers have reason to hide their knowledge of everyday tricks from the bosses.[15] As Ken Kusterer argued in one of the earliest critiques of Braverman from the left, quotation marks belong around the word "unskilled"; almost all work situations involve unpredictability and uncertainty; the skills required to handle the unanticipated are something that management cannot eliminate, no matter how hard it tries.[16] On the other hand, the fact that workers are willing to use their everyday know-how *because* they want to get the work done—contra Marx—often gives management less reason to reorganize work in ways that would require even fewer skills.[17] Rephrased in more pertinent terms, work at the bottom of the labor market may require little formal education, but it nonetheless involves job-related proficiencies of significant degree.

LABOR MARKET SEGMENTATION

Thus, creatively destructive, capitalism maintains its pool of less-skilled though hardly skill-less jobs. But it departs from the trajectory of unilinear development, forecast by the prophets of industrial or postindustrial society, in yet another way. Instability is the bane of market economies, and its producers attempt to shelter themselves from its effects in any number of ways. Firms look for ways to capture a market or as much of a business line as they can. Workers try to build in protection against the vagaries of the business cycle, making it hard for firms to sack them, or forcing employers to heavily cushion the costs of the unemployment they periodically create. However, stability is an option only for some. Firms are willing to tie up capital, and their most valuable labor, in those parts of the production process least susceptible to fluctuation. In reaction to workers' successful efforts to stabilize employment, making labor a fixed—and high—cost, firms with internal labor markets become reluctant to engage new help. Rather than scaling up when demand grows, they "source out," using contractors to absorb the least stable portion of demand. For some firms (including the contractors engaged to handle the unstable part of demand), the nature of the market they face—its small size, the uncertainty of demand, the proliferation of small producers—prevents internalization. Those organizations least sheltered from the forces of competition and most subjected to the vagaries of the market find themselves without the certainty needed to make long-term investments in workers' skills, and starved of the profits needed for wages that would attract a high-quality, strongly attached workforce.

Thus, the labor market divides into segments; of these, there are more than a few taxonomies. The best known, most influential perspective, associated with Michael Piore, emphasizes the difference between *primary* and *secondary* labor market segments. The former is a reserve of higher-wage, relatively stable jobs, where workers progress and learn skills through movement up an elaborated job ladder; the latter consists of organizations that recruit workers from the external labor market and place them in poorly paid positions with limited opportunities for upward mobility.[18] Piore's dualist model seems less applicable to the economy of the turn of the twenty-first century than it was for the postwar, still-Fordist economy, which it originally served to describe.[19] Recent modifications to the model point to additional lines of segmentation, taking note of industrial, salaried, and craft faultlines within Piore's primary labor market segment. Still, the key insights of the segmentation approach continue to illuminate. First, job characteristics co-vary, as Chris and Charles Tilly argue, so that well-paying jobs offer opportunities for on-the-job training and less onerous supervision, and low pay is correlated with frequent supervision, work repetitiveness, and perceived risk of job loss.[20] Second, easy movement from one cluster of jobs to another is impeded, because each segment develops its own institutional practices, attaching to networks that include members of a particular "club" and exclude all others.[21] Thus, to each segment its own labor force. Because the jobs in the secondary sector are the least attractive, and since capitalism's dynamism regularly leads it to exhaust the available pool of labor, vacancies at the bottom of the totem pole recurrently emerge. And so opens a portal of entry to immigrants, who however poorly educated or unskilled in the conventional sense, nonetheless turn out to be wanted.[22]

The Importance of Being Secondary

In this book, our area of concern lies within the secondary sector of the labor market, although not the secondary sector as conventionally depicted. In that image, the secondary labor market serves as a concentration of jobs requiring minimal skills, the nature of which can be apprehended by almost anyone, with little pain. Our objection to this conventional view echoes our criticism of Braverman's depiction of deskilling: it simply goes too far. At the base of the labor market one can find positions that just about anyone can fill. However, as we argued earlier, ethnomethodological competence is required for any job;[23] in most secondary jobs the demand for proficiency is higher still. Organizations may be small, working with outdated technology, using managerial methods harsher and more dictatorial than the modern personnel handbook prescribes; notwithstanding, the inherent unpredictability and uncertainty of the work makes competence of a non-trivial sort imperative.[24] And for a variety of reasons, the necessary know-how is almost always learned on the job: the skills are industry- or occupation-specific; few external agencies provide the necessary training; and the available workers either lack meaningful formal training or possess certificates that contain no signaling value.[25]

This revised view of the secondary labor market needs to be placed alongside another view emphasized throughout this book: migration is a network-driven phenomenon. As Piore saw it, the secondary labor market is a world without structure, its immigrant workers lacking durable social relationships, living and working in a context where they are "divorced from a social setting."[26] As we show in greater detail shortly, the work environment of the immigrants takes exactly the opposite form; newcomers are linked by dense, cohesive connections to veterans, who in turn use their inside information to secure openings for their key associates. As discussed in part 3 of this volume, immigrant networks work so powerfully because they also serve employers' ends, increasing the likelihood that a new hire, recruited through informal channels, will turn out a stable, productive worker. Even at the bottom of the labor market, employers are concerned *and* uncertain about a new applicant's potential to produce. The needed skills are acquired on the job, through training; training entails investment, which employers are loathe to make, absent assurances about a worker's native ability and reliability. Since fitting in with the group facilitates learning, the employer has good reasons to prefer workers who resemble the incumbents who will teach them. This preference spells bad news for potential workers without connections, or for workers who comprise a small minority in industries or occupations dominated by some other group. It yields good news, however, for the numerically dominant group, since a chance to learn on the job in one firm can lead to upward mobility, through movement to another firm. This option counts heavily in the secondary sector, where most organizations are small and job ladders are short or nonexistent, making inter-firm movement a must for the ambitious worker.

SUBORDINATES WANTED

Before proceeding, we note that there is an entire tier of jobs to which the commonsense concept of skill applies awkwardly, if at all. As the

Oxford English Dictionary defines it, "skill" involves the "capability of accomplishing something with precision and certainty; practical knowledge in combination with ability; cleverness, expertness; an ability to perform a function, acquired or learnt with practice." The jobs of interactive service, such as that between sales clerks and customers, often require qualities of an entirely different kind; while they frequently entail pushing, doing, manipulating, transforming, these actions do not lie at the core of the job. Workers who "work on people" have an additional, overriding objective, that of manipulating the self to create a feeling of contentment in the recipient of the service, as Arlie Hochschild has most eloquently explained.[27]

In Hochshild's account, working on people, as opposed to working with things, used to be correlated with class; those in the middle-class or above gravitated to the former, while persons of working- or lower-class background were typically confined to the latter. The demands entailed in working on people are not necessarily trivial. The interactive-service worker needs to alter his or her behavior in just the way that will lead the customer to respond as desired; she or he must know how to respond to subtle cues, and is expected to have the sensitivity to adjust to changing, unpredictable situations. These tasks require skills not imparted by school: the ability to smile, to present a friendly, personable self, and to control one's feelings so that the customer will be pleased. Put differently, the effective interactive-service worker needs to maintain an appropriate presentation of self. In the terms used by employers, the demands entailed in presenting the right front (if not *self*) make "attitude" count as much as, if not more than, "skill."[28]

However, the successful interactive-service worker requires yet another trait that Hochschild, like most students of so-called "emotional labor," somehow ignores. The word *service*, after all, implies a *servant* and there is no servant without a master who needs to be pleased. Not every job of interactive service reenacts the master-servant relationship; the jobs vary greatly in the degree to which subordination to the customer is an essential component. But as one moves down the occupational totem pole towards the jobs with which we are concerned, it becomes more important that the server know his or her place. The lower-level service jobs bear a strong resemblance to domestic labor, from which they are descended, a resemblance signaled by the symbols of service work and by its codes of interaction.[29] Today's interactive-service worker shares more than a little with the household servant of old, wrapped in a uniform, wearing tags that display only his or her first name, expected to address customers as *sir* or *madam*, shuttling from the shabby halls of the "back of the house" to the comfortable, if not luxurious, environs of the "front of the house."[30] Consequently, one's suitability (or willingness) to comply with the customary demands for subordination ranks high among the criteria that employers want. Skills, whether hard or soft, matter a good deal less.

In general, the best subordinates are those who know their place—a generalization that holds with particular force for the tasks and positions with which we are concerned. The job of interactive service requires inversion of the usual codes of interaction; the service provider's task is to defer to the client, who is under no obligation to reciprocate, let alone acknowledge, behavior normally understood as kindness. True, the customer does not always "look through" the service provider, but many are the occasions when it may be better to pretend there is no one there. The messy hotel room, for example, would surely be more of an embarrassment were it to be cleaned by someone with a claim to equality. It is easier for all concerned if the dirty work is done by someone whose characteristics qualify him or her as a non-person, and can therefore be peacefully ignored.[31] And where employers understand jobs to be demeaning, as our respondents often did, they have reasons to assign the task to a worker already unrespected. More difficult is recruiting someone whose personal status—for reasons of nativity, ethnicity, gender, age, or the like—does not fit with the job's, and who may therefore feel entitled to something better. While the experienced boss is an expert in saying no, it is harder to do so with a clearly observable person to encounter—someone, indeed, resembling oneself—instead of an employee whose external traits allow complaints to be automatically dismissed.

Thus, jobs that require willing subordinates motivate employers to have recourse to immigrants. As we shall argue at greater length in chapters 9 and 10,[32] bad jobs are likely to be seen as "best" for people already demeaned, especially in positions where the service expected contains the *servile* aspect associated with the servant role—for which persons brought up to value more egalitarian relationships at work are unlikely to be seen as the most willing recruits.[33] For the moment, we simply assert that employers have a cognitive map that leads them to associate ethnic and national traits with the qualities that make for subordination. Operating from a "theory" of immigrant labor, they perceive immigrants as workers distinctively characterized by a dual frame of reference, in which the evaluation of treatment in the host society is always assessed relative to treatment in the home society. In that view, strangers (unlike the native) are not yet in the know, and not yet aware that the task and conditions of a job are stigmatizing and therefore something against which one should chafe. Understanding that "here" is likely to prove better for immigrants than "there" on most counts—pay, status of the job, type of work involved, or authority relationships at work—the employer is likely to see the immigrants as more accommodating, if not necessarily happier, workers than those "born in the U.S.A."

LEARNING WHAT EMPLOYERS WANT

Even at the bottom of the labor market, the handicaps with which immigrants start represent no mean thing; the newcomers' deficits in educational attainment, English language ability, and American cultural literacy are grounds for any employer to beware. But the immigrants may have some cards to play—most important, their connections to other immigrants who possess the working knowledge needed by secondary firms, and are ready to teach their kin, friends, and compatriots. Further, the dual frame of reference makes it easier for immigrants to produce the appropriate performance in workplaces where displays of subordination are de rigueur. In the following two chapters, we shall put empirical meat on these bones; we shall discuss what we have learned about what employers want and, as importantly, do *not* want. In doing so, we will see how the other half works.

CHAPTER 3

Doing the Job

The vernacular distinguishes between skilled and unskilled jobs. So too does the sociological literature, alas, accepting the everyday, taken-for-granted preconceptions when precisely these assumptions should be put in question. As we argued in the preceding chapter, jobs may be called unskilled but the label oversimplifies dangerously; virtually all positions entail knowledge or abilities neither universally shared nor trivial. Almost regardless of the task, occupants require "working knowledge" to do a job right.

This chapter takes the discussion from the academic literature to the concrete reality of the entry-level jobs in the industries we studied. In our interviews with employers, we sought to distinguish between the qualities demanded by the job and the traits that employers were seeking among new recruits. We first asked about the most important *skill* that the job required: with this question, we sought to understand what a job entailed and which proficiency was most essential for its successful completion. We asked employers to choose the most important among a list of possible skills—general cognitive skills such as reading or writing, communicative skills of different types, or skills specific to the job—and explain why the chosen skill was key. The results of our questioning are shown in Table 3.1 and explored in the remainder of this chapter.

Since so many jobs require training, we assumed that many employers might hire workers who did not yet have the skills to get the work done; therefore, we later also asked about the most important *quality* employers

TABLE 3.1. MOST IMPORTANT SKILL
REQUIRED BY THE JOB (%)

	Reading	Writing	Interaction with Customers	Interaction with Co-workers	English Ability	Job-specific Skills	Other
Department Stores	12	0	72	8	4	0	4
Furniture Manufacturing	3	0	3	29	0	47	18
Hospitals	16	0	38	0	3	34	9
Hotels	0	0	46	3	0	44	8
Printing	20	0	0	22	2	29	27
Restaurants	5	2	64	7	10	0	12
All Industries	9	0	35	12	3	26	15

SOURCE: Skills Study (N = 217)
NOTE: Rows sum to 100 percent.

TABLE 3.2. MOST IMPORTANT QUALITY SOUGHT IN JOB CANDIDATES (%)

	Related Work Experience	Stable Work History	Ability to Relate to Customers	Ability to Relate to Co-workers	Appearance	Skills Required for Job	Attitude	Minimum Level of Education	Other
Department Stores	4	0	72	0	0	0	16	0	8
Furniture Manufacturing	10	15	3	5	0	26	28	0	13
Hospitals	19	13	19	0	0	19	23	0	6
Hotels	9	6	22	6	3	9	44	0	0
Printing	10	10	0	5	0	15	44	2	15
Restaurants	18	0	42	0	3	0	29	5	3
All Industries	12	8	23	3	1	12	32	1	8

SOURCE: Skills Study (N = 206)
NOTE: Rows sum to 100 percent.

looked for in a candidate. By "quality," we meant any skill, experience, or attribute deemed relevant by employers, whether having to do with the specific proficiencies required by a job, or communicative skills, experience, education, and the somewhat more personal attributes of appearance and attitude. The answers to these queries appear in Table 3.2.

Before moving on to a more detailed discussion, we note that the employers we interviewed hire for positions that fall some distance above the labor market's very bottom. The massive cadre employing casual laborers—homeowners using nannies and gardeners, construction contractors hiring gangs of laborers—do not appear here, nor do the garment and related companies that comprise the Los Angeles sweatshop sector. The establishments that we visited were at least one cut above these; the conditions of work were more salubrious and the employers more likely to play by the rules. Still, the jobs were often demanding, requiring considerable physical exertion. Notwithstanding all the talk, the technical skills that "everyone" must possess these days were not often in view. Although it would be wrong to contend that work in Los Angeles's low-skilled sector resembles the work world of yesteryear, it is not that different. Literacy, numeracy, and familiarity with computers do count, but only for some jobs, and only to a modest degree. To a much greater extent, the crucial skills are those that can be learned on the job, through interaction with others.

Some jobs required those attributes often described as "soft skills," a concept invoked to refer to traits and proficiencies "that pertain to personality, attitude, and behavior rather than to formal or technical knowledge."[1] But (as we argued in chapter 2 and shall show in greater detail below) the notion of "soft skills" confounded the proficiencies required to communicate information effectively with the ability to present oneself in the manner expected by employer and consumer alike. At the low end of the labor market, performance of the job required proper demeanor at least as much as ability to communicate effectively. And whether the job involved doing or talking, making or servicing, the demand for productivity was almost always intense. Hence, in the employers' view, the right attitude was likely to be as crucial an attribute as possession of the necessary skill, and a crucial determinant of which types of workers were let through the door.

THE JOBS: AN OVERVIEW

Production: Furniture Manufacturing and Printing

Once upon a time, factories were the places where unskilled city dwellers would get a start and then move up—or so the conventional wisdom about America tells us.[2] The factory of the future may want a good deal more brain than brawn. Still, there appear to be entry-level jobs for the uneducated but manually proficient workers seeking work in the Los Angeles printing and furniture industries. Factory work remains "hard and all mechanical" as one printer reminded us; those workers who start out at the very bottom "have to be able to do repetitive work. What they do, they do it all day long, all week long, all month long."[3]

A capacity for physical exertion was a property of all of the entry-level production jobs we surveyed. For most employers, however, it was not enough. Manufacturers gave the highest ranking to "job-specific skills," "know-how" that would make a worker immediately useful on the job. Consequently, as employers pointed out, entry-level jobs in manufacturing may not be "difficult to learn," but adequate performance of the tasks "involves tricks to make it go quicker," and these are "all experience-based." Even in the pressrooms, where progress toward computerization has gone far, "every press is different [and] has its peculiarities." "Since a pressman needs to know more than just how it works in theory—he has to have enough skills to solve problems that arise"; knowing how to manipulate "old Bessie" makes a difference.

In other words, employers in the manufacturing industries surveyed depended on finding or training workers with a particular set of proficiencies that relatively few persons were likely to possess. The importance of such specific skills varied from firm to firm, with those most tightly linked to small niches the most reliant on workers with a given blend of skills. The fact that the establishment was likely to be small (generally smaller in printing than in furniture) was equally crucial, especially when vacancies arose in more skilled positions. Without much supervisory overhead, the smaller firms were keen on workers who "could do the job without asking too many questions." Size also affected the extent of the division of labor; one printer, for instance, told us "there's no such animal as the entry-level; people have to know the job"; we heard this comment, in one form or another, numerous times. Small or highly specialized firms needing skilled workers often found themselves forced to go outside in quest of workers with the right hands-on knowledge, almost always experience-based. And in printing, the fact that such skilled workers were likely to be operating expensive equipment—"I'm not going to let somebody at my press who doesn't know what he's doing . . . I've got a $200,000 piece of equipment, and he could ruin it in five minutes"—worked in the same direction.

Though the single largest group of manufacturing employers highlighted "job-specific" skills as the proficiencies most important to getting the work done, respondents who offered this answer often admitted that they regularly hired workers with no or little experience. To be sure, employers looking for craft workers wanted recruits who knew what they were doing. But, as Table 3.2 shows, just over one-third of the furniture manufacturers and only one-fourth of the printers ranked job-required skills or related work experience as the most important traits sought. For most entry-level job categories, the required proficiencies simply did not demand a fully knowledgeable worker. Instead, learning would take place on the job. "It's a completely unskilled job," noted a furniture manufacturer. "I could hire a dishwasher. But our plan is to train."

Consequently, "getting along" was most crucial in manufacturing, where it was not the customer but the co-worker who was king. The manufacturers emphasized that "you have to be a team. That's what it's all about." Needing "everybody's goodwill to put that product out the door," managers emphasized the importance of "fitting in" and working together: "We want harmony." Getting along with others "facilitates cooperation [and] timely completion of assignments, improves the quality of work. Even a general helper who doesn't get along will turn out substandard work." Therefore, *interdependence*, the impossibility of completing the required tasks without the participation and cooperation of multiple workers, often led manufacturers to rate interaction between co-workers as the "number one issue in the shop."

Employers further valued the ability to interact with co-workers because "learning [from] each other" was the medium through which newcomers picked up needed skills; it was "what's going to teach them what their responsibilities are." Training was most likely to occur through "the buddy system," for example, when the "supervisors walk [inexperienced workers] through the first jobs. Then you buddy them up with someone who has experience." Under these circumstances, learning, as the classic accounts of internal labor markets have described, occurs through "exposure. You see how [it's done] on the job."[4]

Since much of the learning occurred through doing, it seemed to happen naturally. Feeders could become second pressman because "basically, the approach was, come to this because you've been watching";

pressmen moved up to more sophisticated jobs by "learning larger equipment in their spare time." But there was more involved than exposure; interdependence both gave owners an interest in ensuring that needed skills were transmitted to newcomers, and engaged the skilled workers in the training process. On the other hand, inexperienced workers could learn only so long as the relationships lubricating the training process worked without hiccups. As one informant pointed out, having to train"puts a lot more pressure on the pressman." Getting the skilled workers involved was the key to the whole process:

> *Field notes:* The feeder–second pressman–first pressman ladder is "the whole goal of working on the press." They moved a kid from the shipping department to the pressroom as a floorboy. Then there were pressmen who requested him (over other floorboys) as a feeder because he showed a willingness to learn.

Consequently, entry-level workers have to get along with those further up the hierarchy. "If they can't . . . then [they] can't do the job. I'm not going to get rid of craftworkers if they can't get along with the entry-level worker."

Service: Hotels, Restaurants, and Hospitals

The conventional wisdom about the ills of American cities puts the decline of manufacturing at the heart of its diagnosis, but the industrial city of old provided ample opportunities for service workers, to clean and prepare food in low-paying industries like hotels, restaurants, and hospitals.[5] In a sense, the past proved prologue, since these same industries form a crucial component of the postindustrial urban present, with all three industries still requiring manual effort of their least qualified, entry-level employees.

Proficiencies that either were job specific or involved customer interaction were the only skills rated by hotels as most important for housekeeping and serving (the largest categories of hotel entry-level jobs); restaurants offered a variation, placing greater emphasis on getting along with customers—although entry-level jobs in kitchens involved a completely different set of demands.[6] As the hotel managers described it, housekeeping was a fundamentally manual job, requiring workers who "can lift and are able to push something that has a certain amount of weight"; jobs involving serving or kitchen "prep" similarly entailed a hefty physical component. Physical demands were on the way up when we conducted our survey, with hotels responding to the stiff competitive environment by reducing staff and increasing workloads.

Under these circumstances, many managers rated "job-specific skills" as most important for performing the job. "Basically, all hotels offer the same soap and linens," noted a manager at a middle-range business hotel. "It's how clean your room is. Is the extra care given?" Consequently, "[I]f they cannot clean, they're out the door." And cleaning to the hotel's satisfaction meant doing so "in a quick and timely manner. It's nice to get along with clients, but if you don't clean the room quickly, you're dead in the water."

Not all managers agreed. About half were in fact likely to give their highest rating to interaction with customers, on the grounds that "Guests can excuse the wet towel left on the floor behind the door. They cannot excuse a room attendant in the hallway that is rude or not polite to them. Guest services is what it's all about." The disagreement, it should be noted, was a matter of emphasis, and related to the price segment to which a hotel catered. Managers who emphasized interaction also wanted "high detail" and workers who would "make things attractive." Luxury hotels, in particular, expected that a housekeeper would not just clean rooms: "[H]er primary function is to act as a liaison between the guest and the hotel for any needs the guest may have, be it dry-cleaning, unpacking, shoe polishing. Anything you can imagine." While deluxe service is apparently not the norm, most managers thought that the need for appropriate service provision made the ability to interact with customers crucial.

In restaurants, managers and owners placed even greater emphasis on behavior required to keep clients happy: "stroking," "smiling," and "communicating." In traditional "sit-down" restaurants, servers were akin to sales workers employed in the department stores, expected to talk to the clientele about the menu, to "sell it," and were described by one owner as "salesmen on the floor, not just order-takers."[7] This is not to say that fast-food operators were less concerned about the face they presented to the public, contending that "service is everything. Good service can make up for bad food, but good food cannot make up for bad service."

Communicating information accurately and clearly must rank as a skill. But for the restaurateurs, the desired interaction with customers involved displaying the appropriate *demeanor* as well; retail managers, as shown below, had a similar view. But the hotel respondents saw the balance between skill and demeanor differently, emphasizing proper *comportment*. "Smiles and good attitude" we learned, mattered a good deal more than providing information.[8] One manager stated, "The most important skill is *attitude*. If a person doesn't have the attitude of wanting to work, they won't do the job well. Whether they know how to read, write, or know how to do the job, attitude is the core. Because it's service."

Another hotel respondent, who picked interaction with customers as the most important skill, then distinguished between skills, which "can be taught," and knowing "how to get along. In life, you've got it or you don't." The comments of the HR manager of a deluxe hotel (who also mentioned interaction with customers as the most important skill) made it clear that innate traits stood at the top of her list of "skills": "Hospitality, because that sets the tone for everything else that follows. A hotel—if you look at it, what you have is a museum. If you add people, you have a home. That's where we start. Hospitality is a natural inclination to want to please, help, and serve other people. It's something you can't train someone to be. Either they want to or they don't."

Put somewhat differently, the interactive capacity valued by the hoteliers was essentially performative. To get the job done, one had to display the right face, and maintaining the appropriate front required a willingness to *serve* or, at the very least, the ability to play the subordinate, good-naturedly.

Similar considerations are not absent in hospitals, but are not always primary. Like hotels and restaurants, hospitals employ cleaners and food preparers, but there are distinctive requirements deriving from the specific characteristics of the institution, leading to very different entry-level needs. In contrast to interviewees in the other industries we surveyed, hospital managers were often unwilling to pick out a single most important skill. They often responded that not simply one skill, but rather a cluster of skills, needed to be in place (with at least some degree of adequacy). For example, a manager at a public-sector hospital with a large black workforce described the skill requirements for a janitor's job: "Reading: chemicals, very important, measurements; writing: orders and reports, incident reports, requests, more things to fill out; customers: work around patients, not supposed to say anything, get the nurse if the patient wants anything; co-workers: need to get along with nurses; specific: know how to use the equipment; other: ability to follow instructions."

Many hospital respondents mentioned proficiencies that would fall into the categories of "hard" and "soft" skills (with reading, writing, and job-specific know-how representing the former and working around patients and interacting with co-workers and nurses representing the latter). Consequently, hospital workers whose jobs entail no formal re-

sponsibility for customer service end up having a great deal of incidental interpersonal contact. As one respondent expressed it, janitors or
food service workers "see so many kinds of people, doctors, patients . . .
it's important that interpersonal skills be high."

If hospitals value soft skills, requirements for hard skills matter more.
In contrast to employers of seemingly similar low-skilled help, hospitals
require that more, and more complex, information be communicated.
Likewise, communication is more likely to require two-way exchange.
One consequence of the greater informational demands is that hospital
employers are more likely to view English ability as comparable in importance to other job skills. More importantly, perhaps, hospitals place
surprisingly strong emphasis on skills involving formal communication,
mainly because workers need to understand written instructions of a
complex sort. In this respect, the specifics of the work environment are
conditioning factors; for a variety of reasons, hospitals are dangerous
places to work, and the hazards increase the skill demands of almost all
jobs there, even those of the lowest sort.

Selling: Department Stores

In department stores, getting in at the bottom most commonly means becoming a "sales associate," where the most important skill is "interaction with customers." As the employers told us, selling is "a people business," where "if you can't get along with people, you can't sell." But the
comments of our respondents also reflected the new, harshly competitive
retail environment of the early 1990s; long-time retail chains closed
down, merged, or were restructured, and customers were increasingly
demanding and "a lot more conscious of the dollar." Under these conditions, where "customer service is that thing that will make you or
break you," the "customer is the most important," leading retailers of
all types, whether mass or class, to insist on salespersons knowledgeable
about "how to get along with the customer."

Proper service, naturally enough, involves communication. "If you
don't know how to speak to a customer, you're in the wrong place,"
noted an old-line mass marketer. Retailers wanted salespersons able to
"speak clearly," "give customers alternatives," and help customers "understand what's happening . . . what it is and what it means." Communication skills—being able to listen to the customer, answer customer
questions, and conduct a two-way exchange in an appropriate language—can reasonably be seen as inherent in the job. But, if important,

these skills did not suffice. "I don't necessarily go somewhere because of the price," noted one merchandiser, "but because of the friendly [environment]." Friendliness, "always a high priority for us," and a set of related attributes emerged as a main theme in managers' discussion of the most important skill. A department store manager put it this way: "Customer service is the number one priority. We *dictate* friendliness."[9] One respondent told us that the most important *skill* that workers need to perform the job is "that they're happy, friendly," collapsing the distinction between the position and the attributes of those who fill it. To be sure, this manager might have misinterpreted our question, but in an environment where retail philosophies had changed to the point that managers were instructed to think of the customer as a "guest," satisfactory job performance increasingly required a particular projection of self. As one personnel manager who used the word repeatedly explained, "Now, 'friendly' is a smile on your face. 'Friendly' is talking to the person just across the counter. Real basic things. . . . Someone who doesn't have a smile doesn't belong in our industry any more."[10]

Clerical Jobs: Information Processing in the Hospital Environment

Of the six industries we studied, only hospitals recruited a significant proportion of entry-level workers into clerical positions. Although our inquiry into clerical work was limited to this single industry and our respondents' specification of clerical skill requirements revealed a distinct institutional influence, the interviews illuminated some generic characteristics of clerical work.[11] Like any other general occupational category, "clerical" spans a range of jobs varying considerably in content and skill requirements. Hospitals distinguish the proficiencies required of medical records clerks from those needed by admitting clerks or by typists. Regardless of particular job title, however, any clerical job requires basic or greater literacy.

The need for general technical skills varied from job to job. For file clerks, the benchmark was relatively low: "They have to be able to read the document and know where it goes in the file." The demands on clerk-typists were higher; their jobs required the reading and writing ability to complete "lots of different forms, test requests, draw up forms for labs, financial paperwork." Further up the clerical hierarchy, the "concern is the level of thinking skills," as opposed to entry-level positions, "where they're not coming here with ability to problem-solve." These distinctions notwithstanding, most clerical positions required technical and other skills, as in a Veterans Administration hospital where the medical desk clerk did "some typing, some filing, talking with patients, veterans, filling out forms, typing out reports, giving out information, working with patients' charts, making sure everything was down for the patient, filling out verifications, answering the phone."

READING, WRITING, AND ARITHMETIC

Cognitive Skills in Production Work

Notwithstanding the technological changes transforming American factories, including important shifts in printing, only a small minority of the manufacturers whom we interviewed scored higher-level cognitive proficiencies as most crucial. In general, cognitive skills of the most basic sort sufficed: "If they could read the labels—that is basically what it is." Printers were more likely to underscore the importance of the "three Rs," but requirements for reading and math in the bottom jobs were not exacting. For the most part, manufacturers' requirements for cognitive skills, and for the credentials that might certify such competence, were not high. "It's not Phi Beta Kappa," one manager pointed out. *None* of the furniture manufacturers, for example, required possession of a high-school degree. "We should get only high-school people, but we don't," noted the manager of a branch plant of a major national brand. "Especially with people from Mexico, we are lucky if they have a sixth-grade education." For the most part, employers had no requirement for formal schooling, or settled for levels far below today's national average: "at least eighth grade"; "at least sixth grade"; "at least primary school."

Printers generally wanted more, though again the high school diploma was rarely demanded. The foreman for a medium-size offset printer,[12] mainly concerned that entry-level workers "understand the mechanics of how things work," hired without regard to school completion. "I can cite a couple of cases of people who were high-school dropouts. If a person has a good attitude, wants to work, and can read, isn't color blind, we will give him a chance." The printers who insisted that some cognitive skill was the most important proficiency likewise turned out not to be exacting. "I like to make sure they can read now," commented a supervisor who subsequently confessed that his firm never checks to see whether applicants possess the high-school degree. With experience still providing the foundational base for much skilled factory work, it seems appropriate to conclude that, for most printers, "education is life, it doesn't mean school."

Cognitive Skills in Selling

As selling involved communication to a public of some diversity, retailers emphasized that cognitive skills were required in performing almost all entry-level jobs. We visited a department store where the future seemed to have arrived; in this successful, upmarket chain where "reading and writing is core, . . . associates will send notes to their customers, and call them on the phone." But this case was unusual. For the most part, the job of a salesperson ("associate," in the doublespeak of contemporary business) includes a surprisingly large manual component. "Most of it involves customer service, filling-in and stocking work, replenishing the floor, preparing stock to come to the selling floor, recovering the floor and getting it back to where it used to be. There's preparing displays, making merchandise move on the selling floor." Reading and writing are helpful in "making the merchandise move," but our interviewees conceded that workers performed the job with or without these skills. "People who are not literate find ways of getting assistance," noted a discounter. "They usually get their co-worker to read something for them."

While cognitive skills were important for gaining familiarity with the merchandise, and learning computer systems, it was not clear that demands for such skills were on the rise. Most managers did tell us that entry-level selling jobs had become more complex, but the degree of complexity was in no case insuperable. For the most part, shifts in complexity seemed related to the greater difficulty of the retail environment and the stores' corresponding preoccupation with customer service, an activity that did not necessarily denote skill. "You can honest-to-God be an idiot, but if you are sincere and really care about helping somebody, then the response translates." Neither operating the register nor learning the merchandising seemed to involve in-depth levels of know-how or extensive training. "I think anybody can learn how to be a sales associate," noted a department-store manager, who went on to point out that "they prefer a few years' experience, but they also want them to work real cheap, too." Acquiring the personality traits to function adequately, however, was not always simple. "We train people for our register," a discounter told us. "But we can't train them to be people-friendly."

To be sure, the view that "You can't teach them to be happy or friendly, but you can teach them to give good service" involves some exaggeration; all forms of interactive service work involve impression management, and one can learn the techniques to establish the distance between real and displayed selves usually required by interactive service work. But these techniques do not involve cognitive skills; and they do seem harder to master than the required form of the "three Rs":

> *Manager:* Friendliness is little cues, like eye contact, being consistent in acknowledging the customer, greeting them, making them feel welcome, taking care of customer service problems with even-temperedness.
>
> *Interviewer:* Can you train for it?
>
> *Manager:* It can be developed. It's harder to develop than just work skills. It's much easier to train on skills than personality traits.

The desired behaviors required sales workers to manage the presentation of self, though to varying degrees. At the bottom level, "it takes a lot to even say 'Hi, how are you.' A 'thank you.'" Any service interaction raises the possibility of a confrontation with irate customers. And the greater the opportunities for moneymaking, the more urgent the impression-management problems. "You will have problems," noted one respondent in a revealing piece of doublespeak, "when you have a challenging opportunity with a customer, like when they take a twelve-hundred-dollar suit back."

Not surprisingly, selling jobs remained fully accessible to workers with a high-school education and often to those who had not gone so far. "They don't need a college degree to take care of a customer." Even the store most demanding in terms of skills had "no edict with regard to education." A discounter, who told us, "our philosophy is high school education is preferred but is not required," summed up the policy and practice of the establishments we surveyed. Many firms clearly settled for less, as noted by one manager, who told us, "Well, they can't be in fifth grade!"

Cognitive Skills in Service

When discussing required skills, hotel managers accented simple competencies that almost anyone could be expected to know. But they did not necessarily think that just anyone would do. As one manager opined, "What's clean to them may not be clean to you. Frankly, some of them are a bit primitive. They just got off the boat. Their standard of cleaning is not the same as what is required in a hotel. So they have to be trained, and [have] it explained to them." Nor did the emphasis on the prevalence of basic skills imply that cognitive skills were irrelevant; they did however, seem of low importance. Managers' descriptions of jobs mentioned physical tasks, never responsibilities requiring reading, writing, or arithmetic. Further inquiry did yield a few hints that a job entailed some reading and occasionally a little writing, but by and large the expectation was that "if they can fill out an application correctly, they can read and write adequately for our purposes."

If requirements for cognitive skills were low, they appeared to be edging up, mainly because demands for interaction with clientele were changing. Interaction requires communication, and when staff members did not speak the language of the customer, a common occurrence in hotels dominated by immigrant Latino workers, communication suffered. As the need to increase the quality of interaction with customers increased, the inadequacies of the existing labor force became clearer. The managers were not blameless in creating this situation, a source of much consternation to hotel managers (and presumably to their English-monolingual guests). As we show in the next chapter, the linguistic environment in hotels was largely a by-product of the hotels' labor practices, with the everyday linguistic practices of an ethnically encapsulated workforce generally forcing Anglophone managers to switch to Spanish, not the reverse.

Managers' descriptions of service work in their hotels betrayed only hints of a trend toward cognitive-skills upgrading, but among the cleaners and food servers in a *hospital* environment that tendency was unmistakable. Technological innovations were altering the scope of even the most menial jobs. Greater attention to worker protection also raised skill demands (as mentioned earlier), since reducing exposure to danger meant educating workers about hazards. Greater emphasis on training meant greater preference for workers prepared to learn. For hiring managers, this meant implementing "more of a requirement of skills and ability to retain memory on how to do things." Considerations of which workers would learn fastest and with the least investment seemed to account for management's insistence that literacy and English-language ability were core job requirements.

Thus, skill requirements for hospital jobs seemed high for stereotypically "entry-level" positions; to some not insignificant extent, the level of entry at the bottom of the hospital no longer lies at the bottom of the overall market. Compared to hotels or restaurants, hospitals were therefore more likely to prefer that their lowest-level workers have a high-school degree or equivalent. "High school would be nice. What they really need is the ability to read and write English." As elsewhere, a candidate's school attainment also sent an important signal not always related to specific job requirements: "You see high school [in an applicant], you at least have, if anything, learned responsibility." But employers also recognized that the relationship between the credential and skills required on the job was tenuous; having other means of assessing job readiness, they were often willing to forego mandatory schooling requirements.

Cognitive Skills: Clerical Work in Health Care

Always high, informational demands on clerical help have been steadily escalating. Changes stem from the technological forces transforming clerical workplaces throughout the economy, as well as from the organizational disruptions related to the new economics of health-cost financing and reimbursement. Never simple, health-care organizations have become more complex, with clerical workers expected to understand how their unit fits into the broader complex, and act accordingly. Thanks to changes in financing and reimbursement practices, clerks are expected to process more information than before: "For one thing, ten years ago the insurance companies paid other things. Now they pay nothing, so it becomes a real challenge for people to code in the right code. And there is a real subtle difference. One code would be paid and the other wouldn't be. Now we have very strict standards of how many days an account could be open. And I don't think we had those kinds of problems ten years ago."

With hospitals "big on documentation—It helps keep us out of court," clerks also need to work to standards of greater exactitude. And the health-care finance crisis, afflicting hospitals no less at the time of this writing than at the time of our research, meant that staff was perpetually being trimmed. Consequently, clericals were "making do with less, and sometimes there are shared duties and responsibilities they're taking over from someone else because that person has left, so I think it's a more complex job."

ATTITUDES: "RIGHT" AND "WRONG"

Whether the job involves production or service, it takes place in a social environment, which is why the employers with whom we spoke were most likely to rate "attitude" as the quality most desired in a new recruit (see Table 3.2). To be sure, not all industries revealed the same pattern: attitude was top-ranked by printers, furniture manufacturers, hoteliers, and hospital managers; by contrast, department store managers and restaurateurs were more likely to choose *"ability* to interact with customers." But as we have shown, the interactive trait most valued by employers in these industries entails the ability to present a manufactured self. Since without the "right" attitude, one can provide neither "smiles" nor friendliness, employers in restaurants and department stores line up with their counterparts in the other industries studied.

Although "attitude is very nebulous," as pointed out by a manager for an upscale department store, respondents' extended discussion of the concept helped spell out its meaning. Most generally, managers were searching for workers who "come in thinking positive" as opposed to "somebody, everyday, who nothing they do goes right." They wanted workers with "a good work ethic [and an] ability to get along with people," who were "relatively stable in their approach." These qualities loomed large in the service interaction, where the need to take "care of customer service problems with even-temperedness" and the unpredictability of the encounter made the human factor all the more critical. A hospital manager, for example, described "pleasantness" as the attitude needed to "deal with the angry individual who calls them on the phone, or comes to the counter." A retailer, concerned with a "willingness to be out there for eight hours, talking to people [you] don't like," appeared to equate attitude with "extroversion." A hotel manager, who told us that "attitude is important because the customer is considered right," then described attitude as the ability "to handle a 'problem customer' diplomatically without yelling."

Clearer were the attitudes that employers were trying to avoid. Like the hospital manager who pointed out that "you don't need deadbeats," managers knew they did not want workers with "a bad attitude," who projected "negativity," who were "always defensive," or who signaled that they might be demanding, putting their own interests ahead of those of the firm: "We don't want anybody who might have a gang attitude, a bad attitude, you know, 'What are my rights?' you know. If somebody comes and the first question they ask is 'How much do I make an hour?' you know."

The definition of what employers *did not* want was not simply the opposite of the qualities sought. They looked for eager, happy, friendly recruits, and were therefore likely to reject applicants who seemed "sullen or withdrawn." However, the selection criteria reflected the jobs in question, as with one of our hospital informants, looking for flexible recruits to be placed in a "pretty controlling department . . . it's not . . . creative." In other words, managers were particularly concerned to stay away from those workers likely to say "no." "If they have a bad attitude, they don't want to do anything," noted a fast fooder. Convinced that "if they've got a bad attitude, they're more hassle than they're worth," a printer then specified just how the problem worker sounded: " 'That's not my job,' 'Oh, no. No, I can't do that,' 'Oh, yeah I'll be in later.' That kind of attitude." Even worse were those applicants who signaled that they might be hard to discipline; "[I]f they're told that something is wrong with their room, and they start getting defensive, well, then we have a problem."

How employers described the importance of "attitude" varied somewhat across industries. In general, the retailers were looking for those personal qualities most likely to spell success on the shopping floor, codified by one large discount chain as a "fast, fun, and friendly" attitude. "I'd say the most important things that I look for is somebody with a nice appearance and a smiling face, and someone who knows how to speak to people. Those would be my three main things. Not necessarily skills, because a lot of people that I've seen that come through here don't have a lot of skills."

The hoteliers and restaurateurs had many of the same preferences as their counterparts elsewhere, altered only by the mix of face-to-face interaction and physical labor that many jobs combined. A hotel manager who used "attitude" colloquially as a shorthand for "bad attitude," pointed out that "you cannot be in the industry with an attitude. You have to say, 'my pleasure,' 'whatever you need, I'll get it for you.' "

Manufacturers, by contrast, were also concerned with finding workers who would respond appropriately to unpredictable situations; for them, "attitude" entailed the qualities that would lead a worker to step up activities when the shop was under a "crunch" or let management know if production was not moving well. Still, our factory informants were more likely to emphasize the social dimension of work in giving such prominence to applicants' perceived state of mind. As we have emphasized earlier, production workers "have to work with the whole shop," and if "everybody is working in a team, and if you don't have the right attitude, it is difficult to work and get along with your co-workers. If you don't have the right attitude it affects your work, productivity, and profit."

Under these circumstances, it is little surprise to discover that manufacturers described a "bad attitude" as "contagious, making the environment in the workplace less desirable." They were similar to other employers in their efforts to stay away from those workers who spelled trouble. "It doesn't matter how good his ability," explained a furniture manufacturer, "if his attitude is getting bad . . . he's going to cause other problems." Still, the situation of workers at the entry level was a little different. On the one hand, employers expected entry-level workers to learn on the job, and thought the "right attitude" signaled something about the qualities involved in acquiring the needed shop-floor proficiencies; on the other hand, there was no compulsion to tolerate an unskilled worker who did not see things the boss's way:

> *Field notes*: R. says that "attitude" lumps everything together, including following directions, doing the best job you can, coming to work on time. The lower the skill level, the more attitude becomes important. "To a limited degree," if someone has great skills, you can overlook their bad attitude. "With a jogger, if they give us a little bit of trouble, whhhht [making a hitch-hiking motion with his thumb], [they're] out."

Only a minority of employers rated qualities directly related to prior work performance—stability, experience, and prior skills—as the most important attributes sought in a new recruit. The manufacturers dominated this group, accompanied by a sizable sprinkling of the hospital respondents. The furniture manufacturers were the most likely to prefer workers with either relevant experience or a requisite skill, seeking to reduce training costs whenever possible—an option facilitated by the availability of a large qualified labor force floating among the region's furniture factories.

A considerably larger, more mixed group of employers emphasized stability. "It's hard to measure attitude, it's impossible," contended a hospital manager who talked with us about hiring orderlies. Stability, in his view, provided a more reliable indicator, signaling the capacity both to stick with and learn a job and to fit in with established routines. Since the furniture manufacturers knew that they were not offering much— "hard labor and low wages, they don't last"—a stable work record promised greater longevity. The employers of factory help were particularly concerned with the consequences of interdependency on the job; not wanting to break the rhythm in the shop, managers were particularly concerned with finding workers who would come every day on time. Where the job was likely to involve training, employers also thought recouping their investment in skills more likely through hiring workers with stable records.

WHAT EMPLOYERS WANT

Thus we arrive at a paradox. At the very bottom of the labor market we find workers with little if any formal education, but few jobs that truly lack skill requirements. However, most require a proficiency that the person walking off the street, with no prior experience on the job, is unlikely to possess. And though there are certain clusters of dead-end jobs—housekeeping in a hotel being the best example—many of the unskilled, entry-level positions can lead to somewhat more demanding activities. Typically, workers acquire the relevant proficiencies on the job, which means that learning takes place through social interaction, not formal training or schooling. While some organizations will only hire newcomers already possessing the requisite competencies, anyone who picked up proficiencies on the job must have previously managed to fit in somewhere else.

Somewhat further up the hierarchy, jobs are more likely to be held by persons with what used to pass for a reasonable amount of formal schooling—a high school degree or more. Many of these jobs entail a service interaction. American industry has made an art out of routinizing interactive work, but all unpredictability cannot be squeezed out of transactions between human beings. To the extent that interactive work involves communication of information, it demands a proficiency no less "real" than the skills put to use in production (whether of a thing or of an idea). But interactive service providers are not just disinterested transmitters of information; they are trying to make a sell, a good part of which involves the creation of an impression and the presentation of a self not quite "true." The capacity for impression management is neither trivial nor universally shared, which is why sociologists describe interactive service work as "emotional labor." But the argument that interactive work requires "soft skills" obscures an uglier reality—the degree to which the provision of interactive services is just another con.

Given the modest skill demands of most employers, it is no surprise that "attitude" should rank so high among hiring criteria. To some extent, the importance attributed to attitude derives from the nature of the job; as the service interaction fundamentally involves the presentation of self, employers perceive "attitude" as the best indicator of the self to which the client is likely to be exposed. Even on the factory floor, isolated from contact with the clientele, the personal attributes of the worker influence the potential for task fulfillment, since most jobs involve some significant degree of cooperation and interdependency. And if we recall that the workplace is not simply the locus of an economic exchange but also entails a political relationship, in which management seeks to secure and maintain labor's subordination, then attitude, far better than "skill," signals the traits most keenly desired.[13]

Ultimately, our interests lie in the question of how categorically distinctive workers (e.g., women, teenagers, immigrants, Pakistanis, or African Americans) get attached to different types of jobs. We note that "categorical distinctiveness" is not an inherent property of a social group. Who categorizes, how, and when play a crucial role in determining which types of workers get distributed among positions of varying sorts. However, the fact that employers are looking for intangibles—attitude, propensity to interact with key others—is likely to make them particularly attentive to the easily indexical qualities of the groups with whom they interact. In light of the difficulties in probing for the "right attitude" or for the presence of "people skills," employers may have further motivation to use other characteristics of applicants, most notably ethnicity, as proxies for the qualities desired. Of course, this hypothesis presumes that managers perceive significant interethnic differences in attitudes and behavior—which indeed is the case, as we show later.

The social organization of work also makes membership in a community of some type (occupational, ethnic, etc.) a crucial influence on the opportunities that workers have to obtain skills. As seen, learning one's job and accomplishing one's task are often dependent on cooperation from others; absent acceptance, let alone assistance, one is in big trouble. To the extent that ethnic and occupational communities converge, members of the numerically dominant group not only find it easier to get started, but also find it easier to move up, especially in industries that resemble the cases we are examining, where most firms are small and careers often take the form of moves from one organization to another. Of course, the same factors impede access and mobility for numerical (as opposed to sociological) minorities.

Thus, contrary to conventional views with their reified notion of skills, workers are not simply sorted according to skill (clumsily and inappropriately measured in terms of years of schooling). Rather, getting a job largely depends on whom you know. Contacts matter not only for getting information but also for securing connections with incumbents who can actively deploy in one's support and help out against management and other laterally placed groups if necessary. Equally importantly, the necessary skills are socially constituted, inseparable not simply from getting things done, but from the people involved in the doing. Consequently, as we will see in the next chapter, social relations at the job determine the very language of work.

The Language of Work

The immigration debate seeks enlightenment, but too often involves a cacophony of voices talking at cross-purposes. The economists, for example, have been worrying whether immigrants are of "declining quality," a phrase which, translated into English, means that the skills of the most recent arrivals are less "favorable" than those of their predecessors. Although the controversy shows no clear resolution, we do know that a large portion of today's immigrants comes to the United States without the formal schooling that the typical employer takes for granted, and this lack of schooling, as the economists rightly note, impedes the immigrants' economic progress. What the economists forget to ask, however, is how these workers manage to get started, in the first place.

Ironically, this same unasked question lies at the heart of one of the liveliest immigration controversies, whether immigrants compete with natives for jobs. The question cannot be answered until one can identify groups of natives whom employers perceive to have skills comparable to the immigrants'. Unfortunately, we usually know very little about the task-related proficiencies of workers, a data problem that analysts typically solve by turning to an inaccurate but serviceable proxy: years of schooling completed. But if we go looking, in the capitals of immigrant America, for native-born workers with schooling levels as low as those possessed by immigrants, we come up with practically no one. Organizations employing immigrants must have a need for workers utterly lacking in skills as conventionally defined, or else they want workers whose proficiencies are only tenuously related to years of education.

Scholars studying the migration process evince little anxiety about immigrants' deficiencies in skills. These scholars note, quite correctly, that immigrants show up in the United States with the resources they need most: connections to people who can help them. To paraphrase a key observation from Douglas Massey's influential *Return to Aztlan*, Mexican *campesinos* may arrive without any formal schooling, but they are wealthy in social capital, which they can readily convert into jobs and earnings in the United States.[1] Massey is on target, but one still wonders how immigrants make that conversion successfully. It is good to have inside information about job opportunities; it is even better, as already noted, to enjoy contacts to others who can help one learn the work. But how, concretely, can social capital compensate if one lacks the core human capital required for the task at hand?

This intellectual problem derives from the fuzziness of some key concepts. Often we talk about skills as if they were attributes contained by jobs, with some sociologists telling us, for example, that "skill refers to . . . the level, scope, and integration of mental, interpersonal, and manipulative tasks *required* in a job."[2] But the job is not simply a matter of technique. Rather, it is embedded in some type of social organization, where contingent factors determine how the job is done and by whom. Whether the organization is new or old; how much of an upper hand management enjoys; the number and types of parties involved: all of these considerations affect the competencies called upon to accomplish a particular job. To be sure, technology, understood as the physical infrastructure though which things get done, exercises a powerful constraint on how work is done. However, the degree of constraint is variable: any given technology lends itself to application in any number of ways. So the crucial factor is often context, implying that the skills required will be related to the characteristics of the persons involved.

This is particularly so since the exercise of skill involves social action, as Stephen Barley has pointed out.[3] Skills are worthless if they reside passively in the person; they matter only if used. As the sociologists of work have shown, the crucial skills possessed by workers are frequently tacit, of the "I can do it but I can't tell you how," "I know it works but I don't know why" varieties. "Working knowledge" of this kind is often specific to a particular firm or shop; usually it is learned in concert with other workers; rarely is it freely shared with the boss. For these reasons, "working knowledge" entails power; the boss cannot effectively run his or her business without the cooperation of the incumbents, whose skills have been painstakingly acquired through trial and error on the job.

Of course, even hidden, tacit skills develop to fit the demands of a particular work situation; they are not constructed by workers arbitrarily. Skills also arise in a specific environment; the working knowledge obtained within a given organizational structure, a particular relationship between labor and management, or a set of machines or technologies may become irrelevant when a new way of doing business arrives.

Of course, nothing stays the same. The social order of the workplace is a dynamic equilibrium, shaped internally by relationships between workers and managers, and externally by the ties between the organization and its suppliers, customers, and regulators. When, for example, the minimum wage rises or customer tastes shift, management will attempt to adjust. As the parties negotiate the new arrangements under which work gets done, skill requirements can take an entirely different form.

To highlight this process, we focus on the language of work, since language is at once symbol and indicator of the profound transformations produced by immigration. As the instrument by which communication occurs, language is also a skill basic to nearly any job. Moreover, the language of work is precisely one of those "requirements" to which immigrants are expected to adapt; immigrants enter at the bottom, working in environments where English reigns. For that reason, the conventional view portrays the shift to English both as a sign of acculturation and as a mechanism of getting ahead. But, as we shall see, linguistic patterns change in a far more complex way, with dominants often changing in response to the expectations of their subordinates, and both dominants and subordinates reacting to the demands of other parties with whom they interact. Because language is the foundation for interaction, changes in the linguistic practices of workers and employers also alter the mechanisms by which jobs are sorted among categorically distinctive groups of workers.

TOWARD A LINGUISTIC DIVISION OF LABOR

America enjoys an unparalleled track record for obliterating the languages that immigrants bring, with English prevailing over any number of "mother tongues" in a pattern that is now fully predictable and documented in great detail.[4] In broad brush, the story reads as follows. The first generation retains the mother tongue for most purposes, switching to the dominant language to get by or get ahead, and only where its use is required. The immigrants' children may be exposed to the mother tongue at home, but as the dominant tongue rules in all other domains—the neighborhood, schools, and work—mother-tongue usage lapses, increasingly reserved for the parental home and even there used with diminishing frequency. The immigrants' grandchildren are at best passive bilinguals, retaining a smattering of mother-tongue expressions for use on special occasions but otherwise conversing exclusively in English. At the end of the chain, the fourth generation grows up as dominant-language monolinguals.

In this account, language *shift* is the result of long-term collective language choice.[5] Succeeding generations *switch* from original to dominant language with increasing frequency and across a growing number of domains; however, the process takes hold from the start. Work is a point of great vulnerability for less-skilled immigrants; they enter the new society in a situation of dependency, working under the authority of managers, supervisors, and skilled workers who usually are native speakers of the dominant tongue and expect immigrant underlings to adjust to their ways. Consequently, "the language associated with the means of production" provides the first occasion for mother-tongue displacement.[6] As the eminent sociolinguist Joshua Fishman has written, "relinguification occurs in nonmobile middle and even lower social classes to the extent that they become dependent on direct interaction with [dominant-language] speakers and the rewards that the latter control."[7]

By the same logic, immigrant self-sufficiency (or independence) can retard the process of relinguification. In the economic realm, independence involves some detachment from the mainstream economy. It follows, then, that employment in an immigrant (or ethnic) economy should lessen the pressure on newcomers to learn English, precisely through the reduced level of interaction with dominant-language customers, coworkers, and bosses. Along these lines, Alejandro Portes and Rubén Rumbaut have suggested that disparities in economic exposure to outsiders are likely to yield divergent effects among immigrant entrepreneurs. Immigrant owners of small businesses catering to non-ethnic clienteles—one thinks of Koreans, East Indians, or Arabs—may have to "learn some English to carry out transactions with their domestic customers." By contrast, Cuban business operators in Miami's Little Havana ethnic enclave enjoy "the possibility of conducting business in the mother tongue."[8] This difference leads to faster and more complete language acquisition among the former than the latter.[9]

If ethnic economies provide a protected space for mother-tongue use and maintenance, other instances of economic and social isolation may also reduce demands for use of the dominant language.[10] But circumstances of this sort are the exception, not the rule; more common is some form of economic dependency on dominant-language speakers, a fact that suggests that *switching* and *shifting* are likely to prevail. While foreign-language speakers may choose either to adopt or to reject the language used by the natives with whom they interact, switching is likely to be influenced by such characteristics of the parties involved as who holds higher status, who is present in greater numbers, or who receives the support and approval of the institutions dominating the exchange.[11] Low-skilled immigrants may benefit from strength of numbers in the workplace, but are unlikely to enjoy an advantage when it comes to status or institutional support. Therefore, we may expect that immigrant workers will adopt the language of their bosses rather than the reverse.

But we can also imagine a very different scenario. After all, "language encounters," as Everett C. Hughes wrote, "are a function of social organization," with the crucial variables being the nature of the communication within an organization and the nature of communication between an organization and its "audiences."[12] From this perspective, linguistic choices and behaviors are an organizational outcome, affected by the factors shaping other institutional patterns. Indeed, language policies and practices result from "the forces in play in each part of the communicational network" that exists inside the organization and links it to its environment.[13] Immigrant underlings are likely to come under pressure from native-born bosses to make English their lingua franca, but other relationships in the work setting—the language practices of co-workers and customers and the importance of communication with either—will also influence the language used by dominants *and* subordinates on the job.[14]

The linkage between an organization and its environment underlines the importance of *market*; a shift in the linguistic characteristics, preferences, or needs of the clientele creates an incentive for an organizational response. In general, migrants depend on institutions where communication involves the dominant language. However, dependency flows both ways, leading dominant-language speakers and their institutions, as well, to adjust.

Evidence supporting this view is not difficult to find. Studies of the sociolinguistic environment in cities on the United States–Mexico border add support to this notion. Richard Teschner's study of El Paso, for example, shows that growing Latino density has altered customer-directed linguistic practices in the city's business sector, with more bilingualism in banks and doctors' offices than before, and increasing numbers of retail establishments owned and operated by Mexican nationals, "who typically conduct all business in Spanish."[15] June Jaramillo tells a similar story for Tucson, where Spanish is increasingly used in public contexts, making Spanish "an effective marketing strategy in reaching Spanish-speaking patrons or clientele."[16]

To be sure, some organizations can happily ignore the immigrant outsiders—especially at the high end of the market, where social class is as solid a barrier to new immigrants as is language. But organizations catering to the mass market, of which immigrants are a part, cannot afford to neglect the large portion of their client base that has the option of patronizing linguistically friendlier businesses owned by co-ethnics.

The market and other forces external to the organization, however, are only part of the story. The economic sociology of immigration highlights instead the centrality of *non-market* processes involved in network migration, and thus of *intra*-organizational factors. As sketchily described in chapter 1 (and in greater detail in chapter 6), migration is lubricated by connections tying settlers to members of their home communities. Immigrants get jobs through their contacts; as one immigrant recruits others, and those recruit more, ethnic hiring networks reproduce themselves and grow. They also sever the linkage between the employer and the outside labor market, with hiring opportunities rationed to insiders' referrals, part of a quid pro quo between incumbents and employers.[17] Thus, networks derive both economic functions and social power from their potential to restrict entry into the workplace to insiders.[18]

The language of work, therefore, need not be that of the host country. While studies of assimilation tell us that immigrants learn English as they adapt to the requirements of their new home, an alternative is imaginable: the deep immigrant penetration into the economies of American cities instead brings a multitude of foreign languages into the workplace. Consequently, it is the bosses and supervisors who accommodate to the linguistic needs and preferences of the newcomers, *not the other way around*. The linguistic preferences of immigrant co-workers and customers may have the further effects of driving out native English speakers, who cannot get the work done because the lingua franca is a foreign tongue, or of excluding natives when employers opt to hire workers who can speak more than one language.[19] Thus, growing foreign-language densities can further diminish pressures for English-language use at work, as we shall now see.

ISOLATION AND EMPLOYER ACCOMMODATION

Although part of the "mainstream economy," the hotels, restaurants, and furniture factories of Los Angeles seem to be following a path of linguistic accommodation with their immigrant work forces. Cleaning and cooking jobs "don't require any English skills whatsoever," noted a hotelier. The same holds for production work, where "you could do it without knowing English. Fifty percent of my workers have been here twenty years and they still have not learned English." As employers see it, the workers' encapsulation in a Spanish-speaking world derives from the nature of the jobs the employers provide: "In the case of a steward or dishwasher who hardly has guest interaction, when you can't find someone who speaks English, we would waive the requirement, because, let's face it, there aren't that many English-language people who would be dishwashers."

It was not only grunt work in the service sector that seemed to attract a similar labor supply. Factory managers had the same problem; one respondent, for example, who had been searching for a driver, "couldn't find anyone who spoke English. All the applicants were Hispanic."

Although most managers in hotels, restaurants, and furniture manufacturing grumbled about the perceived linguistic deficiencies of their immigrant workers, most had taken the path of least resistance. "[W]e would prefer that they speak English, but they speak Spanish," exclaimed one manufacturer; "we try to encourage the workers to speak English," noted another, with resignation, "but it is very difficult." The Latino preponderance in a steak-house kitchen ensured that "English is the second language" in the back of the house. A maker of high-priced furniture, trying to make the transition to an English-proficient workforce, as part of an effort to upgrade the product, hoped that "soon everybody will be able to communicate in English" so that the firm could "hire an English-speaking foreman." "While I say that they need to speak English," conceded a hotel manager, "the reality is that their English is very limited." One of the more technologically advanced furniture companies we visited gives basic skills tests in Spanish; in a second, "all the interviews are done in Spanish"; in a third, the lead men, who provide the informal, on-the-job training, are Spanish-speaking. The prevalence of Spanish in these workplaces is such that English attains the status of a "foreign" tongue. "The job that we are talking about does not require communication of a foreign language, *meaning English*," notes one employer. "They really don't have to read much because in many cases the information is given to them in Spanish."

But not only have employers hired foremen and other intermediaries from immigrant communities, they have decided "if you can't beat 'em, join 'em," which in this case means that managers learn Spanish themselves, or make other necessary adaptations. A furniture manufacturer told us that "both floor managers speak 'Mexican,' so it is not that important that the workers speak English." One hotel chain requires managers "to have basic understanding of Spanish," an accomplishment matched, if not bettered, by a furniture factory in the Los Angeles industrial belt, where "everybody is bilingual," including the production manager, who "is Caucasian and speaks perfect Spanish." In an interview that focused on warehouse workers, a department store manager first told us that "English is not required, because we all had to take Spanish to communicate with them" and later commented that "if there were no immigrants, I wouldn't have had to take Spanish!" Speaking about the "tight Hispanic group" that works in the kitchen of one of Los Angeles's best-known steak houses, a respondent reported that "English is the second language. Most of the communication in back is in Spanish." A third-generation Mexican-American supervisor told us: "The language barrier is very important; that is why a lot of people in my position wouldn't make it. You need to speak the language. How could I make them do and understand what I wanted them to do? I didn't know a word of Spanish before I went to work."

Thus, in hotels, restaurants, and furniture manufacturing, reliance on network hiring has had the result that employers must accommodate workers' linguistic practices. *Market* can, however, be a limiting factor. For example, because furniture factories sell to wholesalers and retailers who interact only with sales staff, linguistic practices among workers on the shop floor are of little import. The language spoken by lower-level employees is more important in restaurants and hotels, which cater to a diverse, largely English-speaking customer base, not entirely removed from interaction with the staff. Still, the core of the job entails doing, not talking, which is why management, not ready to pay the freight needed to secure a workforce fully capable of speaking in English, accommodates the linguistic needs of its immigrant employees.

COMPLEXITY, DIVERSITY, EXPOSURE, AND ENGLISH

Printing and the English-Speaking Customer

In other industries, differences in organizational complexity, workforce diversity, and market exposure yielded greater pressure for switching to English. Spanish was the most prevalent foreign language in printing, dominating certain low-skilled areas, such as bindery work. The bindery excepted, Spanish often competed with other foreign languages as well as with English. One firm, for example, reported use of English, Spanish, Thai, Tagalog, and sign language among employees; another mentioned a Chinese supervisor from Malaysia who spoke Malaysian, English, Cantonese, and Spanish with the workers; in a third, English was used for business purposes but Vietnamese and Spanish were employed on the shop floor, where, also, one person spoke Armenian on the phone.

In this complicated linguistic environment, employers made do, but the effort did not create much joy. Some resorted to managing through a translator, a stratagem that produced its share of hiccups:

> *Field notes:* If she can't talk with them because of language differences, she gets her "best translator." One translator makes her seem more forceful, another makes what she says seem less forceful. She tries to communicate through a neutral translator.

Such problems led one manager to remark "I hate it when I have to have a translator." Another observed that "most employers and workers resent being forced to deal with multiple languages on the job"; as his shop ran all training programs on a costly bilingual basis, dollars-and-cents considerations undoubtedly fed his ill-temper.

The imperative for cooperation across ethnic and linguistic boundaries generated a strong push toward English. Many departments had a mix of people and, consequently, numerous printing firms insisted that English be spoken on the job—a policy absent from furniture or hotels or restaurants. "They can't interview unless it's in English. English is for your work. If you want to speak a foreign language, you can do it on your own time." Interdependency made effective communication an imperative, especially since the most skilled workers were most likely to be Anglophones.

> *Field notes:* The respondent says that if he were in Indiana, the matter of speaking English probably would not come up. "If a pressman gets caught in the press, he wants to be able to tell someone how to get him out." Later, he added this comment: "It may sound anti-Mexican, but speaking English

is important. Even when Mexicans become legal, they tend to drag their feet on speaking English." [This respondent] says the equipment is expensive, but the safety factor is the most important: "You have to be very careful because it's a dangerous piece of equipment."

Foreign-language monolingualism also carried a cost in flexibility; a Spanish-speaking feeder, for example, could be successfully deployed alongside a bilingual pressman, but trouble was in store if the next pressman could speak only English. Even a Spanish-speaking bindery worker "could not be left alone by himself without some sort of supervision. I couldn't supervise him," explained a manager, "because I don't speak Spanish. That would be a problem." The fact that jobs were not routinized and were subject to unpredictable changes made precise communication more important. As one printer related, "There are times that . . . the client calls me, they need something to get done, and if I cannot tell [the workers] exactly what I want to say, it isn't gonna work right."

The preference for promotion from within also ran up against the linguistic limitations of the entry-level work force. Language problems tractable at the lowest levels were more difficult to manage when the linguistic context became more complex. "The pressman [must be capable] of reading English; that's when it becomes important. For helpers, English is not so important. But to become a pressman, you better know English." Another respondent similarly told us that when "customers come in for a press check, and if the salesmen's not here, the pressmen have to talk with the customer. I haven't run into pressmen who can't speak English; most are bilingual."

Retail and the Mixed Masses

Pressures to use English are stronger in department stores. To be sure, the retail sector is swept by the currents of linguistic change in the region. Managers made clear that there is no shortage of foreign-language speakers among their employees. One reported hiring "associates who speak Spanish, Farsi," or "lots of Armenian," while another listed "English, Spanish, Tagalog," and added "I have a whole mix of all of the Baltics, Russians; we have some Yugoslavs, Czechs, a little bit of Dutch . . ."

Far less encapsulated than the manufacturers, and serving a mixed public, retailers also respond to the region's shifting ethnic mix so as to attract the newest Angelenos, seeking to "pick up more and more Hispanic customers" by advertising in Spanish and "using the Spanish-speaking [broadcast] stations." The changing clientele leads the retailers to conclude that "the employee base has to reflect the customer base." In one instance, that employee base may be "white, because it matches the demographics of the area," but in another, "to match our store to the people who come to the store," managers "try hard to have Spanish-speaking people and the Middle Eastern language group—Persians, Iranians, Afghans, Armenian." "We do have associates who speak to customers in Spanish, Farsi, et cetera, if the customer feels more comfortable that way," noted a manager of a mainline department store. A discounter, "catering to a high degree of an ethnic background" and trying to "hire from the community," felt that persons with "strong Spanish accents or whatever" could easily fit into the store. Numerous interviewees agreed with the assessment of one chainstore manager that "if the associate speaks a language other than English, that helps."

Thus, in retail, speaking foreign tongues was frequently permissible; speaking English with an accent was also acceptable "if I can understand them and they can understand me." Still, the stores wanted English to remain the lingua franca. Not that they were always successful in this regard:

> R: Language is a major problem. If I went to the North Hollywood store, I would not be able to survive there. The majority of their workforce is Spanish-speaking, and I cannot speak Spanish.
>
> I: Then what does your certificate [mounted on the wall] mean?
>
> R: That I went to class! I didn't say I learned anything there. They have a personnel manager who's bilingual. They couldn't just put any personnel manager in there.

As the final comment suggests, department stores were making organizational adaptations to the new linguistic environment, although not with great effectiveness or as quickly as desired. "We have bilingual management for the most part," a discounter told us—"pretty much all Latino, although not as much as our customer base." Managers also thought it appropriate to "have a lot of bilingual people" interacting with "a lot of Spanish-speaking customers." Most, however, contended that "we wouldn't have people working here with no English ability." "They need to know the English language," said one manager, and "on the selling floor, they must speak English," noted another. As with the printers and the hospitals, English facility had a bearing on successful task completion. Thus, while a store might conclude that "it helps if the person is bilingual—that's better than just speaking English"—the same retailer would insist that "the most important thing is an understanding of the English; it underlies other skills, such as interaction and reading."

Customer diversity provided an even stronger reason for the insistence on English: "We need them to speak English. We have a very diverse ethnic population in our company and in the stores." Clearly, language differences between workers and customers were a potential source of tension, which many managers wanted to alleviate. "We have customers complaining [using a whining voice] that 'they can't speak English and they live in California.'" Part of this customer dissatisfaction undoubtedly related to ethnocentric feelings among Anglos, but Anglos were not the only customers prone to ethnocentric sentiments. "The Baldwin Hills store is definitely an African-American population," noted a regional personnel manager, adding, "from a language standpoint, there have been situations when I've had to tell workers to speak English on the floor."[20] Moreover, adverse reaction went beyond Spanish. One manager fretted about customer complaints "in the downtown stores, [where] the Filipino workers would speak to each other in Tagalog." Another complained about "the Middle Eastern, who is intent upon using their native language instead of English." And when immigrant salespersons spoke Spanish, Farsi, or Tagalog, adverse reactions arose for reasons unrelated to foreignness as such. Sometimes, "other parts of the work force doesn't know what they are talking about"; in other instances, there was "the American customer who gets offended when he or she hears associates speaking in another language, and gets offended, thinking they're talking or laughing about them." Consequently, managerial tolerance of linguistic diversity often had its limits: "I give them a bad time about [using other languages], but I realize that you're always going to go back to your natural source. And Tagalog is spoken heavy here, but I always go up to them and pinch them or tease them and say 'This is an English-speaking country' . . . I give them a bad time about it, but not on a negative level. I will get angry, though, if they're conversing amongst themselves in the cashier environment."

Hospitals: Clear Communication Can Be a Matter of Life and Death

The linguistic environment in hospitals at once resembles and differs from the evolving situation in department stores. In contrast to employers of seemingly similar low-skilled help, hospitals require more—and more complex—information to be communicated. Likewise, communication is more likely to require two-way exchange. In contrast to comparably low-level workers employed on a factory floor or in a kitchen, where contact is limited to co-workers, the least-skilled hospital workers labor in an interactional structure that involves a great deal of incidental contact with people, whether customers or co-workers. This generalization also holds true for those hospital workers whose jobs do not formally have anything to do with customer service.

Moreover, hospitals emphasize formal communications skills, mainly because workers need to understand complex written instructions. Reading English is of major importance; if the housekeepers or other bottom-level employees "can't read what the doctors or the nurses said about this patient's room, that could put them in danger as well." Low-level workers who lacked the ability to read English spelled trouble; one food service manager told us, "I've got some illiterate people and it's very difficult." And, with hospitals downsizing and requiring a more multivalent workforce, there appears to be less tolerance for monolingual workers: "There used to be a time when we could hire someone who could not speak English, but that changed four to five years ago. The system is too fast; there's no time for hand-holding."

Clientele and staff diversity also yield strong pressures for workers to know and use English, even for the most unskilled jobs involved in cleaning or food preparation. As one hospital manager told us, "we're really trying to promote and encourage people to speak English," a prime consideration being that "if there's an emergency situation, you know, these instructions are more often than not given in English." Further, patients "get apprehensive [when] they don't understand what other people are talking about."[21]

While emphasizing the importance of English, many hospitals made allowances for linguistic switching when workers moved from public areas to "behind-the-scenes" settings: "If they talk Tagalog or Chinese, say, on the job, we will not tolerate it long. This is an English-speaking facility. On break, in the cafeteria, I don't care what language they speak, but in patient areas, they should be speaking English." The typical hospital policy allowed for a distinction among domains, granting legitimacy to foreign language use in workers' private interactions, but casting English as the only language spoken by employees in work areas, "so that patients don't feel that they're being talked about," or because English was the "language spoken in the Medical Center, and by customers and supervisors." Yet managers were less than happy to observe immigrant workers conversing in their own language when not conducting business. Given the large number of Filipino immigrants in the local health care industry, it was common to hear management complaints like this: "The Filipino workers that work here are, I would consider them rude, because they get in a group, and they speak their language, and no one else around can understand. And I've heard that throughout the hospital. I just find that to be rude. They're saying it's just part of their culture."

As in the other industries, English speakers, whether staff or patients, evince "a lot of dissatisfaction with people who speak another language" in their presence. Even when workers acquire English skills, communication problems do not disappear. First, hospital managers are apt to observe, as one has: "We have so many different thick, thick accents that sometimes somebody, say that it's Filipino talking to somebody of a different nationality, [they] have difficulty understanding each other's feelings. Both of their accents are thick. They may be speaking English, but it's thick." Second, hospitals in the region have benefited from an influx of foreign-born doctors and nurses who may share neither language nor cultural understandings with native workers or with patients and workers of different foreign origins. Thus, linguistic and cultural translations between patients and doctors may be a process of two or more steps—from the culture and language of the patient, into that of the mainstream culture, and then into words and meanings most clearly understood by the health practitioner.

To some extent, management complaints can be read as a barometer of more general reactions to shifts in the regional (not only occupational) linguistic environment. Consider the manager who told us that "when I see people walking in the hallways speaking Spanish to their kids, it's just one thing that drives me nuts" or the comment by an otherwise liberal personnel officer who worried that "pretty soon, people like myself are going to be required to be bilingual." But the complaints were also motivated by the real problems involved in managing a "Tower of Babel" where neither workers nor customers could take clear communication for granted:

R: When you're working with your employees and English is supposed to be the language in the workplace, that has been a very difficult thing to try to enforce.

I: Because people are talking to each other in other languages?

R: Oh yeah, and, you know, here it's Tagalog, and here it's something else, and, you know, I've approved it in situations to try to clarify something, but you need to get back to English.

Thus, it was clear that hospitals sought workers possessing basic English proficiency, at the least. But hospitals did hire workers who lacked any capacity to communicate in English, who nonetheless proved able to perform their duties. So bottom-level workers could survive with little or no English proficiency, but not without creating difficulties for the organizations in which they worked. Hospitals also faced challenges in serving a clientele with little or no English. The needs to serve this growing population—"We have a lot of Spanish-speaking members that come in, and we call for translation a lot"—resulted in pressure to ensure employees with the appropriate foreign-language skills. "We desperately need bilingual people," reported a manager in a facility with a large black workforce. Many hospitals viewed bilingualism as a plus: "Many of the positions that we have are bilingual. So I will look at, 'Do they speak Spanish?' Yep, well, then they go into another stack. Not that I discriminate based on [being] bilingual, but it's something that is a skill that is used here, required of many jobs."

A manager in a county facility told us that "to a large extent, people who have bilingual abilities are wanted, because our patient mix is heavily non-English speakers at certain of our locations." Interest was still greater at an HMO ardently trying to develop a niche servicing the area's new multiethnic population. "Bilingualism is the big thing," we heard, although our respondent conceded this was "hard to find." Another hospital offered a premium to bilingual employees: "If you translate for 50 percent of your job, we give you like sixty cents extra an hour. You get a lot of money for that. And the badges say, 'Yo hablo Español,' so if they can't find something, they know you speak Spanish, so. . . . It's a plus if you're bilingual."

However, bilingualism, unlike facility in English, was a preference, never requisite. "Being bilingual is not required," reported a manager in an Eastside hospital, "but it is an asset." Similarly, a manager who noted that "it is important to be bilingual" when filling a clerical job also reported that "I have not had a requisition come down that requested a specific person who was bilingual." The rewards of being bilingual, then, were neither typically immense nor always trivial. These rewards, further, were more likely to be enjoyed by second-generation Americans whose English skills met the requisite standards than by immigrants, whose strength in Spanish or Vietnamese did not compensate for a lack of facility in the local tongue.

LANGUAGE AND THE EMPLOYMENT OF IMMIGRANTS

The linguistic shifts described above are both products of and contributors to the processes that exclude less-skilled native-born workers from segments of the labor market.[22] Relying on referrals to recruit workers detaches job vacancies in the industries studied from the general labor market. Where there are few demands to serve English-language customers, the networks powerfully reinforce linguistic isolation, even to the point of requiring languages other than English. "Since the supervisor is Hispanic, you have to speak Spanish to get hired," explains a hotel manager. "You cannot get hired if you only speak English." In sum, network hiring can allow a linguistic minority to establish monopoly control over a set of jobs and, when the characteristics of the job permit, to use language to exclude those who only speak another tongue.

Employers in immigrant-dense industries like hotels, restaurants, or furniture manufacturing make deliberate efforts to widen the linguistic spectrum of the applicant pool, as in one factory that, in a deliberate effort to avoid undocumented applicants, switched from reliance on referrals to reliance on newspapers and specifically advertised for workers who could "read, speak, and write English." However, others have given up efforts to obtain English speakers, even when recruiting from the open market: "We tend to go to the Spanish papers like *The Opinion [La Opinión]* because a lot of these people are Spanish that work in these furniture factories."[23]

By contrast, linguistic encapsulation is not on the horizon in industries or work situations involving contact with an English-speaking clientele or labor force. Here, interdependency links entry-level work to a linguistically diverse population in which English speakers retain dominance, if only for the moment. Thus, demands for English may actually work to the benefit of less-skilled native-born workers, as explained by one hospital HR manager: "The only real difference is that with black men . . . I typically don't need to worry about English as a second language. Whereas with somebody from a different country, I need to be concerned with their ability to speak English. So I might put, . . . I might choose a black man for an area that is more accessible to the public, so that . . . because our environmental service techs are asked directions all the time in our hospital. So I might put somebody with better English in a position where they're going to deal more with the general public." Moreover, most such jobs demand a modicum of English-language speaking and, often, reading ability, with even the lowly "environmental service technicians" (*hospitalspeak* for janitorial workers) expected to communicate with doctors, nurses, and patients and absorb written information relating to environmental hazards and the threat of disease.

Printing departs from both the hospital and department store cases, as it involves much lower levels of client interaction. But, like the hospitals, the printing plants have an elaborate division of labor, arranging jobs such that workers at different levels of the hierarchy labor in tandem. Entry-level Spanish speakers thus fall under pressure to conform to the linguistic practices of the more skilled, generally Anglophone, workers, as both are likely to be working together on the same machine. Even when workers of Mexican origin occupy those blue-collar positions involving the greatest physical exertion, expectations for effective communication with Anglophone clients make bilingualism a condition for the jobs.

If hospitals, department stores, and printing shops maintain a continuing demand for English speakers, they operate in an increasingly multilingual environment, which inevitably adds another facility that low-skilled native-born applicants generally lack. For those monolingual natives already on the job, the new linguistic environment is likely to be yet another source of frustration and alienation (as we shall describe in chapter 10).

Further, while demands to serve non-English speakers will grow, so will the availability of bilingual speakers. Managing the multilingual selling force of Middle Easterners, Filipinos, and Spanish speakers has not always proved easy for Los Angeles department stores, but on balance the staffs' language skills are a plus, since otherwise the stores could not serve the clientele they need. In hospitals, where the children of immigrants with the baseline skills needed to work as dietary aides or housekeepers are entering the workforce in growing numbers, this second generation will, to the extent its members have some facility in two languages, increasingly have an advantage over native-born blacks. "We have a large ethnic patient population and, to an extent, our patients' access to medical care has improved with having people that they can communicate with. So one of our objectives is having a diverse workforce which mirrors our diverse patient population."

The need for bilinguals, touched on above, is particularly acute in precisely that sector where blacks are most overrepresented: the public hospitals, which also are the facilities most heavily used by Latino immigrants. This trend will grow as the foreign-born presence increases, producing yet another factor weakening African Americans' hold on this traditional niche.

CONCLUSION

Thus, the story of linguistic change at the workplace helps explain how immigrant workers with few of the formal skills desired by employers manage to beat a path into America's economy. Of course, immigrants have to adjust, adapting to the needs of the work world around them. But that world changes, as immigrant numbers grow and foreign-born densities thicken. The massive entry of immigrants into the workforce, combined with the hold of immigrant networks over the hiring process in immigrant industries and occupations, yields linguistic accommodation with a twist, as bosses and supervisors adapt to the linguistic needs and preferences of the newcomers, *and not the other way around.* In other parts of the economy, pressures motivate employers to find bilingual or multilingual workers, even while trying to convince non-English monolingual workers to gain familiarity with English. In either case, linguistic outcomes are not determined at the start; rather they reflect the influence of history and context and the ongoing negotiations among workers, bosses, and customers.

PART THREE

From Market to Work

CHAPTER 5

Network, Bureaucracy, and Exclusion

Whom you know has much to do with what you do. Most job-seekers activate their social connections to find jobs. Employers use ties linking the workers whom they know to the new people they may like to hire. Why do social networks so heavily influence the way workers find jobs and bosses find help?

The answer has several parts. First, networks serve as conduits for *information*, telling job-seekers about opportunities and informing employers about the characteristics of applicants. Second, the same social connections function as instruments of *influence*, allowing job-seekers to put themselves on the "inside track" by proxy. Third, social ties can be used to enforce *obligations*, so that the employer is assured that the favors he or she does for the job-seeker and his or her accomplices will be repaid. Fourth, networks, as carriers of both information and obligations, can cement *implicit contracts* regarding the rights and responsibilities of each party to the employment exchange. To the extent that a group of workers feels bound by these understandings, the employer can count on its exercise of social control to keep recalcitrant fellows in line.

So goes current sociological wisdom, emphasizing the efficiency advantages of *social* over *market* forces. The revisionist arguments resonate powerfully with the migration literature, which has come to recognize that the connections between veterans in the new society and would-be migrants in the old provide the matrix in which movement and settlement take place. This chapter builds on these now-accepted understandings but adds a twist. On the one hand, we develop a new conceptual framework that goes beyond the usual efficiency emphasis; underlining the resources gained by immigrants as their networks implant, we explain how immigrants can use these resources to expand their employment base, in ways that yield conflict both horizontally and vertically. On the other hand, we note that social connections, while important, are not everything; immigrants work in organizations whose characteristics still limit potential for network expansion. We conclude that the interaction between network and bureaucracy bounds the potential scope of immigrant employment.

SOCIAL NETWORKS, RECRUITMENT, AND HIRING

Social-network theory represents the most distinctively sociological and the most successful sociological contribution to our understanding of international migration. Although network theory does not explain the *activation* of migration streams, it does identify a fundamental feature of almost all migrations, one that tells us why these migrations, once begun, tend to persist.

The argument is simple. Social networks provide the mechanisms for connecting an initial, highly selective group of seedbed immigrants with a gradually growing base of followers from back home. These contacts rest on social relationships developed before the migration decision. Most important are ties of kith and kin, in which trust is taken for granted; connections of this sort provide the confidence needed to hold networks together and make them function as durable, efficient conduits for the flow of resources, primarily information and social support. With migration a self-feeding phenomenon, almost everyone in the home community enjoys access to a contact abroad.[1]

The appeal of network theory is not difficult to understand. It illuminates the embedding of apparently individual decisions in social structures, overturning older, individualistic views of migration while providing a long-sought linkage between macro and micro levels of analysis. Better yet, it provides a rare item for sociological export to the economists, who for better or worse can be shown that the consideration of migrant networks enriches the discussion of migration while neatly fitting into their usual cost-benefit frameworks, requiring no major theoretical modifications.[2]

Gaps in Network Theory

Positions of Authority   However productive and illuminating, network theory remains incomplete. To begin with, network theory is a supply-side theory of immigration, emphasizing a "universal logic [that] takes hold as the network is extended and elaborated, binding [home country] institutions more tightly to specific destinations in the United States."[3] Perhaps it is true, as Douglas Massey and his collaborators argue, that: "[A]ll that is necessary for a migrant network to develop is for one person to be in the right place at the right time and obtain a position that allows him to distribute jobs and favors to others from his community." But this formulation suffers from its inevitabilism: should we take it on faith that "eventually someone achieves a position of authority . . . and begins to recruit fellow townspeople for work"?[4] More importantly, it begs logically anterior questions. How does it happen that authority positions open up to socially stigmatized outsiders? And when such positions do open up, how do immigrants, often classified among those outsiders, gain the power to hand out valued resources to needy friends and kin?

Part of the problem involves the *explananda*: network theory is an account of social reproduction. We need first to understand how outsiders insert themselves into a structure from which they have previously been excluded; to answer that question, we need an explanation of social *discontinuity*. We have offered just such an account in chapter 1 (with further elaborations to follow in chapters 8, 9, and 11, where we discuss the job preferences of native-born workers).

For now, we note that all workers at the bottom of the labor market engage in extensive churning; applying for entry-level jobs at higher rates than others, immigrants gradually concentrate in these slots. As the number of immigrants able to help a friend or family member get and keep a position increases, the ranks of lowest-level workers increasingly are filled from immigrant networks; given bosses' preference to recruit from inside, the immigrant presence grows.

Such an explanation tells us why there are lots of immigrant floor sweepers and kitchen helpers. However, if, as network theories contend, migration involves a self-feeding process,[5] then the networks must constantly expand. True, newcomers might simply crowd out others at the very bottom, but this would only monopolize the least desirable jobs. So the networks must be expanding upward as well as outward. The question is how.

Fishing the Lake Dry   Migration networks function as "personal information fields," expanding the quantity and quality of information available to newcomers and simultaneously confining them to the options accessible through their necessarily circumscribed ties.[6] Information constraints lead to channelization, which, according to Douglas Massey's influential account, in turn produces immigrant convergence on a limited number of places[7] and, eventually, immigrant clustering in a narrow set of occupations and industries. Given the low skills of many immigrants, saturation should be quickly achieved, and the upper limit for immigrant network penetration rapidly attained.

Comparing various applications of network theory gives further ground to expect trouble. When addressing how immigrants find jobs, the typical network approach tells a story about the "strength of strong ties."[8] In situations characterized by multiplex networks, Alejandro Portes notes, "community norms proliferate and violations of reciprocity obligations carry heavy costs."[9] In highly networked communities, everyone knows everyone else, allowing *enforceable trust* to function as an economic *modus vivendi*, but Mark Granovetter's[10] celebrated hypothesis about the "strength of weak ties" tells us that this supposed virtue can also be a vice: dense, overlapping networks choke off the flow of new information, constraining diffusion and the search for new opportunities. Ronald Burt's theory of "structural holes"[11] also tells us that competitive advantage, whether in the search for new business or in the quest to climb the corporate ladder, involves connecting to nonredundant contacts. Thus, the optimal situation takes the form of connections to others whom one's associates *do not know*: one moves ahead by activating weak ties that cut through structural holes, thus breaking away from the pack.

But immigrant ties are unlikely to work in this fashion. For one thing, network studies tell us that with increased education both the number of contacts and the advantages that they generate increase.[12] Put differently, immigrants' social traits are associated with network structures unlikely to yield the same rewards as those of the middle class. Moreover, immigrant networks link one to associates whom *every* other relevant actor knows. For that reason, immigrant networks threaten to funnel the latest arrivals into a narrow tier of the economy, where they will shortly saturate demand and from which their limited skills will make exit difficult. For these reasons, the channelization of low-skilled immigrants should bring any self-feeding process to a choking halt.

Social Closure   In actuality, immigrants appear quite able to push up the job ladder where they cluster, avoiding saturation. We argue that the term *social closure* best describes the mechanism through which low-skilled immigrants, burdened with disadvantages, manage to steadily expand their employment base, first horizontally, then vertically.

Tying down the meaning of *social closure* is complicated, as the sociological literature employs the concept in two distinct, although related, ways. The most popular use focuses on relationships within a group or community. According to James Coleman, for example, a "closed" social structure would be one characterized by multiple, overlapping contact among all parties to a given interaction. Relationships of this sort produce a "feeling" and "fear" complex that keeps the relationship in place. On one hand, ongoing contacts within the circle generate the sense of belonging that makes it possible to help out the other even when one's own resources are stretched. With time, *you* and *I* become *we*: the greater my sentiment for you, and the more experiences we have shared, the deeper my conviction that you are someone I can trust. On the other hand, the common ties connecting the linked associates rein in any urges toward betrayal or deviation from the group norm. My friends are your friends, which is why I am worried about the sanctions the group might enforce if I break with its expectations.

Migration networks tend to be closed, in precisely this sense. Migration is risky, and the poor, low-skilled migrants with whom we are concerned here have too few resources to extend without care; thus, support gets directed toward one's closest ties and those contacts one knows best. Migrants may have little, but what they have, they can share, making exclusive use of the resources that the network collectively possesses.

By definition, these resources comprise social capital. As Portes has written, "social capital refers to the capacity of individuals to command scarce resources *by virtue of their membership* in networks or broader social structures."[13] The social closure involved in membership in migrant networks helps newcomers precisely because it is also valuable to others. Employers greatly appreciate the social-closure property of the migrant networks through which they hire; the interdependency between migrant veterans and newcomers increases the likelihood that sponsors can actually control the behavior of those they refer. Moreover, the social structures built up through migration can give newcomers an edge in using connections to affect behavior; relative to native-born members of the host society only weakly tied to their associates, migrants may be better positioned to exercise influence, precisely because migrant networks take such a closed form.

Thus, the social-closure potential of immigrant networks generally receives a positive gloss in the immigration literature. Immigration scholars note an additional virtue: closed relationships in the immigrant community ward off undesirable influences emanating from the host society. Such appreciation, however, tends to minimize, if not overlook, a less desirable feature of the newcomers' networks: immigrant social capital is available only for members of the club.

Here, we return to a theme first enunciated by Max Weber: social closure entails the exercise of power in a broader field of social relations. Always concerned about legitimation of the exercise of power, Weber wrote, "One group of competitors, takes some externally identifiable characteristics of another group . . . of competitors—race, language, religion, local or social origin, descent, residence, etc.—as a pretext for attempting their exclusion."[14] Like Coleman, Weber talked of "closed" social structures, but in the context of a broader discussion of differences between "open" and "closed" relationships. In the Weberian view, some interactions are available to any interested participant; others can be accessed by insiders only. As Rogers Brubaker explains: "A pick-up softball game, for example, may be open, while a game played by teams belonging to an organized league may be restricted to team members, and in this sense closed. Retail commerce is usually open to all buyers, though less often, unconditionally, to all sellers. Worship, conversation, fights, neighborhoods, countries—all may be open or more or less closed."[15]

From the Weberian standpoint, then, social closure is defined as much by the external factors governing a given group's relationship to others as by the conditions shaping the group's internal relationships. The ability to close relationships *internally* is useful for spreading resources among members of a deprived group; if relationships can also be closed *externally*, then social collectivities can maximize their own rewards by limiting access to resources and opportunities to those already within the circle.

Exclusionary Closure: Against Peers   Social closure is likely to be most efficiently used against outsiders whose social standing and position is similar, but not quite equal, to the condition of those insiders that have gained control over some rare, valued resource. Where labor is ethnically segmented, closure is exercised against laterally placed groups, circumscribing opportunities to all but members of the inside group. While social relations embed economic behavior in an ethnic community, and thereby enhance the ease and efficiency of economic exchanges among community members, these connections implicitly exclude outsiders. Indeed, the more that ethnic economic actors are embedded in dense, many-sided relations, the stronger are the mechanisms, and the greater the motivations, for excluding outsiders.

Network recruitment offers the opportunity to detach the hiring process from the open market, allowing insiders to ration openings to their referrals; consequently, one ethnic group's ability to mobilize resources through social structure becomes a barrier limiting another group's chances for advancement. The prospects of recruiting others of one's "own kind" provides further impetus for the spread of network recruitment; *exclusionary closure*, to borrow Frank Parkin's terminology,[16] occurs when ethnically distinctive insiders attempt to monopolize job opportunities for members of their core network.

Usurpationary Closure: Against Hierarchical Superiors Employers generally see advantages in the close-knit nature of immigrant networks. So too does the sociological literature, which tells us that informal hiring practices can perform more efficiently than more open, formal processes.[17] But, as noted, these consequences derive from the social-closure *potential* generated by the linkages between newcomers and incumbents; when immigrants actually attain closure over a set of jobs, network recruitment can alter the balance sheet, circumscribing the employer's options and therefore imposing significant costs.

Consider management and labor. Incumbent workers are well positioned to exercise influence over the hiring process, whether management likes it or not. First, established workers have access to inside information and may know immediately about job openings. Second, since many, if not most, work processes involve some degree of interdependence among workers, new recruits have to get along with the old-timers to produce. Third, trainees and unskilled hires usually learn key competencies on the job from established workmates, which means that management must enjoy the cooperation of incumbents to integrate new workers. For these reasons, management ignores the hiring preferences of the core workforce group at its peril.

Of course, these preferences are often compatible with management objectives—but not always. Less-skilled workers are usually hunting for work under conditions of job scarcity. In these circumstances, workers seek to maximize employment opportunities for their kin and associates, a goal unlikely to coincide with management objectives. Consequently, the ties that bind the workforce comprise a resource that workers can use to expand the scope of network hiring *against* management preferences. In this instance, the group attempts to gain what Frank Parkin has called *usurpationary closure,* asserting its power upwards, biting into the resources and privileges of the dominant group.[18]

NETWORK VERSUS MARKET

Factors related to efficiency and power explain why the implantation of ethnic networks among formally "open" organizations enlarges opportunities for low-skilled ethnic insiders while reducing access to outsiders. But if network hiring is extensive, it is not all-pervasive. Networks connect immigrants to organizations; it is the distinctive features of the organizations employing immigrants that set the upper bounds on network penetration.

Emphasizing network over organization is a common sociological theme. The network phenomenon offers proof that the earlier antinomies posited by modern sociology—*Gemeinschaft* vs. *Gesellschaft,* traditionalism vs. modernity, informal vs. formal—do not hold. After all, what could be more *gemeinschaftlich,* more traditional, than the reappearance of entire family groups within a workplace that maintains all the other appurtenances of bureaucratic management? And the pattern at the top of the organization does not necessarily look so different, even if "old boy" connections and club memberships are not quite as important as two decades ago.[19]

We can agree on the reality of a backstage life to organizations, in which social connections among employees—and between employees and the communities to which they are linked—remain alive and well. But it is one thing to argue that networks ward off pressures towards formalization, described so well in the earlier literature, and another to ignore those pressures altogether. Modern personnel management arose, in part, out of an effort to reduce the role of personal ties in hiring and promotion. That effort cannot be judged a full success, and may well be doomed to partial failure, as the modern organizational literature would suggest. However, it remains the case that organizational practices circumscribe the scope for network recruitment—for reasons having to do with formalization, on the one hand, and the maintenance of legitimacy, on the other.

Sponsorship and the Matching of Persons to Jobs

Organizational features affect the conditions under which workers are selected, an issue to which network theory does not attend. Economic sociology provides two variants on the ways workers are matched to jobs, both focussing exclusively on recruitment. The variant favored by the migration literature tells a story, as we have said, about the strength of *strong* ties, emphasizing the ways the information emanating from friends and relatives, and the influence they exert, enhance migrants' prospects for finding work in an unfamiliar setting. Most studies attending to the labor market as a whole, by contrast, accent the importance of *weak* ties—acquaintances, friends of friends, the accidental contact, but *not* the intimate associate.

The literature tells us that weak ties are more likely than strong to diversify the flow of information—ample reason for appreciation by the recipient of help. But the existing scholarship does not illuminate the motivations of the *helper*. Why provide valuable information to someone with whom one has a slight or merely passing connection? More to the point, weak ties are unlikely to serve as two-way channels of communication; they may tell job-seekers about opportunities, but they cannot reassure bosses about the appropriateness of applicants' traits. Thus, the strength of weak ties cannot explain *sponsorship,* an act for which weakly tied associates have neither the means nor the motivation.

Useful as it is to know how weak ties alter the information available to job-seekers, this is not enough. We also need to explain how networks and structures can alter the information needed by employers when making a hiring decision. Strong ties may not diversify information flows, but they do seem to function as conduits for two-way flows of information. Members of dense networks know their associates well; they can also be expected to maintain the pressure needed to ensure that their friends or relatives perform as required. Needing to sift the wheat from the chaff, employers pay attention to the signals sent by sponsorship—all the more so at the bottom of the labor market, where workers lack certificates and verifiable experience.

WHEN NETWORKS ARE NOT ENOUGH

Networks and Bureaucracy

Strong ties may well deliver a job, but not always. Success occurs only when the employer's informational needs are in fact met by the intelligence provided through the referral network. The interests of workers and employers are hardly symmetric; under conditions of job scarcity, as noted above, workers may seek to maximize employment opportunities for kin and associates, a goal that can distort the information provided to employers. Even where sponsors may be impelled by motivations of the purest kind, or identify their interests with those of their employers, they are only imperfect judges of an applicant's qualifications, having limited knowledge of both the job and the applicant's suitability. The nature of the job will also come into play; it is one thing to trust a sponsor's word when the tasks are relatively simple and the work closely supervised, quite another when a function involves greater complexity and autonomy. For these reasons, organizations are likely to *screen* the persons who apply for the job. To the degree that organizations thoroughly screen applicants and apply their own *selection* criteria, they limit the scope of informal, network-based recruitment. The more formal and extensive the screening process, the lower the dependence on referral networks—which, for the subject matter of this chapter, implies that bureaucracy can mitigate the exclusionary effects of network recruitment.

Classical organizational theory tells us that bureaucracy selects with an eye toward prediction; the need to insure consistent performance, according to a set of standardized criteria, drives the substitution of formal, impersonal means of selection for modes based on ongoing, particular relationships among persons. But organizations also need to maintain legitimacy among their clients and workers. From this perspective, network recruitment is a possible threat, yielding excessive, unwanted homogeneity that may signal that the organization treats some groups of people differently from others. Hence, the need to maintain legitimacy provides additional impetus for bureaucratic hiring procedures, which, by their very nature, reduce the scope for network recruitment.

Let us be clear: in highlighting the contrast between network and bureaucracy, we are not seeking to add yet another dualistic scheme to the binary oppositions of primary vs. secondary, formal vs. informal. Bureaucracies are permeated by networks, and, as relatively few immigrants work in the unregulated informal economy, bureaucratic factors influence immigrant employment outcomes. Rather, we invoke network and bureaucracy as sensitizing concepts; we are trying to introduce greater depth to our understanding of the labor market reality in the immigrant metropolis by drawing attention to variations in the mechanisms by which workers are matched to jobs, and to the difference that these differences make.

The "Up" Side of Bureaucracy

Formality implies "fairness," at least if we understand fairness as involving standardized procedures similarly and reliably applied to all. From the standpoint of organizational outsiders seeking to find their way inside, bureaucratic procedures present considerable appeal. First, they can limit the exercise of unfair discrimination, by which we mean *intentional* efforts to prefer one group and avoid another (a topic covered more extensively in the next part of this book). Second, consistent application of hiring rules helps prevent nepotism and cronyism—or, put differently, restrains or even breaks up the power of the networks just described.

The push for formalization of hiring procedures has quite a history. The advent of the modern personnel system had its origin in an assault on the foreman's idiosyncrasies and arbitrary prerogatives, with "modern" managers seeking to replace personalism with systematic means of hiring and recruitment. The same logic fueled affirmative action, which originated as an attempt to introduce fairness into the hiring process by making it more transparent and rule-dominated. The greatest successes of affirmative action occurred in large organizations, where bureaucratization was already far advanced and monitoring at once easy to accomplish and effective as a source of sanction. By contrast, the toughest calls took place in those environments—family enterprises, small firms, craft jobs, occupational communities—where the distinction between person and position was difficult to establish. Should a family-owned firm be compelled to consider all comers, as opposed to giving priority to kin? And even if the familial enterprise should be so compelled, was this an objective on which policy could effectively set its sights? Upsetting patterns of friendship, ethnic, or neighborhood-based recruitment did not pose normative problems of the same sort, but the practical difficulties still proved impressive.

Three decades after the United States initiated its experiment with affirmative action, large firms turn out to be much more likely than their smaller counterparts to hire African-American workers. The best recent evidence comes from a survey of several thousand firms in four U.S. cities, including Los Angeles, that economist Harry Holzer conducted just as our own survey went into the field. Large firms, Holzer found, not only hired proportionately more African Americans than did smaller firms, but proved more likely to take on those African Americans who applied for jobs.[20] A variety of factors—skill needs, wages, location, industry, and presence of African Americans in the customer base—account for the correlation between firm size and the propensity to hire African Americans, but size per se remains the dominant factor. The nature of Holzer's data made it impossible for him to explain this impact of firm size on the propensity to hire African Americans, but his speculations deserve mention. "Overall, it seems quite likely that the much greater propensity of larger establishments to hire blacks largely reflects much more pervasive discrimination in smaller establishments."

We do not quarrel with this conclusion; we would simply like to expand upon it. Formal procedures may reduce the potential for employers, or their agents, to act on discriminatory impulses. But formality is likely to have the additional, possibly more important, effect of weakening the hold of others' networks.[21] As the literature tells us, smaller firms are likely to be the most reliant on network hiring, given the costs, as measured in material and human resources, needed to standardize hiring practices.[22] As we embark on a discussion of the nature of formalization in the hiring process and its likely consequences, we remind the reader that size increases the *potential* for bureaucratization while *not* eliminating recourse to personal, particularistic, or contingent practices and preferences.

Formality   By "formal hiring procedures," we mean active, structured, systematic methods of recruiting applicants, screening applications for acceptable candidates, and selecting new hires from the narrowed-down pool. The ideal formal hiring procedure is well understood by all participants; it gets applied with relentless consistency; it is constructed with the goals of efficiency, fairness, and optimal results. Best-practice organizations will strive to *validate* their procedures—shoptalk for checking that the process assesses candidates for the real qualities demanded by the job, and for ensuring that the ranking any assessment produces correlates with actual on-the-job performance. (Since the details of the hiring process matter, they receive considerable attention in the chapters to follow, particularly chapter 8, in addition to the brief overview presented here.)

Recruitment involves the process, involving any number of steps, by which a pool of candidates is formed. *Formal* recruitment occurs when firms take deliberate steps to generate applicants, as when they place newspaper ads, attend job fairs, recruit on college campuses, hire "head-hunter" agencies, and so on. *Informal* recruitment proceeds through networks ("word of mouth") and more isolated means, such as taking non-network[23] walk-ins, cold-calls, or resumes. From the standpoint of an organization, informal methods involve little expenditure of effort or resources; thus they are often described as passive. Regardless of the mix of formal and informal means, recruitment results in a pool of job candidates.

The next step is *screening*. Here the objective is two-fold: to weed out obviously unqualified or otherwise undesirable candidates, and to narrow the field to manageable size. Screening can take the form of simply making sure that applications are fully and properly completed, or it can mean requiring a minimum score on one or more standardized skill or psychological tests. As a rule, a screening tool must be sufficiently cheap (in terms of time and therefore money) to be applied to most or all applicants.

The line between screening and *selection* can blur, especially when the two proceed simultaneously. If the employer hires the first qualified person who walks through the door, the distinction is hardly worth making. In general, though, selection is the process by which a final candidate is chosen from a small pool of already screened applicants. Screening determines who will *not* get the job, while selection determines who *will*.

The *interview*, too time-consuming and therefore too costly to deploy as a screening tool except where applicants are rare, provides the most common selection tool—much skepticism about its objective value from the academic and practical literature notwithstanding. As a valid, reliable guide to likely performance on the job, the unstructured one-on-one employment interview rates poorly. Consider the following appraisal offered by relatively friendly academic reviewers of the technique: "Essentially, interviewers ignore base rate information, do not pay attention to disconfirming evidence, and over-depend on case-specific information in making their judgments . . . Perhaps the glaring 'black hole' in all previous reviews [of research on the employment interview] and in the current literature concerns the issue of why use of the interview persists in view of evidence of its relatively low validity, reliability, and its susceptibility to bias and distortion."[24] To be sure, the biases and distortions generated through the typical interview can be overcome—through the use of structured panel interviews, for example. But doing better costs money, at least in terms of time demands on managers, and is therefore unlikely to occur, outside the public sector, when hiring entry-level workers.

Organizations enjoy more and better options when it comes to screening, largely as a result of standardized tests, which fare better from the standpoint of reliability and validity; however, the tests have little appeal to employers with few positions to fill or with low turnover. Organizations can select from a variety of tests; when well-designed, general cognitive tests and tests of job-related skills appear to have solid validity.[25] Behavioral tests can be useful, as well, but while those based on experience ("What did you do in such-and-such situation in the past?") appear to possess validity, those that pose hypothetical queries ("What would you do if this or that happened in the future?") do not.[26] Organizations do have the option of using tests for selection; but, with the exception of government, few entities have enough faith in the reliability of a standardized instrument to forego the interview altogether; thus, the potential for bias is almost always present.[27]

Firm Strategies   But why would organizations bother sifting with such care, especially at the low end of the labor market? The material already presented suggests an obvious answer: although sometimes the job is purely dead-end, requiring skills so low that virtually anyone can do the work, and such that incompetence and turnover yield little cost, most often other conditions apply. Entry-level workers interact with others, whose routine can be upset if the bottommost worker cannot fulfill baseline expectations. Even those positions for which the "unskilled" appellation applies often serve as entry for movement into higher-level proficiencies; if today's janitor may be tomorrow's jogger, who may, in turn, be the next day's assistant pressman, it pays to recruit janitors with some care. And, as we have argued from the start, few unskilled jobs are as devoid of skills as their official labels suggest.

Additional pressures push employers of low-skilled help to search in more than perfunctory ways. In the public sector, for example, legitimacy is at stake; workers and taxpayers must perceive the process as fair. In the private sector, legitimacy also matters, but, ironically, it may be best enhanced by being *un*fair. The composition of the workforce is most visible when workers are in direct contact with the public, as in retail sales or various services. While higher-status groups see nothing to object to in a service class composed of subordinates, groups at the lower ranges of the totem pole are apt to look for workers of their own kind, interpreting underrepresentation or, worse, absence, as evidence of exclusion. Sometimes the effort to match workers to customers results in a push for fairness in hiring, but at other times it amounts to "customer discrimination," with the potential for harming a variety of groups, and appears to act as a significant barrier to black employment.[28]

Exclusionary Principles   To choose one worker over another on anything other than a random basis is to *discriminate*, but not necessarily to discriminate *unfairly* (as we discuss in greater detail in chapter 9). The more formal or bureaucratic the procedure, the greater the degree to which discrimination depends on an index of "merit" or "fit." Whether by intent or not, informal procedures discriminate, too, excluding people on the basis of whom they do (or, more importantly, do *not*) know. If recruitment is entirely informal, outsiders may not know about openings and may never apply. If recruitment is entirely formal, those who test poorly or lack credentials will be left out. And woe betide those who have neither connections nor credentials.

CONCLUSION

The social connections among immigrants receive good play in the sociological literature, given the analytic power that the concept of immigrant social networks packs. The networks can be accurately characterized as structures "with history and continuity that give [them] an independent effect on the function of economic systems," as James Coleman has maintained.[29] But there is probably an affinity between the sociologists' professional biases and the virtues they detect in the networks they seek to describe. After all, the dominant picture is one in which embeddedness in ethnic networks and communities leads to cooperative, if not conformist, behavior among ethnic economic actors. While *homo societas* may be preferable to *homo economicus,* an undue emphasis on cooperation, conformity, and solidarity is a source of analytical weakness.

While agreeing with the conventional view that immigrant networks yield their effect through social closure, we have built on a different sociological tradition, one which views social closure as an aspect of conflict and cleavage. We have sought to show how the workings of usurpationary and exclusionary closure illuminate a puzzle in the immigrant employment scene; it is one thing to observe, with Powell and Smith-Doerr, that "even the disadvantaged can turn to networks to provide access to opportunities not available on the open market,"[30] another to explain why those networks should so consistently expand their reach. After all, the network structures are "wrong," in that weak, not strong, ties are the key to gaining access to new sources of employment; the network associates are "wrong" as well, since their (low) socioeconomic characteristics make them unlikely to form those weak ties (to others in positions of influence) that the network literature tells us are a must. But immigrants are rich in strong ties—fortunately, since jobs and job information are too scarce to distribute to those to whom one is weakly connected.[31] Moreover, employers turn to immigrant networks not simply for reasons of mimesis or filtering,[32] but because the social control potential of immigrants' networks generates additional predictive value. Thus, the repeated action of network hiring leads to the cumulation of informal immigrant resources; over time, immigrant workers gain the potential for the exercise of power, as network associates can mobilize connections in ways inimical to the interests of managers and outsiders alike.

Exclusionary closure is of theoretical interest for illustrating a different, less pleasing side of embeddedness than the one sociologists are wont to note. For the most part, the sociological literature casts embeddedness as a social, and therefore positive, container for economic life, rooting transactions in ongoing relations that shift actors' motivations away from narrow pursuit of immediate economic gains though trust and reciprocity.[33] But other consequences may also ensue; in this case, immigrant networks produce a structure inimical to outsiders, who fare poorly because job opportunities get withdrawn from the open market, and ethnic membership implicitly circumscribes eligibility for employment. By yielding a labor market where particularistic ties play an important role, the embedding of immigrant networks within the Los Angeles economy makes ethnic affiliations significant and ethnic boundaries salient. In the end, the implantation of immigrant networks produces a segmented system, providing new incentives and mechanisms for contention over the ethnic division of labor and its fruits.

Exclusionary closure thus highlights the negative aspects of embeddedness. Admittedly, we are not the first to have noted this dark side. Granovetter's pioneering article on the topic, for example, did more than remind us that concrete personal relations generate trust and trustworthy behavior; central to his argument, although less noted, is the contention that "social relations . . . may even provide occasion for malfeasance and conflict on a scale larger than in their absence."[34] Whether or not familiarity breeds contempt, it does open possibilities otherwise closed. From the employers' perspective, employees who recruit kin in the face of policies that forbid nepotism are surely engaged in malfeasant acts. One need hardly accept the "boss's" point of view, but it shows how aspects of network recruitment that initially appear mutually beneficial can later be used for more one-sided advantages.

The employer can, perhaps, find protection in formality. Much of the sociological literature, oriented toward debunking the classical view of organizations, would suggest not. After all, there is a long and established tradition of studying the backstage, "networked" life of organizations, as contrasted to the lines of influence portrayed by the organization chart, to show how informal sources of power can often overwhelm official authorities. We now also know that because organizations are spanned by networks, mobilizing these connections can be exploited for managerial mobility. Still, network studies of the labor market—particularly those concerned with the fate of immigrant workers—have largely neglected the encounter, and opposition, between network and bureaucracy. Formal methods of recruitment, screening, and selection can severely hamper the penetration of ethnic networks into the workplace. Circumventing these barriers is far from impossible, as demonstrated by the public sector, where line workers infiltrate and eventually control the bureaucracy. Even so, the use of formalized procedures in recruitment, screening, and selection inevitably limits the ability of informal groupings to exercise control over hiring decisions.

In the following two chapters, we see how the concepts developed here stand up to the evidence we collected. In chapter 6, we will apply our evidence to illustrate why network hiring is so pervasive, and detail situations in which the employer has lost control. In chapter 7 we discuss the promise and limitations of bureaucratic mechanisms, and draw conclusions about their consequences, especially for low-skilled natives.

Social Capital
and Social Closure

Every business needs to fill positions from time to time. From the organization's point of view, filling a position means *recruiting* a pool of hopefuls, *screening* for the most suitable candidates, and *selecting* a new hire from among the best candidates. In practice, the steps can be collapsed into one, as in the case of the sole proprietor who literally hires the first person through the door, or they can be telescoped into an elaborate multistage process starting with the receptionist who gives out the application and ending with the personnel chief who makes the final decision. In our interviews, we saw this full range, with small print shops and restaurants on the most informal end and public sector hospitals at the most formal and bureaucratic.

From the standpoint of the *idealized* job applicant, an unemployed individual seeking work, the process looks different. He or she is involved in a parallel process of identifying a list of prospective firms and positions, winnowing these down to the few most suitable, and finally applying for those that seem best. Like the employer, the applicant can be indiscriminate, applying for work with each firm she or he encounters, or fussy, applying for only the very most desirable positions.

The idealized job applicant, however, is not the *typical* applicant, and not simply because one tries to avoid the unenviable situation of looking for a position when already jobless. Few of us go on the market "blind," without guidance from past experience and without assistance from friends, relatives, former co-workers, and others who can help.

Work histories generate *path dependence;* one's prior employment does not solely affect the types of skills one can market, but also influences the contacts one can utilize and one's very vision of the available opportunities, since one's understanding of how the labor market works is shaped by the experience of self and friends. Finally, a good deal of job-finding goes on without shopping or searching; whether through accident (the working of gossip chains) or the purposive action of disinterested or self-interested others, information about job openings comes to you.

The renaissance in economic sociology, a phenomenon that resonates with developments in the sociology of immigration, has at its center the "discovery" that economic relations are *not* a world apart; instead they are fundamentally *embedded* in social relations. Economic transactions often involve trust between the parties; at the very least, some fore-knowledge—derived from experience or reputation—of the traits of the participants is required for any exchange to occur. Recurrent social interactions, and the consequent development of stable social relations, are the rule, not the exception.

The literature on ethnic enterprise both illustrates and illuminates the ways economic activities are embedded in social relations. Ethnic businesses burgeon through an ability to mobilize and profit from co-ethnic labor, utilizing pre-existing ties to recruit labor and deploy it, under arrangements that reflect membership in a common community. The paternalistic management style of small ethnic firms emphasizes the fact that the worker-employer connection is not separable, in practice, from underlying social relations, especially when we recall that the "fatherly" ethnic employer must meet non-economic obligations with his co-ethnic "children." The literature has also shown that ethnic economies may be supported, not simply by the self-conscious activities of owners and workers who actively identify with the "community" or group, but through the operation of contacts based on purely social ties that nonetheless facilitate economic transactions. For example, Light and Bonacich developed the concept of "ethnic facilitation," referring to the way the clustering of earlier immigrants in business lines sends signals to newcomers as to the most appropriate economic pursuits.[1] Writing with Thomas Bailey, Roger Waldinger[2] applied the concept of "training system" to show how ethnic networks increase the quality and quantity of information exchanged between co-ethnic employers and employees, reducing, for both, the risks associated with investment in skills. And Alejandro Portes and Julia Sensenbrenner underlined the

impact of "bounded solidarity" and "enforceable trust" in promoting al-
truism in immigrant communities and creating mechanisms to reduce the
likelihood of opportunism.[3]

Thus the scholars of ethnic enterprise have sketched a picture in which
social—not market—processes provide the more effective economic
medium, even when the economies in question bear many traits of the
classic market model. But it also appears that the embeddedness of ethnic economies in networks and communities leads to cooperative, if not
conformist, behavior among ethnic economic actors. As Portes has
noted:

> Ethnic networks are the key source of tips for suitable business sites for
> middleman merchants and for employment opportunities in a developing
> occupational niche. Networks are equally important as a source of capital
> to start middleman shops as well as enclave firms. Bounded solidarity
> underlines the common preference that immigrants manifest for their
> fellows in business transactions. Although buying from co-ethnic firms,
> hiring other immigrants, or bringing them into the same employment site
> may be motivated by self-interest, each such instance also possesses a clear
> altruistic component based on solidarity with one's in-group.[4]

Of course, one can treat social capital as an endogenous group characteristic, existing "in the relations among persons," as Coleman insisted, and varying between groups with the extent of their mutual trust-
worthiness and trust.[5] But, as Portes has also pointed out, "social capital
refers to the capacity of individuals to command scarce resources *by
virtue of their membership* in networks or broader social structures."[6]
Since, by definition, the social structures promoting a group's economic
action belong to that group and no other, membership affects outsiders
and insiders differently. As noted in chapter 5, the interests of bosses and
immigrant workers recurrently lead organizations to source labor
through the social connections of the established workers. But these interests do not always coincide; the networks also provide immigrant
workers with leverage *against* their bosses, who share neither their class
position nor their ethnic affiliation. Likewise, one group's ability to mobilize resources through social structures can serve as a strategy for limiting another group's chances for advancement, with the embeddedness
of economic life generating both pressures and motivation to exclude
outsiders. By the same token, reliance on networks can breed the appearance of favoritism and the reality of nepotism, outcomes that many
organizations find threatening. Recognition of the embeddedness of hiring processes in a social context consequently calls forth, as we shall see

in chapter 7, mechanisms designed to mitigate the undesirable effects of networks.

EMBEDDEDNESS AND NETWORK RECRUITMENT

"Under all values lies the hard cash," reads a famous text in political economy. The employers we interviewed had apparently read the same manual, praising network recruitment because it was cheap: "It does not cost us a penny"; "It saves me having to spend money on ads"; "It's easy and quick." But their interest was not simply to forego an outlay of physical or personal capital; network recruitment seemed to furnish a large, often satisfactory supply of labor—sometimes "an unlimited supply of people"—with little, occasionally no, managerial effort. Existing ties to incumbents provided almost instant access to a latent labor force outside the workplace. "All you gotta do is just *think* about hiring people and then next thing you know you've got several people from other departments saying 'Hey, I understand you're hiring, and I got a friend' or 'My husband's out of work' . . . they just come out of the woodwork. This happens even before the job's posted."

Just as social connections secure jobs for persons not actively looking—a conceptual complication of non-trivial importance for the job-search literature—social networks produce applicants for employers who do not yet have vacancies. "Fifty percent of our people come from referrals," explained the HR manager for a public sector hospital. Since hospital departments were often intentionally kept shorthanded for budgetary reasons, having enough "fresh" applications on hand to fill vacancies quickly was no small thing. "They know someone, tell someone, have a friend fill out the application. We have a lot of people who have friends with applications already filled out; we have encouraged them to do that. If you can't come every day, have someone keep a look-out for you. They will give in an application the day the notice is posted. Then the supervisor could get the person that day and hire that day."

As this example suggests, incumbents keep themselves busy—or are kept busy—finding placements for associates. "If he [a brother of an employee] is not working, they'll approach us. Do you need a new polisher?" "We usually have a waiting list of friends from the existing employees," explained a factory owner. "Most of the time we have people waiting to come to work." A production manager told us that "there are always people looking for a job who know people here and would like to get a foot in the door."

To be sure, securing the right supply of suitable applicants usually entails exertion on the part of management, but often not much more than that entailed in "getting out the word." "I could have a thousand people here tomorrow," exclaimed a factory owner; "we just post our jobs and they come rushing." A touch of hyperbole, perhaps, but, if so, not greatly out of line with the views of many employers we visited. A printer told us: "We put the word out that we're looking for an inspector. Believe me, it gets around in about thirty seconds, and the whole place knows about it. People go to the phones to call others about the opening. If we put the word out at 7, we'll have applicants calling or showing up by 9, 10, or 11."

Networks efficiently activate the labor supply because employees, so managers claim, "always know someone who needs a job." Reliance on referrals capitalizes on an existing set of connections to family and friends. "Everybody," it seems, "always has a cousin, nephew, or brother who's a good worker." A mattress manufacturer contended that "they always have cousins that always need a job"; a fast fooder was more impressed that incumbents "always have friends who need jobs." "Generally for the entry-level positions, we got a lot of younger guys, who need jobs," a printer observed. "[They] say I got a friend who would like this job."

It seems unlikely that our respondents were versed in the social networks literature, but at times they sounded like intuitive network theorists. "You could have all the credentials of the world," said the owner of a small custom upholstery shop, "but without networks you are nothing." The employers often invoked a network concept to explain how they obtained labor. "It's a network they have for letting each other know about jobs," claimed a printer; a furniture manufacturer referred to "a whole network of acquaintances and relatives that people have that we draw on." The personnel manager for a regional fast food chain explained that "in Southern California, you've got a network that's very efficient. If José is there, he knows a brother, Juan, who is ready."

Employers were quick to point to a basic network principle—homophily, the tendency of socially similar people to band together.[7] "Friends of friends, friends of employees, word of mouth, it's as if they've all worked together, they all, it's a community type of thing, it's a networking type of thing." Similarity among persons within the same recruitment network meant that referrals were likely to originate from an appropriate applicant pool. "All these people know someone who has been working in the industry and, when they become aware that jobs are available, they will bring a brother, cousin, or neighbor in." In this situation, word of mouth ensures that information leaks out to the appropriate occupational community. The owner of a trendy Santa Monica restaurant explained that "everybody knows we are hiring, whether through other restaurants and out in the community, or through referrals from existing employees."

Managers appreciate network recruitment for its ability to attract applicants quickly and at little cost; they value it even more for its efficiency. Hiring through connections upgrades the quality of related information, reducing the risks entailed in acquiring new personnel. Owners and managers know more about the sponsoring worker than about any applicant; the operational principle, as one printer noted, is that "birds of a feather flock together."

> *Field notes:* Since they get people through referrals and many people have worked there a long time, so they know the employees, they figure the applicant will be a "carbon copy" of the employee referring them, anyway.

Incumbents' characteristics send a signal on which employers depend. Entry-level jobs are good for persons trying to get a start; but employers are well aware that the work involved is no picnic. "It's a hard job," explained a respondent in our hotel sample. For that reason, an incumbent housekeeper "is more likely to know some one who . . . can also handle it." Believing that good employees produce good referrals, managers "pay attention to the person who is doing the referring," and the "credibility of the person who is referring is looked at." As one restaurant manager said, "If you have workers who are reliable, their friends are probably similar, same skills and metabolism." Operating in a big-city environment where expectations, even experiences, of opportunism are the norm, the ability to draw predictive value from experience with a known entity counts for much. A retailer, noting that using referrals "saves me having to worry about whether or not the person is a good person or not," elaborates:

> *R:* [T]here's a lot of people out there that would just as soon get hired here, and trip and fall and file a worker's comp claim, as to coming here and wanting to do a good job. There would just as soon be people that would want to come in here to have access to equipment so that they could steal it.
>
> *I:* Have you had a lot of experiences with both of those things, the disability and the theft?
>
> *R:* Uh huh [affirmative]. Across the board. And that's why we like to trust a little bit more about a person who is personally referred by an individual. . . . Sometimes it fails miserably, but the majority of the time it works.

But it is not simply probabilistic considerations that lead employers to consider a sponsor's characteristics as reliable proxies for the traits of the worker referred. Even at the bottom of the labor market, job-seekers are a dime a dozen; "there is an abundance of people at any level in the street," noted a printer. While the in-house workforce is rarely short on contacts hunting for a better job or larger paycheck, jobs, especially those providing some chance of upward mobility, are not nearly so plentiful. Job scarcity ensures that "people have a stake in the referral" and a "vested interest in seeing the person succeed," considerations that provide motivation for self-policing. "Most employees don't want to refer anyone they know is a goof-off," explained a hotel personnel manager. "It reflects poorly on them."

A worker's standing with the employer may not be all-important; as we shall show, the referral process involves a good deal of negotiating and exchange of power plays. Still, reputation seems unlikely to be of such trivial significance as to be regularly squandered. After all, employers "pay attention to the person who is doing the referring," responding one way when a "strong individual brings in a family member or neighbor," but turning a blind eye to "referrals from questionable employees because they don't really know the standards." Employers are also apt to remind workers that hiring a friend or relative involves a quid pro quo: "I tell my employees, if you are going to refer someone, that person better be a good worker. Because the way they work is going to affect you. You will look bad if your referral does not perform adequately."

The prevalence of favor trading—as in the case of a printer who hired his pressman's son as a way of bringing the young man into the trade—gave sponsors good reason to "fear they'll jeopardize their standing with a bad referral." Beyond concern over antagonizing the boss, sponsors also had to manage their relationship with co-workers: "The people we have here, many have been here a long time, they wouldn't bring in someone who would flake. They're worried about me and what the co-workers would think. They don't want trouble."

For all these reasons, employers assumed that "the existing employee is not gonna bring in a schmuck." Sponsors functioned as a "screening device," relied on to filter information between the organization and the labor supply, and taking care to recommend only applicants likely to work out.

Employers are concerned also about the quality of information traveling from the organization to the applicant; conveniently, connections between incumbents and applicants improve these flows as well. Incumbents know "what our criteria are about," "know what the store is really like," understand "how a retail organization runs." Consequently, contact with the established workforce generates realistic expectations and knowledge about the responsibilities of the job. As a restaurant manager put it, "The pluses are that the people referred know what is expected from them, because they have been told what the job involves by the existing employees."

Thus network hiring uses community to structure information flow, thereby yielding another advantage: pre-existing relationships originating outside the workplace continue to influence behavior after the hiring decision. For example, a hotel manager told us: "I have also found that because we hire referrals, most of the employees come from one area of El Salvador, they know each other from back there. It's a very cohesive environment, a small-town atmosphere. In a big city, but they know each other, have a high degree of ethics and morality that you get in a small town. It's another advantage of hiring referrals in a city like LA."

Sponsoring also entails subsequent obligations, with incumbents expected to monitor performance ("look[ing] after the friend or relative") and apply discipline if necessary ("push them when they need to be pushed"). Reputational considerations, as noted earlier, control the quality of information flowing from sponsor to employer—and generate an incentive to ensure control after a referral has been hired. A retailer told us: "We feel that it's an understanding between those two people. If I refer you and [you] get hired, my reputation as an employee is on the line so you have to do well and there's no question about it . . . It's an understanding I feel that people have with each other. You can't jeopardize my reputation because you don't want to do a good job. Do you want to work or do you not want to work, 'cause I'm not going to let you put my name on the application just because you want some extra money and you're not going to come in and do a good job."

ETHNIC NETWORKS AND CLOSURE PROCESSES

Thus far, our story about why employers prefer network hiring differs little from the conventional view. The social relations among workers and between workers and employers facilitate economic action. Network recruitment is embedded in concrete social relations and therefore improves the quality and quantity of information that workers and employers need to invest in skills. Network recruitment also shapes the employment relationship by imparting a set of understandings common to workers and employers, reducing the possibility that informal understandings or implicit contracts will be broken. Because migration is a network-driven process, the ability of networks to reduce the costs and risks entailed in hiring explains why the impoverished, poorly educated immigrants who have converged on Los Angeles may nonetheless be rich in social capital.

Network Recruitment as Social Reproduction

Efficiency is to be valued—especially by sociologists when they find a social, as opposed to market, process the more useful. But as is often the case, efficiency involves an equity trade-off; in this case, workers without contacts to incumbents lose out on access to job information.

Exclusion is the natural by-product of reliance on referrals, if only because network recruitment inherently involves a process of social reproduction. While employers often feel that their reliance on the "birds of a feather" principle yields solid employees, it also keeps recruitment channels bounded by occupational and ethnic ties. "All these people know someone who has been working in the related industry and when they become aware that jobs are available, they will bring a brother, cousin, or neighbor in." In this situation, word of mouth ensures that information leaks out to the appropriate occupational community. "Almost everyone who applies here has worked in some other furniture company," explains a plant manager; as for those without comparable experience, "We don't look at them." Both kitchen workers and waiters seem to have privileged access to a supply of qualified workers: "They [my workers] know everybody in the business. It's a very tight community. All you have to do is ask one of your workers or your cooks if they know someone in the market and they'll always satisfy the needs. I don't know someone who comes in through the door. They [the workers] know if a guy's a thief or rude to customers, because of socializing outside." A furniture manufacturer notes that referrals can pull in candidates from other factories. "We rely a lot on employee referrals. Because they know people who work in other factories that are unhappy."

The tendency to hire persons socially similar with respect to occupational background carries over to ethnic background—a matter of no surprise, since predilection for convergence on an ethnic niche steers groups towards some and only some economic specializations. "Once one has one Hispanic, you have two or three more and this brings about

a chain reaction. The same thing happened with our accounting department—once we hired an Asian, they seemed to be all Asian." Hotels display a distinctive ethnic division of labor: Mexicans and Central Americans dominating housekeeping and the kitchen; blacks in security,
parking, and the front office; Filipinos working as accountants, night
managers, and clericals; and whites employed as waiters in restaurants
and as barkeepers. Manufacturing plants tend to be heavily Hispanic on
the shop floor; office operations frequently look different, as in one furniture manufacturer where the "entire accounting department is from
the Philippines." The ethnic consequences of network hiring are even
more vivid in the restaurants; relying on two hiring strategies—walk-ins
for front-of-the-house jobs, and referrals for kitchen workers—yields a
pattern where "the front is a little bit of everything, whites, blacks,
Asians," while the kitchen is exclusively Latino.

   In general, the past served as prologue, favoring ongoing recruitment
from the established source regardless of the group involved. Thus, even
black workers in the hospital industry found that network recruitment
could work in their favor, as in the case of a public hospital in South Central Los Angeles where, an HR manager noted, "At the hospital, in this
area, it's predominantly black. Most people out here are from the area.
It's hard to get into unless you know someone's sister, uncle, aunt." Similarly, a private hospital employed a large black workforce and experienced a high black applicant rate, but could only secure Latino workers
through active recruitment efforts and an affirmative action program.

   Though all groups displayed a tendency toward convergence on particular occupational or industrial niches, employers emphasized the immigrant factor. "Many are immigrants and they seem to look out for each
other. These immigrants network much more than any other group."
Given the demographic diversity of Los Angeles, "immigrant" can refer to
any number of groups. But our interest involved entry-level jobs, and when
we asked about referrals, employers were most likely to respond with reference to the Mexican and Central American workforce ("the Mexican
mafia" to quote a regional fast food executive) that dominated the bottom
ranks and that "nine times out of ten, provides someone the next day."

   In explaining the growing dominance of Latino immigrants in specific
occupations, employers highlighted two factors. First, a preference for
ongoing relations, for accepting the referrals produced by incumbents
with track records, simply led to "more of the same." "When we do the
networking with our current Hispanic workforce," noted one furniture
manufacturer, "they are bringing in other Hispanics." Another explained

that "90 percent of our workforce out there is Hispanic, and all of these people know someone who has been working in the related industry, and when they become aware that jobs are available, they will bring a brother, cousin, or neighbor in."

Second, the ability to furnish referrals was related to the structure of the networks and communities to which Mexican and Central American workers were attached: Latino immigrants tended to have larger families than do most natives. A furniture manufacturer told us how "over the years, reliance on referrals has led us to a largely Hispanic workforce. They are very social. I don't want to sound racist, but I never met a lonely Mexican. They all have extended families." A printer struck the same note, explaining that "a Hispanic household has extended family—friends, neighbors. They always know someone who needs a job." A restaurant manager told us: "The back is filled almost strictly from referrals. The kitchen workers have a lot of friends and cousins. And we don't have much turnover. They have ten people waiting in the wings. We opened a new restaurant this summer. I hired all the waiters from walk-ins; all the back-of-the-house workers came from referrals."

Employers valued strong ties for their predictive value; for that reason, if no other, groups with more extensive strong ties were more likely to benefit from a preference to hire from within. Whatever the precise motivation to mobilize connections to the Latino workforce, one result was a work world where "everyone knows each other," to quote an Anglo factory owner. A manufacturer described furniture as a "grandfather, father, son, situation." "We have a very large Hispanic population," recounted the production manager in an East Los Angeles printing plant, "and they all have cousins and uncles. Everyone in the open-web department is related. The sisters are in the bindery and some of them are related to people in the open-web department." A production manager estimated that "almost 60 percent of the workers are family related. Many of them are *compadres* and *comadres* because they have known each other for so long." The degree of connectedness can be such as to take the employer by surprise, as on a Christmas eve when management of a medium-size hotel had the following experience: "[W]e gave everyone turkeys [before] realizing that we gave the same family twenty turkeys. At least half of the maids are from one family, and the other half probably is from another. The executive housekeeper's assistant is her sister."

By definition, social reproduction implies exclusion. Operating on the "birds of a feather" principle and motivated by concern for the efficiencies generated by reliance on the contacts of established, proven workers, employers recruit in ways that exclude those groups who lack ties to the community of the plant, facility, or shopping floor. Once in place, network recruitment has a further excluding effect: the linguistic majorities put in place, for instance, in furniture plants and in the back of the house in restaurants and hotels make it difficult for English-language speakers to function, assuming that they could find a job there in the first place. In addition, the evidence shows that workers also exclude by intent, rather than only from not knowing or befriending ethnic outsiders.

While the social structures of ethnic communities breed a *tendency* toward encapsulation, boundary maintenance is problematic. *Self-segregating* processes are generally weak; while more skilled workers develop distinctive occupational attachments, less-skilled persons hunt less discriminately. And, by definition, the competitive industries in which immigrants and other minorities cluster pose low barriers to the entry of newcomers. Thus, there is often some degree of "niche overlap," in which the search for employment leads outsiders into conflict with established groups, a phenomenon that exemplifies exclusionary closure.

Exclusionary closure occurs when established groups withdraw the support that outsiders need to learn and do the job—a vital resource, since so many jobs are interdependent. Chapter 10 provides a more complete discussion of exclusionary closure, as a specific instance of interethnic conflict on the job; for the moment, we simply note that, while we found considerable evidence of exclusionary closure, it was far from universal. Hostility most often came from Latinos and Latinas and was usually directed towards African Americans, but active hostility was not necessary for *maintaining* closure; once one group attained dominance over an occupation or department within an organization, that area became "alien territory" to others.

USURPATIONARY CLOSURE

That hiring patterns are embedded in social relations generates additional pressure to hire through incumbents' networks, pressure that employers often do not want. As noted, network hiring reproduces the characteristics of the existing labor force, and not all employers pursue this goal. In wresting effective control over hiring away from management, workers exercise *usurpationary closure*.

"With referrals you get very homogeneous groups," noted the owner of a South Bay furniture factory. "There is a problem with [having] only one group." One problem was of particular concern to some employers—the exclusionary results that network hiring seemed to produce. As another factory owner explained:

> R: If you are not careful you end up with all Hispanics. And I am a little
>   bit nervous that I have too many Hispanics and not enough blacks.
> I: Nervous in what sense?
> R: Are you familiar with affirmative action terminology? We will end up
>   with a concentration of Hispanics and a[n] underutilization of
>   blacks. And I think in areas I have that. I don't have any government
>   contracts, I am not an affirmative action employer, but it is some
>   thing that I am sensitive about.

Anxiety was not high enough to drastically change practices in this factory, although the employer took pains to insure that the Hispanic clerical workers did not control the flow of new hires in their part of the business.

Many employers do lose their grip over the hiring process, and for them the problem begins with a loss of control over information about vacancies. "Referrals occur before the vacancy appears," a printer told us, "Everybody out there knows about it before we do. People put an application in on the first day, and then the brother reminds us of it." Shopfloor knowledge—"They know when they are short of people, they actually feel it"—is one factor allowing workers to preempt their employers. "They come to me and tell me that they are short of two people, but they indicate to me that they know these two people. So I see [the two]."

In larger, more bureaucratic establishments, contacts between incumbents and job-seekers are crucial for learning of a place before the rest of the world finds out, but in smaller establishments, where workers have access to more information than bosses, incumbents take care of recruitment before even the employer realizes that a vacancy may arise. "Around here," noted one respondent in our hotel sample, "someone says 'I'm going to resign in two weeks' and the next day I have applications for a job that may or may not be vacant." Often the workers know better than their bosses, who report that "the least amount of knowledge the [workers] can share [with their employers], the happier they are." According to a furniture factory manager, "I have people coming to apply for jobs and I say there are no openings out there, and they say, 'but José is going to quit'; they have already heard about it before I even have the job posted."

Field notes: The respondent tells me a story about how workers will know about vacancies before management finds out. "Someone comes up and says, 'Jaime's going back to Mexico,' and I say, 'Oh really,' and Jaime says,

'Oh, I forgot to tell you.' So the new guy says, 'You have an opening, and if you train me I'll be ready by the time he's gone.'"

Response to workers' spontaneous referrals depends on a tacit continuing negotiation in which employees' cooperation depends on their employers' willingness to hire their contacts. The expectation that referrals will be hired, or at least considered, when possible, seems a common part of the bargain. Thus, managers complained about employees who felt that vacant positions were "owed" to their friends or relatives, or about workers who "expect some favoritism or to be at the top of the list" and are upset when their referrals do not get the nod. "Most of the time, a friend thinks their friend should be able to get in without skills," complained a hotelier. "They think it's unfair if we don't hire them." This hotelier added: "We can't always guarantee the employee that made the referral that their person will be hired. Sometimes that's difficult to explain to employees, because if you have a good employee who refers someone, they're automatically going to assume that that person is going to be hired based on that referral."

Thus, employers were quite conscious of the perils run when violating implicit contracts, even if not quick to allow that a worker's retaliation was a rational action. "If you don't hire a person that is referred," recounted a furniture factory manager, "the existing employee will be upset. Because this person is upset, then he does not work to his potential and then we suffer in productivity." One of our HR hospital informants similarly noted that "it becomes difficult if you choose not to select the [referred] employee, because then you may have another employee relations issue."

Where the top brass is weak and has limited leverage over its employees, as in a hotel where management admitted its inability to move beyond network recruiting, workers' expectations serve to keep hiring within the ambit of the incumbent group:

I: What makes it difficult to develop other recruitment methods?
R: Resentment. They feel that "we brought an applicant in first, why has someone else been hired first?"

Although stronger or larger organizations are unlikely to succumb to pressures of this sort, they recognize an implicit set of obligations that bind them to the existing labor force, and act accordingly. Thus, for all the advantages of network hiring, a hospital manager explained,

R: [T]he bad part is when you know everyone and their relatives is laid off of work right now. And so you just get so many of them [applying]. And then in most cases they're not as qualified as what you're looking for. And the courtesy does need to go out to them, especially when they're family or relatives of your current employee.

I: So do you have a policy of always interviewing the referral?

R: We try to keep that policy, especially when it's family members. It's difficult to do that, especially when the people are not qualified. My main policy is that I'm the only one that does the prescreening. If the person is qualified and they were referred, they'll definitely get an interview. If they're not qualified and they were referred, they're going to get a phone call, explaining why they're not going to get a second interview, if they're not among the most qualified people.

The self-activating nature of network recruitment made it resistant to management's efforts at short-circuiting the process, regardless of the formality of the hiring process and the particular organizational context. One of the hospitals we visited surveyed its employees twice a year and found that 95 percent of new hires came from employee referrals; the personnel manager explained that "we do place a lot of ads, but it usually ends up that somebody is a friend of somebody who works here, and that's how they've gotten in." Similarly, a small community hospital posted jobs with the local Private Industry Council[8] and the state employment service, but applications from in-house postings arrived first: "The employees really keep a good eye, 'cause they want to bring their families and friends in." For reasons of equity—"It's not fair to just go out there and tell the good worker about a vacancy"—a furniture factory put a help-wanted sign in front of the plant when new workers were needed. But, as the plant manager noted, "it's the same as telling the employees." One factory owner did switch from network recruitment to newspaper advertising to upgrade the labor force, but this required running a blind ad (with no mention of the factory's name, address, or phone number). "When the name of the company was in our ad," the owner pointed out, "the existing referrals would bring the people in." Ties between incumbents and applicants were so powerful that a reliance on formal recruitment methods often failed to shut down the machinations of informal hiring networks. As an HR manager at a public hospital admitted, "We have a lot of family members that work [here], you know. Everybody's cousin works here, and sister and, you know, brother-in-law, and stuff like that." As she noted, as soon as notices were posted regarding examinations for open positions, "people call up all their friends and go 'Hey, they're hiring.' So probably there's a lot more referrals than we know of."

An employer did not need to totally lose control of network hiring before running the risk that "you possibly could be creating a clique." "Cliquishness" was a source of worry, for reasons concerned with maintaining comity among distinct groups of co-workers and between labor and management. Wherever a staff was connected by social relationships, ties at the job site involved "more than a co-worker relationship"; consequently, conflicts within the clique might get out of hand, transforming a dyadic dispute into one where "about twenty others get involved." Alternatively, existence of a clique might shift allegiances from management to members of the set. Patronage ties within the network posed one source of threat, as noted by a restaurant chain manager generally upbeat about the quality of his heavily immigrant staff: "[W]hen you get the 'Spanish,' who are very tight, sometimes you get a guy who is boss of all the people because he got them a job. You have to be careful of that syndrome." More troubling to employers were solidaristic relationships among network members, grounds for one manager to conclude, "I prefer if everybody work here be acquaintances. It's not to our advantage if they're good friends."

Hiring Kin

Many employers still eagerly hired incumbents' friends and acquaintances, but they were far less comfortable about kin. The view that a preponderance of family "does not make for a good environment" echoed frequently. *Fairness* was one source of caution, especially since the imbalance between job supply and demand made it difficult to accommodate all employee requests. "There are so many people who are referred that there's often resentment that 'his relative is hired and not mine,'" explained a hotelier. The same problem worried a department store manager, otherwise positive about referrals, who pointed out that "everyone has friends and family looking for work. They can say to us, 'you hired so and so, why not my friend or relative?'"

More pressing was the perception that "family pressures change the motivation among workers," as one manager noted. "The loyalties [extend] to each other, not the hotel." Hence, deploying relatives proved a vexing issue, with some organizations accepting kin-based referrals but opting for separation on the job to reduce the likelihood of networks diffusing conflict throughout the organization. For example, a hotel prohibited relatives from working in the same department, as did a discounter, and a department store employed still more rigorous rules, hiring relatives but not allowing them to "work for the same supervisor, nor for the same senior supervisor." More difficult to manage were familial ties linking supervisor to staff—a concern that, incidentally, signals the movement of immigrants into positions of authority. For example, a personnel manager in a religious hospital, who told us that "referrals are best," went on to note, "All policies state that it's fine to have a family member working in the hospital, but they can't supervise [another relative]." Allegiance was in question when supervisors brought in their own kin, as a factory owner noted, who was "especially careful when I have recommendations from supervisors; that is the most risky situation. If the person they recommend doesn't work out, they will definitely cover it up." Kinship connections that crossed authority lines also raised equity issues: "[Referrals] can be bad in the sense that we can possibly hire someone's family member, without them telling you, into the same department, which can be a problem further down the line. If a supervisor hires their niece or nephew and employees find out, they may feel that the niece or nephew is getting preferential treatment. They may feel it's unfair. And it is unfair."

Managers identified additional dangers in kinship recruitment. Kinship networks among employees increased the likelihood that information about conflict would travel quickly. Strong ties also threatened to bond workers against managers, with unfortunate consequences. Noted one employer: "Sometimes [having] more than one family member leads to cronyism, and also to protect each other to hide their inefficiencies. It's hard to punish a bad employee if their relative is a good one, because you don't want to lose the good one. That's the risk you have by getting referrals. Sometimes you have to bite the bullet and say 'This has got to stop.' If the other person wants to leave, then [let them] leave. If the other employee is sensible and realizes the other person has shortcomings, things work out."

Just as the self-activating nature of network recruitment subverted employers' authority, workers' determination to place family often overpowered policies to keep kin from crossing the workplace threshold. "We look down on families," noted a department store manager, before conceding that "we have them, though." The personnel manager for a small hospital in the San Fernando Valley noted that hiring family members was a matter of sensitivity, "but I will hire them anyway." Thus preferences bent in the face of the pressure to hire kin; rules too were violated. A hotel, for example, maintained a policy of not accepting referrals, but our respondent told us it was "not enforced." Similarly, a hospital was "very strict about not hiring relatives to work under the supervision of family members, [but] rules get broken and you find out later it's a daughter."

Rule-breaking occurred for reasons of both the costs entailed in enforcing antinepotism restrictions and the asymmetric interests of workers and employers. Antinepotism rules or preferences simply encouraged workers to keep relevant information to themselves: "In the entry-level classification, it's word of mouth through them. And rarely do we hear about it. But we just find out when they come to work that 'Oh, yeah, my sister works here and I have an aunt and a brother-in-law.' "

Curious employers had to work hard to uncover kinship connections, as noted by a furniture manufacturer who explained that "especially the Spanish-speaking workers, they have the habit of using the mother's name or the father's name, so you get two brothers using two different names." Consequently, determining the connections between incumbent and referral demanded extra care: "Unfortunately, employee referrals that I've seen in the Southern California area tend to be relative-oriented. You may not know that, initially. But, if you check, it's the husband, it's the wife of the husband, cousin, the cousin's cousin. It's not 'someone I worked with before who I know is good.' So sometimes you run into the nepotism trap, I'd say a considerable amount here." So, while not "want[ing] to ever be accused of nepotism in a small little hospital like this," an HR manager conceded that "that is the risk I run. You're always hiring family members." And a production manager with years of experience in the furniture industry evinced the same note of resignation, stating that "Hispanics will try to get their relatives and close friends hired, regardless of whether they're qualified. The thing I found out is that you'll get relatives whether you like it or not."

While such suboptimal situations were not necessarily intractable, they demanded additional managerial effort. For example, a printer hired relatives, but noted that "somebody has to have the intestinal fortitude to fire the employee if they don't do a good job." Better yet were techniques to head off trouble; one of these involved specifying the nature of the implicit contract. If the person giving the referral agreed to abide by the employer's judgment, the firm had made a big step toward maintaining or regaining control:

> *Field Notes:* The employee referring the applicant has already been asked if the applicant will fit in. Management says, "You won't be upset if she doesn't work out? [In other words,] if we have to fire her?"

Striking the right balance between company and familial and ethnic loyalties was a tricky game, however, with much at stake. For the smaller organizations, like restaurants or printing shops, any disturbance to a core kinship group could have a devastating impact. "If you have any family crisis," noted a printer, "they've all got to go through that." Numerous respondents voiced concern over the possibility that "something happens in Mexico to one of their family members and then they all leave." Accidents were another worry: "[I]f Juan had something in his eye and he wanted to go to the clinic, he would then ask his brother to take him and then they would both go. They would sit at the clinic for four hours on the company's time." To be sure, however, even a sudden loss of personnel could be handled without disastrous consequences, as the managers of a steak house discovered.

> *Field notes:* When something happens within the family, a fairly high percentage of the workforce can change. The father of four of the kitchen workers passed away and the restaurant let them all go home for the funeral. "The decision on the funeral did more good than anything [else] we could have done. We put it to them that they could rearrange schedules, but that a couple of them had to be back as soon as possible. So two came back in a few days, two came back several weeks later." A lot of people worked six days so they could do it. "They're indebted to you. 'Look at what they did for us.' It's probably one of the greatest things we could have done. The chef had to work an extra day. It generates lots of loyalty." If they come back, they're going to stay.

Still, this case demonstrates that reliance on extensive kinship groups did heighten organizational vulnerability; and the source of the potential shocks is not always so benign. Take workers' compensation, an item looming large on managers' minds, in some instances, to quote a furniture manufacturer, a "nightmare. . . . [W]e were basically paralyzed, afraid to hire people." The general view among managers was that people were "trying to defraud the system," and kinship networks were perceived as one means by which fraudulent behavior would spread: "If the relative files a worker's comp claim, the other relatives watch. If the insurance settles and gives them an award because it's a nuisance case, then you've opened a Pandora's box. You can multiply the number of workers' comp injuries."

Kin and Unionizing

Sounding a note well known to labor historians, an old-time factory owner reminded us that "families lead to unionization"—ample reason, in his eyes, to be careful about hiring relatives.[9] A hospital manager, otherwise upbeat about hiring through referrals, concurred.

I: Are there other drawbacks to referrals?

R: Probably, if you have too many family members, 'cause a lot of times most, that's what most referrals are, recommend one, recommend a brother or sister or something like that. Too many family members at one location creates problems. So that's one of the most serious drawbacks.

I: What kind of problems do you get with too many family members?

R: Well, if, if, if you do something to my brother then we're all gonna walk off, that type of situation.

Although relatively few employers appeared worried about unionization, the hoteliers fretted that ethnic solidarity might yield "infection" from the militant hotel local headed by a charismatic Latina, a condition that increased anxiety about the consequences of disciplinary action directed at workers linked to a kinship group: "The back-of-the-house and banquet service is where the Hispanic concentration is found. The [union] leader is the Cesar Chavez of the industry and the housekeepers is their stronghold. Because the people come in with so little skills it's easy to convince them to distrust us."

Managerial anxiety notwithstanding, labor uprisings were not exactly on the horizon at the time of our survey, when union decertification was more common than successful unionization. But appreciation of labor peace was no reason for our respondents to forget its fragility—which is exactly why they worried about the connections among their workforce, and the ways these connections could be turned against them.

CONCLUSIONS

Network hiring is at least as pervasive at the low end of the labor market as it is for more highly valued positions. Employers do not always hire through the connections of incumbent workers; sometimes they go to great lengths to avoid relying on the social ties of incumbents, to achieve goals incompatible with network hiring. Nonetheless, network hiring ranks as the most important of employers' recruitment mechanisms, as this study and many others have shown. Network hiring prevails because the benefits it provides are too great to ignore, and the effort needed to curb its excesses requires more resources than many employers, especially the smaller ones, can afford.

But as much as sociologists find something to admire in the connectedness of the networked labor market, it is not entirely a pretty scene. One might be pleased to find sociality and solidarity playing central roles in the labor market, but we note that these can be turned to more than one end, with exclusion a common and sometimes intended result.

From the employer's standpoint, the contacts between established workers in the organization and the labor market may be too much of a good thing. Nepotism creates the appearance and sometimes the reality of unfairness, threatening an organization's reputation as well as its ability to function. "Birds of a feather" may be recruited because they have similar, desirable, job-relevant qualities; for the same reason, they have at least some common interests unlikely to be shared with the employer. If many, most, or—in the employer's worst case scenario—*all* of the underlings understand themselves as members of a common group, the employer may find that management's room for action has been circumscribed to no small degree.

But organizational passivity need not reign supreme. Employers can avail themselves of a variety of tools to counter the power of ethnic networks—which are, after all, hardly the invention of the latest wave of immigrants. As we shall see, bureaucracy provides another means of traversing the threshold separating organization from market, limiting the penetration of immigrant networks—in ways that the scholarly literature has not yet acknowledged—while producing exclusion of a different sort.

CHAPTER 7

Bringing the Boss Back In

Family and ethnic ties are alive and well within modern organizations, for reasons having to do with the efficiency consequences of network hiring. The persistence of personal relationships signals that particularism has not been destroyed by universalism—far from it. But we cannot conclude that particularism is again triumphant. Rather, particularism and universalism remain in tension; the social ties among workers can threaten managerial authority, fail to provide the predictability desired by organizations, and threaten to weaken organizational legitimacy, a threat especially important when the clientele consists of a multi-ethnic public. Thus, the slicing of the ethnic pie is not merely an "ecological" matter, where "invading" groups use whatever resources they have to compete over jobs and struggle to control niches. Bureaucratization limits the penetration of immigrant and other networks into the workplace, introducing a set of screening and selection criteria applied universally to all comers. To the extent that universality implies equity, this is good news for those who find themselves outside the dominant network. On the other hand, universalism is far from universally applied, with the subjective preferences of recruiters and hiring agents crucial. Consequently, the back door is always open for the introduction of stereotypes and prejudiced views, the impact of which depends on a range of factors including the structure of the organization, the nature of the clients, and the preferences and power of the workers already employed.

Rephrased, our story thus far is a tale of networks and the ways in which the penetration of ethnic social ties into formally "open" organizations enlarges opportunities for ethnic insiders while reducing access for outsiders. In some cases, organizations make little or no effort at recruitment, relying on incumbents to find and select the firm's new hires. But often they do otherwise, implementing formalized screening and selection procedures, techniques that inevitably reduce the range of network penetration, as we show below.

FORMALIZATION

Textbooks tell us that organizations manage the intake of personnel in the more or less structured fashion suggested in chapter 5, first, *recruiting* to form the pool of candidates, then *screening* to pare down the pool, and last, *selecting,* often through an interview, the worker or workers to whom an offer is made. The network story, recounted in chapter 6, shows that the social connections linking established workers to their communities often bypasses or circumvents the first phase, sometimes with the consent of management, sometimes against its wishes. Where powerful or trusted networks are in place, efforts at screening and sometimes even at selection are likely to waver, with the information conveyed by established workers either dispelling doubts or at least relaxing the level of scrutiny. In effect, management moves directly to the selection phase.

There are other reasons why the neat sequence of stages often is altered. As noted in chapter 5, organizations screen to quickly and efficiently sift applicants, almost always through processing written applications and resumes, and often through employing standardized tests. But the screening process also allows for the more informal types of evaluation usually involved in the interview. Organizations pick up on the cues that applicants send when making an inquiry about a job or filling out an application—checking for grooming, demeanor, helpfulness, and dress—and dispatch those who do not meet minimal criteria, without further ado. Any interaction affords an occasion to weed out ineligibles, as when an interviewer calls an applicant to schedule an appointment: "Um, when I talk, call people on the telephone, I listen to what kind of an attitude they have on the telephone, 'cause that usually lets me know how people are going to answer the phone here. If I call somebody and they answer the phone '*What?*' first, I usually will hang up on them or something, I won't even pursue it." In general, each encounter between the applicant and the organization—or rather, its agents—offers an opportunity to strike someone off the list, often for reasons that have little or nothing to do with codified procedures.

At the same time, the effort to standardize hiring practices is subverted by, or subordinated to, the imperative to satisfy key actors—the relevant line managers charged with supervision of the performance of basic functions. The views of line managers count; rare is the personnel functionary with the power or desire to force an applicant on a skeptical manager. Chefs, for example, are notoriously individualistic, not likely to do things the way top management wants. Yet few restaurant managers exclude them when considering a hiring decision that may affect how the kitchen runs. Factory owners and managers often delegate the hiring process to line supervisors or at least take account of their views. The management may also show sensitivity to the wishes of key skilled workers. In hotels, the head housekeeper, typically a non-managerial "lead" worker only slightly elevated above her or his charges, may decide who is hired or not.

The key point is simply not to fall into the trap of reification, of treating "the" organization as a *thing*. Line managers are likely to have internalized the firm's ideals, and thus there may be alignment between the hiring preferences of individual managers and the human resource goals of the broader organization. But organizations are made up of people who do not necessarily act in the lockstep fashion suggested by the organization chart. Rather, they enjoy a considerable degree of freedom within the broad parameters established by the institution. Put differently, the organization's agents are charged with implementing a set of (sometimes highly, sometimes less) standardized rules, but since they do so in their own way, both procedures *and* the idiosyncratic preferences of individual actors affect the ways workers gain access to an organization.

Formal Recruitment Procedures

Social networks linking established workers to their family and friends seeking work universally generate referrals. Almost all the establishments we visited (93 percent) used referrals from incumbent workers to help build their pool of candidates (see Table 7.1), with relatively little variation from one industry to another. In general, the employers we surveyed sought to hire referrals, when available; more than half rated network hiring as the technique that produced the highest quality applicants, with restaurants the most enthusiastic and department stores the least. The majority of restaurants (58 percent), printers (59 percent), and

TABLE 7.1. PERCENTAGE OF FIRMS
USING RECRUITMENT METHOD, BY INDUSTRY

	Restaurants	Hotels	Printing	Furniture Manufacturing	Department Stores	Hospitals	All Firms
Referrals from employees	95 (44)	93 (40)	95 (44)	95 (39)	92 (25)	88 (32)	93 (224)
Walk-ins	93 (44)	90 (39)	66 (44)	74 (39)	100 (25)	97 (35)	85 (226)
Advertisements	30 (43)	56 (39)	55 (44)	46 (39)	60 (25)	54 (35)	49 (225)
State employment agency	27 (44)	44 (39)	11 (44)	44 (39)	72 (25)	55 (33)	39 (224)
Academic schools	36 (44)	34 (38)	14 (44)	24 (38)	76 (25)	56 (32)	37 (221)
Community organizations	7 (43)	56 (39)	20 (44)	15 (39)	56 (25)	55 (31)	32 (221)
Trade schools	14 (42)	29 (38)	50 (44)	26 (39)	32 (25)	35 (31)	31 (219)
Private employment agencies	5 (43)	18 (38)	11 (44)	14 (37)	8 (25)	13 (32)	11 (219)
Other	19 (31)	37 (27)	67 (36)	24 (34)	44 (18)	43 (21)	39 (167)

SOURCE: Skills Study
NOTE: Actual number of firms is given in parentheses.

furniture manufacturers (66 percent) used referrals as the primary recruitment method.[1]

However, employers recruit with a varied tool kit, of which network hiring is just one component. As Table 7.1 shows, organizations can employ a plethora of techniques, activating any number of sources. In reality, however, they tend to go with a limited set of the available options; we found considerable variation from industry to industry. Virtually every organization accepted applications from walk-ins, but only department stores, where the workforce is frequently churning and the nature of the business naturally generates applicants coming in from the street, rated walk-ins as the most important recruitment technique (see Table 7.2). Few were content with reliance solely on a passive source. Many took more active steps—advertising, contacting the state employment agency, working with community organizations. Printers frequently made use of a unique option, an industry association that served as a referral agency, thus providing an institutional container for occupational networks of a more informal kind. Only among department stores and hospitals—that is, large entities enduring high levels of turnover—did a majority of establishments utilize a full set of active methods.

Formal Screening and Selection Procedures

Thus, our survey found a pattern neither inconsistent, nor perfectly aligned with, the network story. But recruitment simply refers to that process that brings workers to the employer's door. To some extent, informal recruitment is paired with equally informal screening and selection. Indeed, many organizations we visited had dispensed with bureaucratic screening and selection, if for no other reason than that networks could often provide more and better information than that obtained through bureaucratic means. We were told on more than one occasion that, although some bureaucratic forms were observed, bureaucratic checks were mostly cursory.

> *Field notes:* The [printing company] supervisor does an interview—a "marginal" one. The employee referring the applicant has already been asked if the applicant will fit in.

Most organizations, however, scrutinized prospective workers with—somewhat—greater care. In printing shops and furniture factories, referral networks clearly gave applicants with connections a "foot in the door." In some cases, as suggested above, employers made no effort to screen referrals; that the candidate had the sponsorship of an incumbent worker sufficed. Most manufacturers did more, almost always choosing

TABLE 7.2. MOST IMPORTANT RECRUITMENT METHOD, BY INDUSTRY (%)

	Restaurants	Hotels	Printing	Furniture Manufacturing	Department Stores	Hospitals	All Firms
Referrals from employees	58	46	59	66	0	26	46
Walk-ins	37	21	0	6	96	42	30
Advertisements	2	15	21	16	4	13	12
State employment agency	0	3	0	6	0	3	2
Academic schools	2	0	3	0	0	0	1
Community organizations	0	5	0	0	0	3	1
Trade schools	0	0	0	0	0	6	1
Private employment agencies	0	0	0	3	0	0	0
Other	0	10	18	3	0	6	7
Total	100	100	100	100	100	100	100
Number of firms	43	39	39	32	24	31	208

SOURCE: Skills Study

to interview, but rarely made more than a rudimentary effort. Screening procedures were apt to be informal, relying on a manager's or owner's intuition and varying from one situation to the next. Smaller manufacturers, in particular, rarely maintained a specialized personnel function, decentralizing hiring decisions—often to a supervisor, who was likely to have come up from the ranks. Still, more than one-third of the printers we interviewed, and almost half of the furniture manufacturers, did subject applicants to some sort of test (see Table 7.2). Even so, the testing seemed less designed to assess the match between applicant and job than to check for physical ailments in an effort to ward off workers' compensation cases. Some firms also engaged in an informal, skills-related assessment, as with a printer who gave promising applicants an opportunity to work half a day, saying, "I'll pay you [for] a half day; you show me what you can do." The nature of work at the entry level rarely demanded more intensive selection; "You can tell in a day if they are going to be any good." And this statement seemed to hold true for the many bottom-level production jobs "where, if you don't cut it in a week, you're gone."[2]

Screening procedures were likely to be more elaborate in the hotels, with efforts to assess an applicant's potential increasing among larger and pricier hotels. As sizeable units of very large, often international, chains, hotels typically maintained a human resources office, and the presence of a personnel function yielded considerable standardization in screening efforts. To be sure, referral networks played an important role in recruitment, but then "personnel" took over. Although the jobs were unskilled, they offered ample opportunity for theft and some, such as in housekeeping, involved work of considerable autonomy. Consequently, hotel managers consistently checked references, even though that procedure yielded little information. Moreover, the interview served as a crucial selection tool, one that hotel managers wielded with more care than did their counterparts in manufacturing. In most cases, the personnel department screened applicants, making an initial recommendation to a functional manager who would then interview candidates and select the new hire.

Department stores went further in the direction of formality than did hotels and most of the other surveyed industries, frequently administering formally validated tests and performing thorough background checks in addition to the reference checks and interviews. Again, an interpersonal situation such as the interview always involved considerable informality, in which decision making usually occurred by rule-of-thumb—a matter to which we return shortly. Even though the interview and the final selection process were not always standardized in format, the department stores interviewed consistently, systematically, and at great length, a great contrast to the manufacturers, in particular. Screening typically involved multiple steps, which reduced advantages enjoyed by members of a referral network. Typically, successful candidates first underwent a review by a lower-level personnel officer, next an interview with the HR manager, then an interview with the relevant department manager, and, in some cases, final interviews with the "big bosses" themselves. In the following exchange, a store personnel manager (R1) and a regional personnel manager (R2) for the same discount chain describe their process, which is not atypical.

> R1: I take the application and review it, and if they meet the requirements I'm looking for, I go and call SPA [Store Protection Agency].
> R2: We "SPA the app." The [discount chain] loves paperwork!
> I: You do this before the interview?
> R1: Right, if they don't even pass the SPA, I'm not going to waste my time interviewing them. Second, we call them in for their first interview, usually with the personnel manager. Then, if I feel that they're qualified for a specific job, then I would direct them to a second interview with the supervisor of that area. During the interview, I give them our [discount chain] screening inventory. I call it, like, an "honesty test."

Thus, for reasons having to do with organizational features and job characteristics, screening among department stores took a highly elaborated form.

Hospitals presented a similar pattern, with the industry's division into private for-profit, private non-profit, and public sector segments introducing interesting variations. In the private sector, informality often rules, in spite of the size and complexity of the institutions, when it comes to methods used in selecting bottom-level help. "If it's an entry-level person," explained a manager for one of the region's major non-profit HMOs, "more often than not, the manager or the supervisor that's interviewing those people, he's going to, you know, get a fairly good gut feeling for that individual," and simply decide on this basis. Although tests are not commonplace for such entry-level jobs as "environmental services technician" or "dietary aide," they are the norm when clerical help is sought. For low-level filing jobs, the tests may be as simple as being "asked to write out the alphabet in block letters" (and applicants often "get that wrong, if you can believe it."), but typing tests are still mandatory for any keyboarding job.

Public sector hospitals are somewhat different. The only one of our six industries with a sizable public component, hospitals offer a particularly good example of bureaucratized selection procedures and their effects on hiring outcomes. The county-run hospitals,[3] in particular, follow rigid civil service procedures for almost all jobs, screening applicants in large cohorts, administering job content–validated examinations to the entire group, and ranking members of the cohort by performance on the examination. While reliance on interviews provides an escape hatch from the rigidity of pen-and-pencil tests, the system only allows for panel interviews that administer a fixed set of questions, with rankings based on predetermined criteria and selection limited to the test-takers passing the examination with the highest marks.

Thus, the civil service framework gives individual managers limited flexibility in hiring; it therefore severely limits the influence of ethnic networks. In extreme cases, employment managers can lose autonomy altogether, as in the case of a hospital where the Federal Office of Personnel Management "took away direct hiring, because people started looking to work for the Feds. We weren't using OPM's [the Federal Office of Personnel Management] people. None of us were." Even when hiring does not use examinations, other restrictions, such as an imperative to hire veterans wherever possible, constrain managers' decision making.

More importantly, perhaps, the civil service framework keeps job requirements high, partly because the high volume of applicants yields no pressure to lower demands. In the exchange below, two public sector health system managers told us about the responses for a set of temporary clerical positions that did not require typing.

R1: [W]e got 800 applications in two days.

R2: But that doesn't mean. . . . We only have probably 30, 40 vacancies, if that.

R1: It was just amazing that we got that many applications.

R2: Because typically we would like a little bit more of a skill, because that gives us the flexibility of utilizing someone. And almost everyone needs them to have some kind of keyboard knowledge.

R1: But even on the exam process, even though we got 800, only 140 passed the exam.

    I: Is that the normal ratio?

    R1: Well, it wasn't in the past, but today it is. Yeah, that's reading and comprehension and spelling, and it becomes a major issue in terms of having these skills needed just to pass an exam. Shows a change in skill level. Coming out of the schools.

    R2: Coming out of the schools. And it is unfortunate. And it's something we're concerned about.

Although these managers were satisfied that, since the examination had been officially validated, it tested fairly for the competencies required by the job, other respondents were not so sure. A personnel official at a hospital in the same system told us that "the clerk [test] is a high rate of fail, probably the highest," and noted that "people would get so bogged down with the math, they couldn't get to the end of the test." Likewise, an HR manager in a Veterans Administration hospital contended, "Some people with reasonable clerical skills don't take the test well," and lamented that "when we were able to examine directly, the quality was better."

Of course, reliance on formal civil service procedures made it hard for most immigrants to get through the door. Rules are rules, and they generally work well in excluding newcomers who lack the credentials, experience, or English-language facility that public sector hospitals seek. Notwithstanding elaborate efforts at validation, some of the best test-takers did not have the oral communication skills to actually function on the job:

> The only requirement is they pass both the tests and then they're put on the eligibility list. So we have some people who have made out the application, passed the test, passed the typing test; we send them to interview, and they're absolutely, we don't know, we can't figure how they passed the test. They can't even talk. I mean they, it's kind of like, especially Asians, we don't know how they passed the test. Because it's kind of like they can't speak English. You ask them a question and they don't know what the hell you're talking about. Yet they pass the exam, they can read. Because the exam is held under very strict, we have proctors there to make sure that nobody takes the test for somebody else. And we have to have their driver's license there. I mean it's a very extensive closed exam. And we sit in on interviews and we get people and they say, "How did that person pass the test?"

Thus, in the end, the test *does not* conquer all; when managers encounter candidates who "can't put two [English] sentences together," they ensure that "they don't ever get hired, ultimately hired." Thus, screening alone bars the route to native-born workers who lack the skills to do well on the tests, while the combination of screening *and* selection deters immigrants.

In sum, screening and selection procedures range widely. At the very bottom of the labor market, it is "catch as catch can," with some organizations not bothering to test, "because they normally don't have the skills anyway," while others screen "when we have the time" but, if pressed, only want to find out "who[m] do you know that could come in today?" Larger, more bureaucratized entities—most commonly hospitals and department stores—employ far more complex procedures, which they deploy in a standardized way. Although these organizations often fall back on informal recruitment practices, they secure much, if not most, of the labor force through formal means. Not using networks for information exchange, they need to learn about and screen workers more formally.[4] Many of the differences in screening and selection procedures have their roots in the content and structure of a job, while others have to do with a firm's environment.

LEGITIMACY: TOO MANY OF THESE, TOO FEW OF THOSE

Searching for the applicants most likely to meet the expectations of the job, organizations find virtues in the bureaucratic mechanisms for matching persons with positions. Formality has attractions extending beyond its predictive power, as it helps protect against developments that may threaten the organization's legitimacy in the public eye. Because it leads to "the 'like me' syndrome," as the manager of a fast-food chain pointed out, network hiring often yields a workforce where everyone "looks alike." The possibility that employees would be ethnic clones of one another was not always viewed by employers in a positive light. "I try to keep a pretty broad spectrum of ethnic groups in the kitchen so we don't get too many cliques," explained a hospital dietary services manager concerned that "it would be real easy to have an all-Filipino kitchen." While conceding that referrals were more likely to be "good workers, they're usually just, I mean, real reliable, dependable," hospital managers knew that dependence on referrals would inevitably, and undesirably, give their workforce a distinctive cast.

> R: Sometimes it gets too tight, like the old boy network . . . and we have to remember to remain diverse. So that's one problem, because a lot of times if you're just referring certain ethnic groups or something like that.

I: But so you take steps to deter that from happening?

R: Right, right.

I: What kind of, so that would just be not taking any more referrals?

R: Or no, not necessarily, but if some, if you just start getting a lot of referrals, then your affirmative action goal is something else, you just have to do outside recruiting. You can't take those referrals.

Particularly concerned about the face they presented the public, the department stores and hospitals took pains to avoid duplicating the pattern of single-group dominance found in the back of the house in kitchens or hotels and on furniture factory floors. Both industries sought to serve a diverse clientele, an imperative that pushed them toward outreach while breeding an aversion to reliance on hiring through workers' contacts. "Diversity is in both our customers and our workforce, and we want to bring [more of] it into our workforce," explained a department store manager. A unit of one of the region's most important HMOs saw diversity "as a reality based on, from the personnel standpoint, our applicant pool, [and] from a business standpoint, from our membership. You want to have a workforce that's representative and can respond to the needs of our members." A department store manager told us that clientele and employees "parallel each other steadily. You need to truly understand that you have a melting pot in your workforce and you have to look at your workforce and clientele objectively as a marketing group." Another department store manager expressed the desire to "hire 10 percent black, 10 percent Filipino, 8 percent white, 7 percent Hispanic, and really get it in line with what's really going on, as far as how people live in this area," concluding with "what more could you ask for?"

This evidence notwithstanding, one should not think that hospitals or department stores had been bitten by the multicultural bug; rather they were simply listening to the marketplace telling them that sensitivity to ethnic matters counted. Customers "don't just notice the merchandise," explained a manager at an old-line department store, "they look at the people who are working there." This consideration made diversity desirable: "When you are out hiring folks . . . make sure that we have a wide variety of people working at the store, so many blacks, so many Hispanics, and that seems to help business a lot." Not only do customers pay attention to the composition of the people trying to service their needs; they are willing to complain when not happy about the faces they see. A top-of-the-line department store in the South Bay received "letters from African-American customers asking 'Where are the African-American employees?'"; the firm is "now training to focus on an African-American base." Noting that "the biggest challenge I have is getting the right candidate into the store," a manager underlined the impact of customers' ethnic preferences: "I have customers in Huntington Beach who do not want someone who is Korean and Vietnamese waiting on them [and] conversely I have a customer in West Covina who is East Asian or Hispanic, and sometimes they are extremely uncomfortable in being waited on by someone who is Caucasian."

Considerations such as these led stores not only to recruit among a diverse pool but also to engage in monitoring to ensure adequate representation of the components of the customer base. "I like to have a balanced workforce," explained a department store manager. "It's always on our mind. We get monthly printouts on hiring and diversity, so we know if we're short."

Thus the search for a workforce that mirrors the customer base necessarily leads employers away from reliance on network hiring. Dependence on referrals yields a homogeneity that is doubly unwanted, as it reduces organizations' ability to deal effectively with their diverse clientele and makes the clientele suspect that the organization treats some groups of workers and customers differently from others. But the need to achieve balance can still have exclusionary consequences in a context where one group's numbers are at best holding steady while another's are swelling. Such is the case in hospitals, where, as discussed in chapter 4, the need to serve a growing non-English-speaking population swells demand for a skill (bilingualism) unlikely to be evenly shared among the region's demographic groups.

INTERACTION: IMPRESSIONS AND GUT FEELINGS

Thus, *bureaucracy* and *network* entail two different mechanisms for moving across organizational thresholds. Although social connections between established workers and potential applicants propel the latter, the former involves an active process of sifting in which organizational needs and criteria play the dominant role. By their nature, bureaucratic mechanisms tend toward standardization: regardless of personal characteristics or preferences, hiring agents, whether as clerk or manager, follow a common set of procedures. But the difficulty of assessing applicants' suitability leaves ample room for employment of subjective criteria; many applicants lack verifiable benchmark traits or work histories that could inform a more objective reading. Skills, as we have noted, matter less to employers than do the attitudes judged appropriate. What formal procedures do best, and in faceless fashion, is to determine whom *not* to consider. The positive step of deciding which specific person to hire almost always results from a face-to-face encounter, in which the intangibles of interaction are key.

Indeed, cues derived from interaction can affect the process from the start, as we pointed out earlier in this chapter. Job seekers who talk inappropriately when filling out application forms can be struck immediately off the list; that they did not observe the "no talking" signs in the waiting room provides sufficient evidence that they will not listen to authority on some other, more important occasion. The application provides biographical and work history information, but blanks, too, are sufficiently meaningful so that incomplete applications can be rejected out of hand, with failure to complete the form serving as an indicator of future failure to follow through. Content counts, but so does form: neatly completed applications send a signal about an applicant's personality to which employers attend. "If the application is messy," noted a printer, "it's not a good sign of an eye for detail." While multiple checks make it difficult for any single hiring agent to select the person he or she prefers, they also yield the opposite effect—that is, of increasing the number of agents who can screen applicants out. For example, the job of a department store screener principally entails referring applicants to the appropriate official higher up in the organization. But it is enough for her to write "psycho" on an application, and it falls into the trash.

Appearance makes a difference, from the moment that a job-seeker enters the organization's door. "I can usually tell in the first couple of seconds," reported the manager of a discount chain, "whether I want to hire someone or not." Depending on the organization and the degree of scrutiny it provides, applicants will not get a moment's consideration unless they "get past that [initial] look." As our respondents saw it, meaningful information could be gleaned from the full range of applicants' outer display. Hygiene mattered: "If you see someone coming in dirty for the interview, you know that they really don't give a damn." Clothing, "whether sloppy or nice, clean, or folded neatly," similarly signaled relevant traits. One manager responded allergically to torn pants; a retailer did not "hire people who walk in off the street in a pair of jeans and a tee shirt"; a hotelier who thought that she could infer attitude from appearance had an aversion to those "messily dressed"; a public sector hospital manager did not insist on "gorgeous or handsome, but somebody that is clean and kempt," especially for positions involving customer contact. "It's presentation," noted a manager of a small hospital in the San Fernando Valley, in a comment amplified by one of our most liberal hospital informants, who pointed out that "a nose ring turns people off" and not only for aesthetic reasons: "There's more fear than prejudice. Because sometimes you call someone in and you didn't know that they were a homeboy, so suddenly you have these gang people walk in." And for those managers aware of the prohibitions against discrimination against particular classes of people, "appearance" provided a last, crucial sphere in which purely subjective assessments could be legitimately applied:

> The very first thing I look at is their appearance. If they are coming in here looking like a tramp, they will not get hired by me. They will not be interviewed any more than maybe two minutes. That's the way I am. We are a Catholic-based organization that has certain values, and I try to project those values into what that person looks like. And there's been no reason, or there's no law that says that I can't discriminate against a person based on their appearance. And if they smell, or if they, you know, are not groomed and they come in wearing sloppy clothing, or whatever, I just turn them right away. Because I don't want to hire them. They have no place here in this facility because we are dealing with patients. We are a service industry. You have to look sharp, you have to look clean, neat, and presentable. And those are things that, you know, we just have higher standards here, that's all there is to it.

The interactive setting of the interview allowed employers to gauge all aspects of demeanor—"little things, such as how applicants use body language"—they deemed relevant. Managers frowned on job seekers who chewed gum during the interview, looked for eye contact, or screened out applicants who lacked a "pleasant voice." Tone of voice also denoted qualities of interest. "If you ask them a question and they become indignant, I know I'm going to have a problem with that person," related one manager. Similarly, "You can pick up on how a person reacts to a question, [to the] tone of the voice through the whole interview process. When you've been doing this for ten years, you should know."

The retailers, as expected, used the interview to look for smiles, enthusiasm, and friendliness. Although the "smile quotient" hardly struck us as an objective criterion for selection, managers thought otherwise, contending, as did one hotelier, that "the behavior of being able to easily smile [in the interview] falls under something called 'service attitude.'" In general, managers had visualized an ideal presentation of self (as so-

ciologists would put it), and that ideal provided an extensive baseline
against which to compare candidates' behaviors:

> Does a person look me in the eye? Is a person polite? I've had people use
> foul language during an interview. Has the person made some effort to
> dress nicely? Are they clean? Have they taken a shower that morning?
> Do you look me in the eye? That's a big one. I always feel that if a person
> doesn't look me in the eye, "What are they hiding? What are they afraid
> of?" Do they smile? Do they have some personality? I don't mind shyness,
> but are they going to fade into the wall when a guest walks by? Do they
> have any energy at all? A little bit of enthusiasm? Anything that suggests
> that, when they are confronted with a guest, they're going to be able to
> hold their own? I'm looking for personality, because without that it
> doesn't matter what else they have. General overall attitude. How their
> handshake is.

Of course, the actual interview—content as well as tone—provided
plenty of material of interest to the manager. While reconstructing a
work history helped assess an applicant's likely stability, it also could
throw light on general attitudes towards superiors. Managers heard loyalty when applicants spoke highly of past employers; they spotted trouble when job-seekers spoke ill of superiors or complained of failure to get
a desired promotion. As we noted above, many respondents engaged in
behavioral interviewing, attempting to assess how applicants would respond to the scenarios that they were likely to encounter at work: "You
can tell, how the interaction [is], whether they really want to work or
not. For instance, you can ask questions like, 'What level of service do
you think our customer expects at retail?' If they say 'My feeling is that
they should help themselves,' that is not the type of applicant that we
want. So they would be 'does not meet our requirement.' "

Thus, the intangibles of applicants' attitudes and propensities to interact well with customers and co-workers loom high in the final hiring
decision. As the economists note, hiring is an investment in uncertainty,
which is why so many of our respondents conceded, "I go by gut feeling," "So much of it is just a gut feel," "Basically, it comes down to an
extra sense." In the end, even the most test-ridden and -ruled environments make use of the information obtained in the human interaction.
"It's personal interaction that makes or breaks you," noted an official in
a Veterans Administration hospital. "The person who doesn't present
well doesn't get selected. The selecting official can say 'I don't want this
person. Their attitude stunk.' " While some organizations do reduce the
scope for personal intuition, preferences, tastes, and experience through

the elaborate procedures described earlier, substantial room for subjective, idiosyncratic judgment *always* remains.

> *Field notes:* Re screening, respondent taps her head and says "right here,"
> adds that she goes by whatever she feels through her experience, intuition,
> interaction with the applicant, what her lead people tell her. It's intangible.

CONCLUSION ·

As we have shown in previous chapters, the implantation of immigrant
networks tends to detach vacancies from the open market. Bureaucracy
has a different effect, potentially opening doors that networks close.
From the standpoint of immigrants—and many who study them—networks generate social capital for newcomers poor in all other resources,
and, for that reason, deserve applause. But the repeated action of network hiring favors those with ties to insiders—an outcome that those
lacking such connections are unlikely to view as fair. Not only is it hard
to quarrel with this judgment; those organizations serving diverse clienteles are in no position to do so, as the customer base will not tolerate a
workforce dominated by only one group.

Selecting an appropriately mixed group is easier when the hiring process has undergone a degree of formalization. As we have noted, intensified screening and selection efforts are related to organizational size
and complexity, with the larger organizations more likely to have established formalized selection procedures. While size has an effect regardless of industry, size and other organizational characteristics do
correlate strongly, in our sample, with industry: screening efforts are
more extensive and more formalized in hotels, hospitals, and department stores than in printing, furniture manufacturing, or restaurants.
The nature of the job matters as well: regardless of size, organizations
take more care in filling jobs entailing autonomy and some level of unpredictability. While efficiency concerns can thus motivate organizational
behavior, bureaucratic mechanisms can have an additional, unintended
effect—yielding more equitable outcomes among formally qualified
applicants.

But formality has its downside as well. If fairness means proportional
representation, then bureaucratic selection procedures signal future difficulties for blacks, since African Americans comprise a decreasing portion of the local population and, worse, depend on employment in a
number of sectors servicing a heavily immigrant clientele. Moreover, few

organizations function as Weber suggests they should. Selection almost always involves a personal element; these personal interventions allow considerable scope for discretion, and thereby, for the intrusion of bias—which, in the current climate, is unlikely to favor African Americans.[5]

Even the more impersonal means of selection may not do much to assist those low-skilled African Americans displaced by the workings of immigrant networks. Any effort to check for a criminal record—a screening activity common to almost all department stores we surveyed—will have the greatest negative impact on the members of the group with the highest rate of arrests. In Los Angeles, African Americans comprise the group most vulnerable to such checks, more so than their foreign-born Latino counterparts.[6]

Further, bureaucratic means of selection tend to artificially raise hiring criteria, just as Weber noted. Selection is most impersonal in the civil service, making public employment less permeable to immigrants but also to less-skilled African Americans. Moreover, the ramifications of the civil service system and its requirements redound with much greater force among blacks, given the degree to which the public sector has long been the most favorable source of African-American employment. Referrals, as noted, work less well in accessing public sector jobs, making the build-up of African-American employment in such government workplaces as hospitals relatively inefficient as a source of useful information and assistance to job-seekers. Since the sector's high job requirements exclude the least-skilled members of Los Angeles's African-American community, they also hurt the chances of those persons most exposed to immigrant competition elsewhere in the labor market. And the attractiveness of public sector jobs yields an additional source of competition—from not immigrants but a broad pool of better-skilled natives who seek the security and compensation available on the public payroll.

In the last analysis, network and bureaucracy can both be characterized as systems of social exclusion, although each operates according to its own principles. Neither eliminates the human factor, with networks privileging those possessing connections, and bureaucracy allowing scope for the idiosyncrasies of decision makers. If network hiring involves discrimination in favor of known quantities, and bureaucratic hiring discriminates in favor of those presenting themselves "properly," employers' preferences for willing subordinates leads to discrimination of still a different sort, as we see in the next two chapters.

PART FOUR

Prejudice, Preferences, and Conflict

CHAPTER 8

Whom Employers Want

Social science thinking about discrimination grew up in a simpler, if uglier, America of binary Euro-American/African-American relations. In that *b/w* world, to borrow language from Gary Becker's pathbreaking treatise, *The Economics of Discrimination*, the relevant questions had to do with the consequences of *w*'s aversion for interacting with *b*'s. Whites might prefer to avoid contact with blacks, as the economists thought, in which case *w* employers enduring psychic discomfort as a result of hiring *b* workers would deduct the costs from *b*'s wages; similarly, *w* skilled workers would insist on a wage premium to offset the unpleasantness of coexistence with *b*'s.[1] Alternatively, as the sociologists tended to insist, Euro-Americans would be concerned with maintaining social distance and preserving status and power differentials, in which case occupational and other forms of segregation were likely to ensue.[2]

Although the debate over the motivations and mechanisms of discrimination has continued, we have now moved to a more complicated, less certain world. At this new century's beginning, a new ethnic order is slowly emerging, in part out of the civil rights revolution but also more directly, out of the reemergence of mass immigration. Coming mainly from Latin America and Asia, the newcomers have produced a growing population that sits athwart the twin poles of black and white. Yet, as happened with previous waves of migration, less-skilled labor migrants loom large among the new Americans; stigmatized by foreign tongue,

distinctive physical features, and, often, undocumented status, these outsiders are consigned to positions at the bottom of the labor market.

In this chapter, we ask whether new principles for allocating jobs to
categorically different groups are emerging as America's lower-level
working class diversifies. In this, we build on a growing body of research
regarding the ethnic preferences of employers in America's largest cities.
Researchers Joleen Kirschenman and Kathleen Neckerman pioneered
this line of research when they took the logical, but until then neglected,
step of asking employers which groups of workers they preferred.
Among the Chicago-area employers they interviewed, Kirschenman and
Neckerman found that ethnicity and nativity often played an important
role in the hiring process. The modal boss held to a hierarchy of ethnic
preferences in which native whites stood at the top, followed by immigrant whites, immigrant Hispanics, and, at the bottom, native-born
African Americans. Employers, contended Kirschenman and Neckerman, unfairly engaged in "statistical discrimination," using the ascribed
characteristics of groups viewed through the filter of inaccurate stereotypes to predict individual behavior on the job.[3] Further, employers were
not so unsophisticated as to assume that all persons with the same skin
color were created equal; they also engaged in "address discrimination,"
taking particular care to avoid candidates from the least desirable neighborhoods and housing projects.

Kirschenman and Neckerman did not have the last word on the subject. Wilson Julius Wilson, their mentor, took a look at the same set of interviews and came away with a very different conclusion: the employers
operated with the preferences described by Kirschenman and Neckerman,
but for good business reasons, not out of prejudice. As it turns out, the
black employers in the sample described the African-American workforce
in terms similar to those used by their white counterparts (even though
they were more likely to hire black workers than were white managers);
the apparent consensus between black and white bosses, argued Wilson,
undermined the contention that whites' views were simply motivated by
stereotypes and prejudgments. If both black and white employers could
concur that black workers presented management with its least tractable
group of labor, then reality was unlikely to lie far from perception.[4]

Of course, the relationship between perception and reality is complex.
Wilson may well be correct that black managers' attitudes are immune
from the influence of widely held racial stereotypes, and that the consistency between their views and those of whites validates the latter. Perhaps—but it is equally possible that black managers' perceptions, like

those of whites, reflect widespread, socially accepted views, representing an internalization of the broader society's perceptions of their own stigmatized group—a phenomenon that would hardly be unique to blacks.[5]

Absent direct observation, one can at best hazard questionable inferences about the correspondence between employers' views and the world. To be sure, we would like to have collected such systematic observations, but that goal went beyond the scope of our investigation, which relied on managers' *representations* of new workplace realities. Like everyone else, managers' understandings of groups encountered are filtered by prejudices and preferences, ensuring that their views have an uncertain relationship to the "actual" behavior of the groups. A more crucial point, however, and quite different, is that employers' behavior is shaped by the intergroup distinctions and orderings they make; for this reason, employers' views are as much a part of the labor market reality we seek to analyze as is anything else.

Most of the existing literature focuses on the ethnic attitudes and preferences of persons who happen to be employers; this preoccupation misses the point, which has to do with the preferences that employers act upon as *bosses* selecting *workers*. In emphasizing the linkage between preferences and authority relations at work, we preclude neither the possibility that managers might import beliefs about particular groups into the workplace, nor the likelihood that such beliefs could affect their preferences as to the most or least desirable recruits. But we highlight the context, in which primary importance is placed on the likelihood that labor, once hired, will comply with management's dictates. The word "manage," after all, derives first from the Latin word *manus*, for hand, and more directly from the French word *manège*, to handle, train, or put a horse through his paces. As Braverman pointed out years ago, management is certain to rein, to spur, and to use carrots, sticks, or any other implement that might be necessary to keep labor in hand.[6] But the best strategy is to find the labor that accepts management's wishes with the minimum of bridling. Thus, when asking which workers bosses prefer, understandings of groups' suitability for subordination—as opposed to employers' ethnic attitudes, independent of content—will be the crucial, if not determining, consideration. Consequently, sensitivity to the jobs in question and the type of worker—*not* person—sought will do much to illuminate the attitudes that employers hold toward the increasingly diverse workforce that they encounter in America's immigrant cities.

Although this chapter is informed by the broader literature on the social psychology of prejudice, it diverges in one fundamental respect.[7] As we read it, the scholarship on prejudice involves inquiry into the mechanisms that prevent people from seeing others as social equals.[8] Views as to the identity of those groups whose members may be one's equals undoubtedly influence employers' preferences as they decide whom to hire. Yet, the relationship between manager and employee is inherently unequal, which means that when hiring, the employer has a specific question in mind: "Who's the best underling?" A group's perceived capacity for subordination may well preclude its fitness as a source of colleagues, neighbors, friends, and spouses—but be no issue when deciding which groups of workers get added to the payroll. The greater the demand for subordination, the more likely it is that fitness for subordination, even subservience, will loom large in the employer's eyes.

The literature in social psychology quite correctly notes that attitudes bear a very uncertain relationship to behavior. Common sense may tell us that discriminatory treatment in hiring stems from prejudiced managers entertaining negative stereotypes of this or that target group. But the common sense approach forgets that discriminatory outcomes in hiring result from a process involving any number of individuals, whose ethnic attitudes and preferences may fall all over the board. The employer—or his or her hiring agent—often has to take into account the possibly differing views of other parties, for example customers or coworkers, as to which group does or does not deserve favored treatment. No employer is utterly indifferent to availabilities on the labor supplyside: when there are no alternatives, the least desired worker is almost always taken on. Moreover, institutional factors within the organization also come into play; if the person conducting initial screening rejects all female applicants, the person handling interviews may not have a chance to exercise her preference for female workers. But, as earlier chapters have already discussed the mechanisms by which workers are hired, our concern here lies uniquely with the attitudes that employers entertain. And while attitudes—whether preferential or prejudicial—will not *always* affect hiring outcomes, they are likely to have at least *some* effect most of the time. For this reason, they deserve our attention.

DISCRIMINATION: THE DISTINCTIONS EMPLOYERS MAKE

All employers discriminate—and how can they do otherwise, since to discriminate is to make distinctions, and without distinctions employers would have no basis on which to choose one applicant over another? Indeed, they would have no reason not to hand the job to the first person walking through the door. To be sure, hiring all comers is not inherently objectionable—quite the opposite in a value system starting with "from each according to his means, to each according to his needs." But this position, while possibly worth taking seriously, seems to want adherents. In any case, in a class society, acts of "normal," everyday discrimination are appropriate and unobjectionable. It is normative to sort workers with the requisite skills from those who have little, if any idea, of how the job should be done, and to hire those most likely to hit the ground running. One expects employers to try to distinguish among applicants on the basis of ability to learn, and to then select those likeliest to catch on in the shortest time.

In practice, as we have seen, making such distinctions seems part and parcel of the hiring process. While employers are looking for recruits who can lift, make, do, process, transform, or communicate, the inherently social nature of the work environment ensures they search for more. In particular, employers want friendly workers over surly ones, deferential over rebellious, cooperative over combative—sifting and straining to select the former and screen out the latter.[9] In short, employers discriminate in favor of those workers seen as most likely to get the job done *on the employers' terms*. Put somewhat differently, high among employers' preferences—and hence, among their criteria for selection—rank workers who are accepting of their station, and are least likely to challenge the employers' definition of the situation.[10]

Needless to say, an employer's life is one of trade-offs, which means that the preference for deferential workers is never absolute. The employer usually needs at least one or two workers who possess proficiencies that are in short supply, workers who for this reason are likely to feel free to "throw their weight around." The skilled worker has even more leverage when there is a union or other organized collectivity putting additional pressure on the boss. Thus, the eccentricities, hassles, and *lip* of the key worker are tolerated, as long as he or she does the job. But if the balky worker can be replaced, then better, the employer thinks, to seek out one who does not complain than one who thinks that talking back to the boss is his or her right.

At the bottom of the labor market, employers are unlikely to tolerate workers who insist on "doing it my way." Yet low-skilled workers are relatively plentiful, so why bother weeding out the difficult cases when tomorrow there will be no problem in finding a replacement for the worker discharged today? The rejoinder is that workers at the bottom of the totem pole usually interact with others a little further up, potentially disrupting work or sowing discontent, making it to better to keep the "bad elements" out. And employers know that the least desirable jobs provide so few rewards that it is hard not to grow discontented—the reason that a propensity for subservience is likely to strike the employer as a particularly desirable trait.

For the most part, the scholarly literature on discrimination "discriminates" with regard to which actions by employers it chooses to highlight. Although rarely made explicit, the literature implies that discrimination of the type described above does not merit rebuke. The employer has the full right to discriminate in the pursuit of private interests; problems only arise when that quest crosses a fine line that suddenly transforms quotidian, unobjectionable discrimination into something "unfair" and possibly criminal. While employers hew to the rules when selecting friendly, compliant, cooperative workers, they play foul when they pay attention to certain other personal characteristics and use those traits as criteria for selection and rejection. The list of inappropriate traits keeps growing, indicating the social, hence arbitrary, hence negotiated, conflicted, political nature of which discriminations we accept and which we reject. At the moment, age, sex, religion, ethnicity, and race comprise traits that employers *cannot* legitimately or legally consider when deciding whether to put an applicant on the payroll or not.[11] Nativity,[12] however, can serve as sometimes an acceptable, sometimes an unacceptable, basis for discrimination, with much give and take in the degree to which the law has sanctioned "alien" status as a criterion for acceptable or unacceptable discrimination; the same holds true for disability status and for sexual preference.

Unfair Discrimination and Caste

Having identified employer discriminations that are "fair" and "unfair," we now tackle the question "Why do they do it?" The literature answers in several ways. One tendency places individual predispositions and prejudices at the base of discrimination. The prejudiced manager exercises her prerogative and hires only people she prefers, for reasons that have to do with either her feelings toward the relevant in- and out-groups, or the perceptions ("stereotypes") that she entertains toward these groups. This view can easily extend to take into account the prejudices of individuals who have power over the manager: the unprejudiced manager may act discriminatorily to please incumbent workers, customers, or the community, while the prejudiced manager may shun discriminatory practices, in response to pressures in the opposite direction.[13]

A more radical view contends that discriminatory actions stem from well-understood social hierarchies that all members of a society are expected to recognize and uphold. Where social collectivities enforce rigid distinctions regarding the proper place for members of specific social categories, a society possesses castelike qualities. In a pure caste society, ascribed (inherited) characteristics are definitive, and group membership is synonymous with, for example, the pursuit of particular livelihoods. We typically contrast such a *caste* society with a *class* society, where what you *own* (skills, capital, land) completely overpowers what you *are* (male, Buddhist, Chinese), at least in theory. The more castelike a society, the more likely it is that personal background yields a particular assignment in the social and economic landscapes. When employers make flat statements that group A is good and group B is bad, they conform to the prejudice model. When they indicate that group A is good for type X jobs while group B is not good for type X but is better for type Y, their views imply a castelike model of society.[14]

While some observers have argued that the American system is entirely class-based, few who disagree would claim that it represents a pure caste system. Although Clarence Thomas remains a token,[15] his confirmation as a Supreme Court justice still confirms that maintaining pure caste lines is not a political priority in this country. There is little question that blacks and other minorities have some level of access to all positions; what is at question is how much access, and whether their level of access is lowered by efforts to maintain caste lines. The forces maintaining caste lines may be propelled not so much by attitudes of an unmixed negative sort, as by views limiting particular categories of persons to the roles and positions to which they "belong."

When researcher Karen Hossfeld, a youthful white, native-born woman, tried to obtain employment as an electronics assembler in Silicon Valley firms—a job held primarily by immigrant women—employers told her that she "didn't want" that work, that it was not right for her.[16] By applying for a job "below her station," Hossfeld unsettled the personnel managers with whom she spoke.

Hossfeld's experience evokes Herbert Blumer's concept of "race prejudice as a sense of group position."[17] Going beyond simple in-group/out-group distinctions, Blumer's conception allows for a more developed and even multidimensional hierarchy of groups. Blumer's discussion serves us particularly well because he addresses social situations in which several culturally distinct groups are attempting to coexist, exactly the pattern we find in contemporary Los Angeles. Blumer argues that all groups agree on the identity of the dominant group in the overall hierarchy; each group also possesses an understanding of its appropriate position in the hierarchy; however, subordinate groups do not necessarily agree with one another on their relative positions. Blumer's view thus identifies the distinctive element in a multi-ethnic hierarchical situation of a fluid type, as opposed to a caste society where the hierarchy is universally understood and regarded as objective. His formulation also suggests that the appropriate "place" for workers with origins outside the dominant group will prove a subject of conflict and contention.

In a system where the focus is on group position, *attitudes* and *preferences* may come into conflict. Attitudes comprise two parts: a feeling relating self to object ("I don't like cilantro"); and a link connecting that feeling to a rationalized justification ("because it tastes like soap").[18] A preference contains these affective and cognitive elements, but orders one object relative to another ("I'd like the Merlot, not the Chardonnay") with context strongly affecting that ranking ("but only because I'm ordering the filet"). The relationship between attitudes and preferences is indeterminate; for example, a negative *attitude* towards a particular group ("I don't like Hispanics, because they are dirty") may turn into a positive *preference* for that group when hiring for jobs that require "dirty" work. Likewise, a positive attitude towards social equals does not, as noted above, preclude an aversion for equals as candidates for low-wage, low-status jobs.

Thus, the individualistic, and the more social (Blumerian) conceptions can offer dramatically different predictions of the relationship between, on the one hand, the cognitive and affective components of prejudice, and, on the other, the behaviors involved in discrimination. In the first view, I won't hire you because I despise you, and I want to stay as far away from you as I possibly can. In the second view, I might hire you, but for the same reasons I despise you: the jobs in question are not suited for people of *my* kind, but are perfectly appropriate for people of *yours*. Of course, there is a point of intersection: the Blumerian factory owner will not object to putting an out-group worker on his payroll, but guess who's *not* coming to dinner.

Categories and Stereotypes

Whether it is attitude or preference that explains the actions of employers, the cognitive processes by which they apprehend the world affect the way they view the groups that they encounter.[19] The world is a confusing place to the unorganized mind; to treat each person, place, or thing we encounter sui generis would be impossibly overwhelming. To order our everyday experience, we employ categories, most of which were transmitted by our parents, learned from our friends, or picked up in school, on television news, or from other sources. These categories, like "chair," "apple," "friend," and "Catholic," are tools to make sense of and track our moment-to-moment experiences. The cognitive need to label the world, and to attach meanings to the labels we create, underlies stereotyping. Stereotypes are widely shared understandings about the features of categorically distinct groups. While stereotypes are often regarded as "faulty" generalizations,[20] they have parts that are statistically correct and other parts that are not subject to empirical testing. For instance, it is true that Chinese Americans are, on average, relatively affluent, but a Chinese person chosen at random may be a sub-minimum-wage worker in a Chinatown sweatshop. And in no circumstance are we likely to be able to scientifically test whether the French make better lovers than, say, the Norwegians or the Swiss. In a society where each individual is ideally judged on her own merits, stereotypes are always "wrong," in the sense that they encourage us to see the *group member* rather than the individual.

Stereotypes become prejudices when they become infused with feeling; a person who thinks lawyers are sneaky is not prejudiced against (or towards) lawyers unless he thinks that "sneaky" is a bad thing. Prejudices need not be unambiguously positive or negative. Stereotypes also possess the property of proving resistant to contradictory evidence, even while consistent evidence is seen as confirmatory; this characteristic makes stereotypes difficult to dispel. The intensity and nature of feeling toward a target group influences the degree to which stereotypes are amenable to change; the worst situation is one in which the perception is uniformly negative and the feeling attached to the perception deeply held.

Statistical Discrimination

Both individualistic and Blumerian perspectives link effect—unfair discrimination—to cause—perception of, and feeling, toward, an out-group. Outcomes looking quite similar to those of unfair discrimination, however, may stem from other, less obviously objectionable practices; for example, "normal discrimination" might easily—perhaps even automatically—lead to behaviors that look similar to discrimination of the type conventionally labeled unfair. As we noted above, employers are looking for the workers most likely to do the job well. However, "fair" selection practices are easier to describe than to adequately pursue. To begin with, the employers do not always know which personal traits and experiences best predict performance on the job, and, even if they knew, it is time-consuming and expensive to collect all the relevant information. Thus, employers select on the basis of other traits that *seem* correlated with the characteristics most likely to predict job success.

The reader already knows this story, since these are among the motivations we invoked to explain employers' reliance on the networks of incumbents to provide a ready supply of new recruits. The employer possesses far more information about ten-year veteran Joe than about almost all new applicants, especially if most come without credentials and with references that are hard to confirm—the usual experience at the bottom of the Los Angeles labor market. Under these circumstances, it seems better to ask Joe to bring in his cousin, and bet that Joe and the cousin are workers of the same type, rather than wager on some unknown.

While such network hiring involves making distinctions, and thus discriminations, this does not necessarily imply that the employer makes distinctions that constitute discrimination of the sort that law and today's customs designate "unfair." Where incumbents' networks essentially seize hold of the recruitment process, employers rarely, if ever, have the opportunity to consider applicants who differ from the workers whom they already employ. Under these circumstances, out-group workers find themselves excluded, but not as the result of actions motivated by prejudices of employers.

The issue gets more difficult when the employer does not simply activate the personal networks of the incumbent workers, but rather uses the characteristics of these incumbents as proxies for the traits desired among new hires. The employer is looking for a worker like Joe: someone who comes in on time, shows up every day, works hard, finishes the job with few complaints, and does not sign the union card when the organizer comes around. But since the employer does not know exactly how to fish for workers with just those traits, it is easier, and not irrational, to hire workers of Joe's "kind," that is, members of group A.

In this instance, the employer does indeed make use of the prohibited traits—age, sex, ethnicity, etc.—as screening or selection criteria, but not for reasons of aversion for, or distaste toward, any group as such. It is just that she cannot afford to do otherwise; having only imperfect information, she opts to pick workers from group A and not from group C, about whom she knows so little. Here, discrimination results from past practices; the impact is all the more severe when the employer is also burdened with preconceptions that favor only some groups, since continued selection of group A inevitably implies exclusion of group C. Under these circumstances, how could the employer ever obtain the experience with C needed to contradict the weight of stereotypes acquired prior to, or outside, the work setting?

But assume, for a moment, that the labor market takes an open, competitive form, only weakly structured by the types of social ties highlighted in our analysis so far. Add the possibility that groups A and C differ, *on average*, on some set of productivity-related traits. Under these circumstances, rational employers will evaluate the worthiness of *individual* members of A and C on the basis of the average statistic for each group. In so doing, they engage in what economists call "statistical discrimination."[21]

Discrimination of this sort may not be appealing but is not unreasonable. It may well be that the average member of group A attended higher-quality schools than did the average member of group C; it would also not be surprising should the quality of education correlate closely with on-the-job performance. While some C's possessing the high-school degree may have learned more than some A's, this is irrelevant, since the employer has not the time or funds either to sift carefully or to absorb the differential costs associated with training the (on average) less qualified C's. What counts is the average, which produces a reasonable prediction, more cost-effective than carefully scrutinizing every applicant. Since the average C applicant arrives with poorer productivity-related characteristics than does the average A, eliminating all C's from consideration increases the quality of the effective pool. Thus, under profit-maximizing conditions, employers will engage in *rational* (that is, *statistical*) discrimination in favor of A, not because they dislike C but for reasons of cost.[22]

The quest for cost and risk reduction provides powerful motivation for employers trying to fill positions in which workers receive a good deal of training on the job: the danger of mistaking an unstable worker for one expected to stay long enough for a return on the firm's "investment" in skills provides ample reason for caution. But it is quite another matter when the skills in question are limited, or when little training is likely to be provided—precisely the characteristics that apply to the jobs here studied. Under these circumstances, groups A and C may differ in some underlying trait, but that attribute is likely to prove more relevant to authority relations at work than to the actual skills needed to get the job done.

Research and theorizing about "statistical discrimination" has mainly been content to focus on the ways such traits as ethnicity, "race," or gender serve as proxies for characteristics clearly related to "getting the job done," such as schooling, experience, or the ability to learn. But as already pointed out, work in a capitalist society gets done under a particular type of labor-management regime—an observation that returns us to the more social, Blumerian view of discrimination. One can apply the Blumerian terminology also to describe *class* as "a sense of group position," without doing damage to the root concepts: class relationships at work bear many castelike qualities, starting with the distinction between white-collar and blue-collar and continuing to the differences in appropriate dress, the separate parking spaces for managers, and so on.[23] As we've already argued, management prefers workers who come equipped with an understanding of group position that takes workplace authority relations as givens, not as matters for dissent—who have, in other words, a worldview accepting of workers' subordination. Less desirable are those workers who comprehend their position in the stratification and also contest it (albeit in varying and always limited degrees).

All this matters because, in any one place, at any one time, groups differ in the propensity to accept their status. Some worker groups tend to be more assertive, others more deferential, motivating employers to engage in "statistical discrimination" of a different kind than that envisioned by the conventional hypothesis. In the scenario we have in mind, employers can also use group membership as a proxy, not for workers' skills, but for their willingness to accept authority without question. And who could rightfully complain? As noted in the beginning of this section, employers who try to keep the workplace clear of militant, union-prone, or combative workers are simply engaged in normal—that is, "fair"—discrimination.

These considerations apply to our concerns precisely because disparities in workers' expectations of treatment on the job are neither given nor permanent; rather, they are situational. In particular, the arrival of some new outsider group, perhaps through international migration, tends to yield between-group differentiation of just this sort. As we have argued, immigrants should be understood as workers distinctively characterized by a dual frame of reference, in which conditions in the host society are always assessed relative to conditions in the home society. If "here" is better than "there" on most counts—pay, status of the job, type of work involved, or even authority relationships at work—then foreign-born employees are likely to provide a more accommodating, if not necessarily happier, workforce than the native-born alternatives. One can thus easily imagine that employers will take nativity as a proxy for workers' attitudes towards authority—ironically producing a preference for out-group rather than in-group members.

Employers will have further reason to pursue such intergroup sorting if immigration alters the normative associations between groups and positions. In Blumer's initial conceptualization, groups were more or less fixed, as were the positions to which they were "appropriately" assigned. But the advent of new groups through immigration should easily change such normative expectations, especially when the workforce in an occupation or industry shifts from a mainly native-born to a mainly or heavily foreign-born group. Under these circumstances, jobs previously in the in-group ambit become stigmatized as positions mainly fit for the "out-group," a change unlikely to be viewed with equanimity by in-group members with the bad luck to hold out-group jobs. If one attribute of in-group membership was a high level of expectations, then the type of shift just described would only make members more rebellious, more demanding, and more discontented than otherwise.

However, the lines between "in" and "out," "us" and "them," "established" and "outsiders," are always shifting. At the workplace, for example, the African-American worker, one of "us" when everyone is griping about the "foreigners jabbering" in their own language as if "they weren't living in America," turns into one of "them" as soon as it comes time to leave the job for home. In the case of African Americans or any other stigmatized native-born group, the duality of in- and out-group status—"two souls, two thoughts, two unreconciled strivings, two warring ideals," as Du Bois put it long ago,[24] comes into play. In their status as natives, and thus in-group members, members of a racialized minority aspire to the average standard and treatment of the society in which they have grown up. But their status as out-group members simultaneously generates a sense of disenfranchisement and grievance, as Lawrence Bobo and Vincent Hutchings have argued.[25] Thus the rebelliousness experienced by all native-born bottom-level workers, fueled by the mismatch between expectations and the very different reality of their work, will be sharpened by the greater alienation that native-born members of any racialized minority are likely to undergo.

Of course, we have now fallen prey to the danger highlighted at the beginning of this chapter—entangling perception with reality. But we can save ourselves by arguing that employers are no more stupid, indeed are probably smarter, than professional social scientists. At the very least, they are practical sociologists, operating with a theory of the labor market that guides their thinking about which workers should be picked and why. If employers intuitively, sometimes even explicitly, understand their world as we have just described it, then their cognitive map is no less a part of labor-market reality than are the characteristics and behaviors of the workers that their theory purports to describe. All that we need for now is to assert that employers have an everyday theory of immigrant labor, perceiving immigrants as the class of worker that evaluates conditions "here" in light of how bad they are "there," and, given the right conditions, is to be preferred for precisely this reason.

As we shall show in the next chapter, this is just how our employers understand their world.

CHAPTER 9

"Us" and "Them"

For the most part, the literature on discrimination tells a story about actions taken because of aversion towards specific "others." But it might be better to begin with an understanding of preferences for those like oneself, in which case the sociological literature that has emerged from the study of ethnic enterprise provides particularly fertile terrain. In general, we anticipate a preference for insiders over outsiders on grounds of ethnocentricity alone. The sociological research concerned with ethnic entrepreneurs and their workers actually is somewhat different, painting a picture of an employer whose preference for others of his or her "own kind" stems as much from rational calculation as from intragroup solidarity. Yes, the employer is motivated by a sense of obligation to co-ethnics, but he or she also knows them better than outsiders—and is influenced by this factor, since the indexical qualities of persons like oneself yield considerable predictive power as to how an applicant will actually perform. In addition, the employer's pulse is quickened by the knowledge that group members—both from solidarity and from limited options—can be squeezed that much harder.

This literature is helpful, but only to a point; the problem is that it takes a particular "us" and "them" relationship for granted, when in fact those distinctions fall out in a variety of ways. In the nineteenth century, for example, Benjamin Disraeli wrote of "two nations," having in mind Britain's "respectables," on the one hand, and its workers, on the other.[1] A century later, the famous union organizer James Matles returned the compliment with a book about the militant electrical workers union and the capitalists it battled, *Them and Us*.[2] Whether the view is from the bottom or from the top, managers and workers may look at each other and find only differences, putative ethnic commonality notwithstanding.

Moreover, nativity and ethnicity crisscross in paradoxical ways. By definition, the United States is a consensual nation, now distinguished, at least in theory, by the irrelevance of ethnic origins to attainment of full citizenship. "We Americans" provides a category for organizing and grouping persons of all ethnic stripes—in part by opposing them to the immigrant outsiders, who have not yet shifted their ways and affiliations from "there" to "here." But like any category, "American" can be associated with valences of a positive or negative kind, depending on the context. In particular, employers looking for low-wage help may be attuned to qualities of Americaness ill-suited to the tasks at hand: doing difficult, unpleasant jobs in return for paltry compensation. Under these circumstances, do employers seeking to fill vacancies see the work as better fit for "them" or for "us"? In the pages that follow, we examine how employers define "them" and "us," and the difference that these definitions make.

"WHITE WORKERS JUST DON'T WANT TO GET THEIR HANDS DIRTY"

In our sample, a substantial majority of the persons in positions to make decisions about hiring were of Euro-American background, but that trait hardly exhausts their relevant characteristics: they were also all managers or owners (the occasional foreman excepted). As our concerns involved the low-skilled labor market, the hires in question were always quite different from self—issues of ethnic background, nativity, language, or gender notwithstanding.[3]

Indeed, for the most part, those making decisions about hiring were reluctant to take on those workers who were least removed from their own social status. We saw this most vividly in our interviews with managers at restaurants and retail department stores, especially in the San Fernando Valley where many reported receiving applications from former aerospace workers. Managers proved reluctant to hire men and women who had been earning upwards of twenty dollars per hour for jobs that would pay little more than the minimum wage on the grounds that these formerly highly paid workers would be too unhappy with low-wage work to stay long.[4] However, employers might have also had an unspoken worry: "overqualified" workers might cause trouble, resisting paternalistic control, fighting for conditions and wages more commensurate with their felt worth. In sum, these usually white, highly skilled, but displaced workers came with relatively high social standing—and this turned out to be the chief factor disqualifying them.

Thus, when managers did hire white applicants, such workers were usually "them," that is, of a lower-class background, possessing a good deal less education and skill than the person making the decision. Usually, no job seeker answering this description knocked at the door; to a large extent, whites had fallen out of the labor pool for such entry-level jobs. Many employers complained that, from looking at the applicants they did get, "Most of the white people don't want to work." "Take your Caucasians, they get fat and happy," noted the chief engineer of one factory we visited. "They take things too easy. A lot of people around this area don't want to come in at the five-dollars-an-hour level. If you take people who have just arrived in the [United States] a short time [ago], they want to get ahead. Same as our grandparents did." Whites were particularly scarce on the production floor; referring to natives in general, one furniture manager observed that "nobody wants a job in a factory here." According to the furniture makers, whites had largely dropped out of the industry's labor supply, reflecting the stigmatized character of the jobs and not just their low wages: "White workers just don't want to get their hands dirty. That is it. People prefer to work in McDonald's all their lives for the meager salary of five dollars. We only have one person that earns [only] five dollars. Our whole society discourages for people not to work in these type of [manufacturing] jobs. People are not supposed to get their hands dirty."

Although positions in furniture manufacturing certainly stood near the very bottom of the job hierarchy, other industries employing low-level labor were also bidding adieu to their Euro-American help. The owner of an Italian restaurant recalled that whites were available to do any job when he had lived "back east"; now, "the American or Anglo is not a great dishwasher—unless he's an 'alkie' just doing it to get off the street." "We don't have a lot of whites applying or being hired for entry-level jobs," was the view of a manager with a large public hospital. When the dominant pattern was reversed, the unexpected entry of whites only served to underscore the norm, as in the case of a regional chain that had opened a restaurant in a newly developed area in San Bernardino County: "Anglos don't work at [this restaurant chain] any more. The only problems finding workers are in 'lily-white' communities. We opened a new store in a 'white flight' area a year ago. We had three hundred applicants for thirty jobs, most of whom were Anglos. It was incredible, like going through a time warp. A throwback."

Of course, many managers still recruited from a white labor supply; in these cases, their evaluations were colored by their understandings of the appropriate relationship between the labor supply and the particular positions they were trying to fill. Seeking "the traditional American values—be on time, be clean, do what your employer tells you," employers often found that at the bottom of the labor market, non-white groups were more likely to come with the desired traits. Asians, in particular, often edged out whites as the labor force of choice. "I would say it's a little tougher to find today white workers with as high a work ethic as Asians. But that doesn't mean it's impossible. . . . I would say that twenty years ago there were [more]." And employers who would concede that "white workers are good workers" would nonetheless go on to say that "overall Latinos are much better workers. They have a loyalty towards the company that white workers don't have."

The white worker "problem" involved a contradictory relationship between (dominant) group and (lowly) position: "White people . . . feel that they can achieve more, so therefore entry-level or lower levels are beneath them. Like we talked about it earlier, we paint this picture of the ability to achieve success, and success in this country is measured by expensive things. Big houses, expensive cars, all the things you can't get at entry-level jobs. And they want it now." The immediacy of whites' expectations was certainly a matter for grumbling. "They [whites] are not as hardworking as Hispanics. They want to get to the top rung quickly," noted a manager in a public sector hospital. As pointed out by a number of employers, especially those in manufacturing, white workers employed in jobs that were now "right" for some different group were not simply impatient; worse, "a lot of white males in entry-level positions have the attitude that they're better than this and don't need to be doing this, whereas someone with a different ethnic background wouldn't think that." To express the point a little more politely than the pungent quote that follows, white workers had a different understanding of the proper equation between effort and reward than their employers thought appropriate: "The white factory worker is a whining piece of shit. They [feel that they] never make enough money, they always work too hard, they never want to work over eight hours a day and they feel that, as soon as you hire them, you owe them." Another remarked with equal pungency: "Their [whites'] work ethic is a little bit lower. Because they feel that they should not be doing this type of work because they are Americans. 'I shouldn't be breaking my back.' Whites are worse than blacks, they are always complaining. They tell me that they are not 'wetbacks.' "

As these comments suggest, in-group status was exactly what made "in-group" workers undesirable. Moreover, the lines demarcating "ins" from "outs" varied with the situation. Since the reward-and-effort equation is mainly affected by relative expectations, whites were likely to be disqualified because they insisted on "American" standards. As a restaurant manager opined, "They're lazier. They don't work as hard as immigrants in this market. They'd rather earn the same wage for a less strenuous job—this is hard work." For that reason, whites were seen by a hospital manager as "more like the blacks." He elaborated: "You know when you offer them a job, they want more money, they expect more. The Asian groups, a lot of them just really want a job. These immigrants, they come in from their country and they just want to work."

Of course, those employers most likely to rate white workers negatively were also those recruiting for the least desirable jobs. Relatively few managers placed whites at the bottom of the heap. Situational factors also heavily influenced the negative assessments. Hotels and, particularly, restaurants were often way stations for actors or "spoiled Valley kids"[5] working in the front of the house; in hiring whites, managers were aware of, and irked by, the likelihood that "the minute they get a call from an agent, they drop us like a hot potato."

As further evidence that context matters, whites' work ethic was generally viewed more favorably where job ladders were more extended and opportunities for career employment more abundant. Some managers, for instance, were positively disposed toward white workers, but their dispositions were often functional, as when they had a preference for hiring native whites because these workers could speak English. Often, the critical assessments of whites would have had a positive valence in some other context. Sometimes, situational considerations had the opposite effect, as when managers noted that white workers were the most eager to get ahead, a trait that also made them a poor choice for jobs with few outlets upward. In the end, relative considerations heavily influenced employers, who were more likely to assess fitness contextually than in the terms of ethnic attitudes of a more abstract sort. That whites were often found unsuitable tells us much about the factors influencing employers' views of the other groups making up the labor pool.

A NEW ETHNIC ORDER?

Latino Immigrants: "They Like to Work"

One might imagine, especially in the immigrant-dense regions of Southern California, South Florida, or New York, that apprehension over the political and demographic consequences of immigration might lead Euro-Americans to revise their long-held racial antipathy for blacks. Yet Euro-American employers still prove reluctant to hire African Americans, even if the alternative involves recruiting Mexicans or Central Americans, toward whom the same Euro-American bosses often evince considerable aversion.

The distinction made earlier between attitudes and preferences does much to illuminate the characteristics of the emergent ethnic hierarchy, as well as the factors influencing employers' selection and ranking criteria. In Los Angeles' multi-ethnic labor market, nativity serves as a crucial marker, although only one of several, distinguishing "us" from "them." As noted earlier, individualistic understandings of the issue link discrimination to an aversion to others not like oneself: "we" do not hire "them," because "they" are different, hence to be kept at a distance from "us." But, from the employers' perspective, "we" lack those characteristics that make for a good—that is, hardworking and uncomplaining— low-level worker. Although the employers seemed unlikely to think of themselves as "un-American," they often viewed "American" as shorthand for those qualities to avoid in a worker. "The American people, *we've* been spoiled." Part of the problem was a general disinclination for hard, menial labor: "The American workforce does not want to do physical labor." But the problem lay deeper: "Americans are too damned spoiled and lazy to work. Fifteen, twenty years ago, I wouldn't have said this. Their outlook has changed completely."

"Spoiled" American workers held to the belief that "it's a birthright to have good jobs and good pay. Why on earth would an American clean a hotel for five-fifty an hour? But immigrants see them as good jobs. There's a willingness to take jobs that Americans see as demeaning." Managers were enchanted neither with the American approach to work at the bottom—"It's 3:30, I've done my job. It's 'me, me, me.' "—nor with the prevailing work ethos. "When you say to an American person, 'Do you want to work at McDonald's?' they'll say, 'No way. I don't want to flip burgers,' due to the general laziness of American culture." Worse still was the fact that, as Americans, the native-born workforce was likely to talk back: "And American workers are more concerned with their rights, as opposed to immigrants who just want a job and will settle for minimal pay without a fuss. [Without immigrants] we'd have more problems managing workers that would be more difficult and more demanding."

Lack of the experiences, and therefore, expectations, shared by natives made the foreign-born workers different. But this was not such a bad thing, since "having gone without meals gives you motivation," as a fast-fooder explained: "These people have a drive. From where these people are coming from, they are not given the opportunities that they are granted here, so the workers are very motivated to work, and work hard. Even though they are earning low wages."

Rephrased in the language of our respondents, the disparities between *here* and *there* made all the difference: "Where *they* come from, five dollars an hour, at home, is a lot of money to them, where five dollars *here* is nothing"; "From where *they* are coming, working for these wages— *they* think it's great"; "For *them*, the basics is a lot; for people raised *here*, it is not worth it." Or, as clarified by one of our more sophisticated furniture industry respondents, "If *I* consider that relative deprivation,"—the "that" consisting of unskilled work at "six-to-seven-dollar rates"—"*they* consider this a very good opportunity."

Thus, immigrants *were* different from "us," but their differences served as a *positive* signal for selection; the immigrants' "otherness" was associated with a set of behavioral characteristics that employers generally liked. "The 'amigo'," a fast-food manager said bluntly, "comes to work." Noted others:

> Yes, the immigrants just want to work, work long hours, just want to do anything. They spend a lot of money coming up from Mexico. They want as many hours as possible. If I called them in for four hours to clean latrines, they'd do it. *They like to work.* They have large families, a big work ethic, and small salaries. The whites have more, so they're willing to work fewer hours. Vacation time is important to them. They get a play and want to get two months off. They want me to rearrange a schedule at a moment's notice. These guys in the back would never dream of that. They would like to go back to Mexico every four years for a month which I [let them] do. The back-of-the-house workers take vacation pay and then work through their vacations. I try to get them to take off a week once a year. But most of them plead poverty. The kids in the front of the house are still being taken care of by their parents. I'm not trying to disparage them, but *they're spoiled.* (Manager in a French bistro)

Immigrants are here to work, and they're not afraid of hard work. There are a lot of young Americans who don't want to work. If they want work at the minimum wage, they go elsewhere. Immigrants will work for minimum wage and *won't complain, even if you keep them there forever*. They're used to this kind of job. (Coffee shop manager)

They're real good workers and they work lots of overtime. I mean they work and work and work. . . . Maybe some of your natives would say, "Wait a minute, I've already worked, you know, eighty hours this week. I'm kind of tired." Well then, you know, your Asian will go, "Oh yeah, you need me to work? No problem." So I think that the work ethic, you talk about work ethic, is there for them. Because, I mean, compared to what they came from this is paradise. (Public hospital human resources manager)

They're willing to work for a dollar. They don't have an attitude of "you owe me a job." They'll give eight hours work for eight hours of pay, *and they're happy doing it*, especially Hispanics. (Print shop manager)

As indicated by the comments above, employers' assessments were most likely to be couched in contextual terms, praising the immigrants for traits especially valuable in the function that the newcomers filled. As a furniture manufacturer put it, "I think that immigrants as a whole are generally suited for the type of work that we do"—hard, menial, poorly remunerated, and not likely to be seen as suitable by many other, native-born groups. Indeed, the employers tended to describe group character-istics in terms of jobs held, as did the furniture manufacturer who told us that "the Hispanic will work on a repetitious basis," the printer who ob-served that "Latinos seem to be good with their hands," or the manu-facturer who told us that "Hispanics are good in this type of industry." Not only were immigrants considered well-matched for the tasks in-volved, they also were seen as possessing understandings of the re-ward/effort relationship that an employer would be especially likely to appreciate. "They are willing to come and do whatever job you tell them without question." Unlike the natives, the immigrants were fully cog-nizant of the importance of a job, and therefore less likely to quit in search of better prospects. "We have very little turnover in positions that I would think people would not want to stay in for a long period of time, like the Environmental Services Tech position [janitor]," said the HR manager of a large HMO. "The [immigrants] . . . are content to have, to continue working in those positions. So, often we have people who've been here for twenty years."

Even better, the newcomers were unlikely to scoff at the employer's coin: "I think immigrants are very hardworking, they are responsible, and most importantly are willing to receive meager salaries for the work they put in." Finally, they knew their place in the social hierarchy of the workplace, proving more accepting of subordination than were natives, as suggested by the white personnel director of an Asian fast-food chain: "The Latinos in our locations, most are recent arrivals. Most are tenuously here, and here on fragile documents. I see them as very subservient. I see the Asian restaurant managers call them the 'amigos.' That's their name for them. The Asian kitchen people are very hierarchical. There's a place for everyone and it's clear where their place is."

"I Don't Know How They Do It"

As argued above, the managers were quite capable of preferring immigrants to fill the low-level jobs that few others found attractive without actually *liking* the immigrants, or (as we note below) favoring immigration, or holding the immigrants' ethnic groups in high esteem. To some extent, the stigma associated with the job spilled over to the group, with suitability for undesirable work signaling incompatibility with higher functions. Thus, the appreciation involved in a typical comment—"Lots of Spanish people, if they're working for you and feel that they have a fair shake, they stay forever"—had its nastier accompaniment, in the form of respondents' "amazement" over workers who persisted in dead-end jobs for years. "I see a lot of complacency," noted a respondent, referring to "people contented in housekeeping or entry-level jobs and remain in them. I don't know how they do it." Likewise, managers glad to find somebody to fill their entry-level jobs nonetheless looked down on those persons, whom they saw as "not all that interested in responsibility and advancement." One hotel manager nicely expressed the Janus-faced nature of the evaluations involved in the preference for immigrant labor: "The dishwashers don't have to speak English. They're not driven, not motivated. They don't want to better their life. They're happy, doing a good job, a whole group of non-promotables."

Thus, contrary to what follows from more individualistic perspectives, a preference for immigrant labor could go hand-in-hand with an aversion to immigrants or their communities. "There are so many of them," said a department store personnel manager, who happened to be a native-born woman of Mexican descent. She referred to the immigrants in terms that echoed the protests of many other Californians: "There are also a lot from Mexico that come up to get social services. They're exploiting California's welfare system. They come here and think we should support them. They get Social Security. Especially from Asia. They come in with an immigrant status and they get more money than Americans on Social Security."

A printer who saw no alternatives to hiring immigrants, since "I can't seem to hire whites right now," still thought that immigrants "should be kept out, enough are here already." A furniture manufacturer with a heavily foreign-born workforce conceded that immigration "creates the quality of my life," but also told us that "on a personal level where we live, a lot of us see the quality of life deteriorating and a lot of us feel it is because of immigration." A manager in a printing plant could laud the newcomers as *workers*, but go on to describe the immigrants as *people* in quite unflattering terms:

> *Field notes:* The respondent first tells me, "A lot of people come to me from working in the fields." She goes on to say that they've picked vegetables, milked cows, done whatever they could do to help their family, and are used to hard work. "There's very few lazy immigrant workers." But she then notes that Thais are industrious, more eager to assimilate into American culture than are Hispanics. "Here, everything is set up for Hispanics. They don't have to utter a word in English and can get along fine. Thais want to learn English." She tells me that she lives near a Tianguis supermarket [a subdivision of a major supermarket chain, designed to serve the Hispanic market] and has to make a two-city drive to get to a market where people speak English and she can recognize the food.

Similarly, a contextually related preference might not exclude a negative stereotype or an implied, more abstract, aversion: "[The immigrants are] all pretty much hard workers but relatively lazy when it comes to the language." In general, resentment of the symbolic and cultural changes associated with immigration—as well as of the prominence of Spanish and other "foreign" languages in the workplace and public space—were frequently echoed by managers who had nothing but praise for the immigrants' work ethic.

The Hierarchy of the Bottom

By the same token, as immigrants' "otherness" progressively disappeared—a process quaintly described by the social sciences as "assimilation"—employers came to feel differently about the newcomers, without, however, any gain in affection. Hardly multiculturalists, the managers were ambivalent about Americanization. "[T]he more Americanized the [immigrants] become, they start getting a little bit lazier, once they start to learn the system," said a furniture manufacturer. A hotelier had a similar complaint, praising the "new immigrants, [who] tend to be the most aggressive and hardest workers," but chastising "the more American ones, [who] tend to be less productive." A printer thought that "immigrants come here trying to survive," but that "those who've been here a while see that there are ways to get by." Asked about the second generation, managers were even less enthusiastic: the children of the immigrants were "too damned Americanized"—that is to say, too much like "us." One remarked: "If the sons are raised in the old way of raising children, they are just like their parents. But if they are Americanized, a *pocho*, the majority of them turn out to have an American work ethic."

Managers looked askance at assimilation—"Americanized Mexicans . . . that's the problem"—because the process changed the benchmarks by which immigrant children evaluated both jobs and the terms of compensation. The second generation was seen as not so willing to cooperate with authority: "We tell them that we need you to sweep outside," said a printer; "They say 'that's not what I was hired for.'" Nor were they willing to work as hard, having other options. "The children of immigrants are more cocky. This is probably as a result of the American system. They have an attitude, they are also more familiar with their environment. Confidence is more apparent in the children of immigrants. They are also more inclined to leave the job and not work for a considerable time," said one white furniture manufacturing manager. "Many of the Mexican Americans acquire an education and they don't want to work in these types of jobs. Also the Mexican American is bilingual, so he has other opportunities to work in other settings earning better salaries," said another HR manager, a Latino, also in furniture manufacturing.

Of course, the same characteristics could fit managers' needs in other ways, as noted by a manufacturer who told us that "they are not as hardworking as their parents, although they speak both languages, which is an asset." Consequently, depending on the dimension and its relevance to the tasks at hand, the fading of otherness could make immigrants' children preferable as workers because they had become "like us," just as it could make them unwanted for the same reason.

Since the preference for immigrants was so often contextual, it did not necessarily generalize beyond the workplace or even the specific set of jobs for which particular immigrant groups were thought suited. Whereas employers associated foreign birth with an "otherness" conducive to desired work habits, many were also aware of other distinctions among the immigrant population, providing the basis for a more elaborate ranking. In the words of one furniture manufacturer:

In Southern California, if I had to rank workforces, and give you four racial areas of Caucasian, Asian, blacks, and Hispanics—I would say if I had to rank them I would probably rate the Caucasian with the Asian equal, but for different reasons. The Caucasians because of the communications skills, the flexibility skills, and the comfortness that we would have culturally. The Asians would be here on the basis of hard working, long hours, the ability to do detailed work. The Hispanic would come underneath them, on the basis of their ability to do tedious work over a long period of time, and reasonably good quality, but lacking in flexibility, communication skills, education, and drive. This leaves us with blacks at the bottom, who have no flexibility, no drive, massive personal problems, and no feeling that they want to contribute to the well-being of the company.

Most managers thought that "immigrants are hardworking people, anywhere they come from." Still, their discourse about race and ethnicity at the workplace pointed to a distinct and often quite elaborate hierarchy. Asians vied with whites as the most preferred group; Latinos, taking into account distinctions based on generational status and national origins, were arrayed towards, but not at, the bottom; and blacks were generally the least liked *and* least preferred group. Said one manager, after a long pause: "Based on my observations, I could generalize by saying that Asians are very well-organized and regimented. They are quality workers. They don't distract easily from their work. Hispanics, on the other hand, are more casual, have less intensity. You also have to be motivating the Hispanic group so they will arrive on time. Tardiness is a big problem. Blacks, on the other hand, are even less productive. This is from the very limited experience that I have with this group [blacks]."

As suggested by these remarks, rankings often involved the invocation of prejudices having little if any relationship to the work context, informed only by broader social stereotypes. Employers' praise of Asians took the familiar form of the superego stereotype. They heaped encomiums on Asians' hard-work ethic, desire to get ahead, drive, goal orientation, and so on, only to arrive at the inevitable comparison: "They're able to trade dollars with the best Jewish salesman you ever saw." As displayed also in the quotes above, stereotypes of Hispanics revealed ambivalence with a more negative twist. Wanting a compliant workforce, some employers discovered that there was such a thing as workers who were *too* subservient. As one department store manager said, "[T]he Hispanic people don't seem to really want to improve themselves as much as some of the other groups do." Of course, stereotypes invoking the image of the dumb and unambitious but eager-to-please worker seemed to entail considerable projection; it was far easier to blame underlings for their lack of skills than oneself or the "bigger bosses" for the pinched purse and unpleasant conditions that deterred more-qualified workers and allowed no outlet for the ambitious.

On the other hand, differences in education and skill between most Asians and Hispanics meant that employers' preferences regarding the two groups were unlikely to enter into hiring decisions for entry-level jobs. Employers were indeed likely to prefer hiring Asians over Hispanics when given the choice, but this opportunity only rarely presented itself. Skill differences ensured that workers of Asian and Hispanic background were typically assigned to different jobs. Asians were found in the office, not in the shop; employed as supervisors, not line workers; involved "in sales and work with computers, while Hispanics are in the pressroom"; "stealing the jobs at the technical level," according to a hospital manager, but never applying for housekeeping positions. Even if many respondents agreed with the printer who contended that "Asians are more productive," this assessment was normally irrelevant to entry-level hiring decisions. As the African-American owner of a small print shop told us, the ethnicity of the worker "depends on the job function. In the United States, you wouldn't find an Asian running a press."

Although employers were also aware of national origin differences among Latino workers, no comparably clear set of feelings or judgments had crystallized around these characteristics. Some respondents did seem to entertain a ranking system, but there was little intensity or much consistency in their comparisons. For the most part, social distance complicated the job of making the fundamental perceptual distinctions needed for such discriminations. "They are all Hispanic to me. I can't distinguish between nationalities." Occasionally, the employers noted a behavioral difference related to some disparity in the immigrant settlement experience, as pointed out by a manufacturer who told us that, "[w]here we see the difference, the Mexicans, during Christmas, tend to want to go home, because it's closer." Such niceties apart, the traits that might distinguish Latino immigrants from one another were not seen as so impressive as those that made these immigrants different from the native-born. As a department store manager tersely responded, "[They are] all hard workers to me."

AFRICAN AMERICANS: DISLIKED AND NOT PREFERRED

If employers prefer immigrants without necessarily liking them, what considerations influence their views of blacks, and with what effects? Dislike for African Americans does a reasonable job of explaining white avoidance of blacks as neighbors, but it obviously cannot explain why some people who will not tolerate a black neighbor will happily employ a black servant. Economic theories of prejudice provide plausible accounts of how white owners can get away with paying lower wages to black than to white workers, but these accounts are of limited help here. As we discussed in chapter 8, standard economic theory casts owners as motivated by the desire for profit maximization. Instead, however, the economic theory of discrimination contends that they may be driven by a "taste for discrimination," a modification introduced ad hoc and without justification.[6] At its best, the economic theory of discrimination illuminates the trade-off between the psychic benefits of discrimination and the monetary rewards of hiring without prejudice. However, this trade-off only applies to capitalists, not to their agents—that is, managers—who may well put their comfort ahead of any profits foregone as a result of discrimination. In any event, the economic framework is largely irrelevant to the issue at hand, which is not wage inequality *within* any given occupation, but occupational segregation. We want to know why employers have generally been willing to hire blacks as janitors and hotel maids, but far more resistant to engaging them as bank tellers or salespersons—not to speak of higher-level, more prestigious positions in the professions or management.[7]

Where Do African Americans Now Fit?

An alternative to the economists' view might be that employers hire under the influence of stereotyped notions of the jobs for which blacks are most fit. But any such hypothesis suffers from circularity, since the fit between traditional stereotype and historical position has been too tight to determine which came first. In the past, long-held stereotypes proved no obstacle when other considerations became important; the historical record shows that employers who previously excluded blacks could quickly turn accepting, particularly when blacks could be deployed as replacements for union-prone and strike-happy whites.[8]

In any case, it is not clear how traditional stereotypes of African Americans would influence decisions in today's labor market. On the one hand, we are asking about factors that affect entry into jobs that have generally been considered right for persons considered inferior, so it is unlikely that views of African-American inferiority would render them ineligible for jobs denoting inferiority (such as janitorial or other unskilled jobs). On the other hand, we are also interested in explaining the declining African-American presence in positions or industries (e.g., hotels and hospitals) where they were previously overrepresented. Since a constant cannot explain a change, one cannot invoke traditional stereotypes as an explanation of why employers of low-skilled help suddenly developed an aversion to black labor. And as these stereotypes served to explain why blacks were confined to the low-skilled sector in the first place, we are locked in circularity.

It may be that employers are impelled by a new set of stereotypes. As Lawrence Bobo, among others, has argued, there is a new form of Euro-American prejudice in play, in which "laissez-faire racism" has replaced the "Jim Crow racism" of old.[9] For Bobo, laissez-faire racism functions as a stratification ideology, explaining black/white inequality in terms of deficiencies of individual blacks, as opposed to the persistent effect of racialized social structures; laissez-faire racism includes *symbolic racism*, a view that "blacks violate such traditional American values as individualism and self-reliance, the work ethic, obedience, and discipline."[10] *Laissez-faire* racism also draws from contemporary conceptions of African Americans bound up with media-popularized notions of the "underclass"—which, to the extent they attempt to explain persistent black poverty, have increased the salience of stereotypic views of blacks as unwilling to work. As opposed to older stereotypes of inherent inferiority, the "underclass" label ascribes the problems of poor African Americans to misguided government attempts to do good, the suburbanization of the well-behaved middle and working classes, and the birth of a "culture of poverty" among those remaining in the urban ghetto.[11] Lingering images from the Black Power movement of the 1960s, videos from the "gangsta rap" movement of the 1990s, and age-old fears of "black thugs and rapists" have combined, within the "underclass" rubric, to identify opposition to authority as the principal expression of black identity. Whereas traditional stereotypes of blacks impeded movement into higher-level positions, while supporting continued black employment in menial jobs, underclass stereotypes may have the opposite effect. Equipped with the new stereotypes, employers filling professional positions may consider well-educated middle-class African Americans, but those seeking deferential less-educated workers are cued to scratch African Americans off the list.

This argument brings us back to the Blumerian concept of race as a sense of group position, and to our related discussion of class. Traditional stereotypes of African Americans told employers where black workers belonged, producing a contextual preference for persons otherwise disliked. The new stereotypes, by contrast, signal that this earlier fit no longer holds. Black workers should not be assigned to bottom-level tasks, because their sense of group position no longer supports the subordination that such low-level roles require. The new stereotypes associated with low-level labor groups typically combine negative traits (too stupid/too smart, not sufficiently ambitious/too competitive) with some positive evaluation (hardworking). Thus past and present diverge. Employers in the low-skilled sector previously held *negative* attitudes toward blacks as *people* but *positive* preferences for blacks as *workers* for the least desirable jobs. Today, however, both attitudes *and* preferences are negative. Moreover, the weight of the antiblack animus reduces the likelihood that employers' experiences with blacks will be sufficiently common or powerful to undermine the new stereotypes' baneful influence.

"I Hope This Doesn't Sound Racist"

Our interviews show that the aura of negativity associated with African Americans deeply affected employers' views toward applicants from this group, as our respondents' many frank admissions of *pre*judgment make amply clear. Predictably, employers' disquisitions on the qualities of black workers sometimes began with a preamble disclaiming any prejudicial intent, as in "I don't want to sound like a racist. I don't think I am. But . . ." or "I don't want to sound like I am stereotyping this group, but . . ." or "I hope this doesn't sound racist," the last statement intoned by a Central American immigrant manager. However, we find our respondents' admission of their racialized views far more telling:

> From my standpoint, and I'll be very, very honest with you, I have a difficult time dealing with the black man. . . . And that probably is a part of my own social upbringing, because my mom was very much a racist person. So she groomed me that every black person in the world—and that is not true, because I have known numerous black people and they have been very great people and have enjoyed their relationships. (White male furniture manufacturer)

> I don't think racism really comes into play with us, though there are stereotypes. Especially after the riots. To be honest, they say that black people scare white people; they do. I confess. You know, I see young black guys walking on the street and I look twice. It is not fair, because I don't think these individuals have anything to do with it, but as a group that is a perception. We don't have a perception that is formulated from a business experience, you know, because we have not been exposed on this level. But

we did employ a black truck driver for years and we deal with an all-black company that does our delivery out to the desert. So it is not really that, it is just that there are stereotypes about work ethic, dependability, and things like that, that are with us all. We all try to be individuals and judge people on an individual basis, but that is when stereotypes come true. (White male furniture manufacturer)

Such sentiments may fade under the impact of experiences that contradict them. But, as suggested above, prejudices are known to be reality-resistant, and the intensity of antiblack feelings increases the likelihood that belief will resist reality—and this is precisely what our informants often told us. "My black secretary was excellent," recounted a furniture manufacturer, who simultaneously insisted that "blacks have no work ethic and an attitude."

> *Field notes:* A printer had several longtime black employees on the payroll, with whom he had no complaint; nonetheless, he was of the impression that blacks "are not serious about wanting to work." Hard work is acceptable to a lot of Hispanics. He's hired a young black, and he'll say, "It's not my job." He'll have this kind of an attitude.

Sometimes, negative views expressed themselves in stereotypes that drew on those traditional elements in American racial culture depicting African Americans as inherently inferior. Whereas employers lauded immigrants for their hard-work ethic, they were far more likely to describe African Americans as lazy. A fast-fooder insisted that there was a "big difference" between immigrants and blacks: "They're lazy. Black men are lazy. Immigrant men are more willing to work and do the job right. Black men don't care what the outcome is." Comments of this sort, tapping into one of the oldest Euro-American prejudices against blacks, were not infrequent, although we should note that they were not delivered uniquely by Euro-Americans, as with the Chicano manager who told us, "They are lazy, they don't show up on time, you could just see the attitude." Employers' descriptions linked laziness to other identifying traits, making blacks responsible for their own difficulties. Sometimes, laziness implied lack of ambition: "They don't want to come up in life. They just want to stay where they are." More often, the employers depicted laziness as lack of effort: "They don't try hard enough. They want everything to be handed down to them. They don't want to work for what they get." *Laziness* also served as shorthand for *attitude*, of which blacks were often perceived to have the wrong kind, as in the quote from the Mexican-American manager just cited. And laziness was invoked to describe the perceived deficiencies in blacks' work ethic: "The blacks have less work performance. They don't work hard; they're just lazy. They have less work ethic. It's because of their upbringing."

Self-Presentation and "Attitude"

The "laziness" theme was actually a minor note, although complaints about effort and performance resounded throughout the interviews. It may be that our respondents were engaged in heavy self-censorship, aware that comments associated with a view of inherent racial inferiority have become too socially unacceptable for mention in public. But as the employers seemed otherwise uninhibited in their willingness to expound on the deficiencies of black workers, one suspects that we picked up a real, rather than artifactual, dimension to their "racial" views.

We begin with a back-handed compliment, noting that managers often resembled social scientists in a preference for multidimensional depictions and multivariate explanations. For example, a manufacturer insisted that "there is a real problem," but then threw the sociologists' own vocabulary back at them to highlight its complexity: "There is a perception out there and it might be a vicious circle, there is the perception that they are lazy, that creates a resentment in them which I think makes them lazy, which makes the perception more real, and somewhere you are going to have to break that cycle." When asked whether lack of skills, discrimination, or something else was responsible for the labor market difficulties of young black men, the foreign-born black HR manager in an upmarket hotel covered all the bases: "Difficult to answer because all the factors play a role. When there's a weak economy, those at the bottom suffer the most, because there's no safety net. Skills are important. Discrimination unfortunately has been with us for centuries and it has not left. It does play a big role. Attitude, I regret that the attitudes of the person looking for employment has turned into one of arrogance. The street mentality is very unfortunate, a certain arrogance that you sometimes see in young black males."

Comparable phrasing emerged from another hotel HR manager, whose views also explicitly echo social-science thinking on the topic:

> Attitude is a root cause, but the three [attitude, skills, and discrimination] interrelate. If he perceives he is being discriminated against, he is going to have an attitude. Therefore he is not going to get the skills. I'm hesitant to say blatant discrimination. But I'm not a fool to believe it doesn't exist. If he thinks he's not going to get the job because he is black or that he should

get the job because he is black, I'm not going to hire him. He's got a bad attitude. In the end, to believe that you're not going to get the job because you're black, then you portray that attitude, and you don't get the job, [it becomes a] self-fulfilling prophecy. Young black males who do not portray that attitude succeed. I see "because I'm black" as a cop-out, a way of blaming someone else for failures. I don't buy into that.

Each element above—skills, discrimination, and especially attitude—was repeatedly sounded in our interviews. Many managers depicted black applicants as less likely to know, or at least to display, the appropriate demeanor for getting the job. "In the less educated," a furniture manufacturer pointed out, "I've noticed that they don't carry themselves well. In other words, they will come in [seeking a job] looking like a gang member." More common were comments directly related to the skills actually required on the job, but these were most likely to be offered by respondents in organizations where entry-level requirements were higher than the average in our sample. "We have lots of black males applying for jobs who haven't finished high school and have either no work history or very poor work history," noted a manager in a nonprofit hospital with a workforce characterized by high ethnic diversity. "Their disadvantage is no skills. And the fact that they don't go out and get them." A manager in an HMO with a large black workforce and a mainly black applicant pool complained that "lots of people coming out of high school don't have basic skills. One of the questions [on the test for chart-room file clerks] is to write out the alphabet in block letters, and they get that wrong, if you can believe it. We test ten to twelve people at a time, and only three pass it." And as a printing manager perceptively noted, basic skill deficiencies could easily produce interactional frictions that would make it difficult for less-skilled black workers to hold, if not to obtain, a job: "More because of, because they'd get frustrated, because, for one, they weren't taught basic skills. A lot of what they should've learned in high school, they end up having to learn on the job. If an undereducated twenty-two-year-old has to be talked down to, to make sure he understands things, it would be frustrating for him. Even for a mechanical job, it could be necessary to be able to fill out purchase forms."

As intimated by the extended quotes above, having the wrong (or lacking the right) "attitude" was a particularly frequent criticism, one as frequently made in context as in isolation. A hospital environmental services manager, for example, who evaluated black workers and applicants unfavorably, noted that "lack of skills makes people hostile, hard to deal with." "My gut feeling is that they're not stable," echoed a public sector manager, in reference to black men.

> *Manager:* It's a combination of attitude and lack of skills.
> *Interviewer:* What do you mean when you say attitude?
> *Manager:* They're mouthy.

The Latina human resources manager in a discount chain store told us: "In this store, we haven't had any luck with young black men. From past experience, I'd say it's their attitude. I couldn't say it's their skills, because there's no real skill required for the job. And this goes for some of them, but not for all. It's attitude. They felt that they didn't have to work, didn't have to put effort into it, because they were black. And that's a quote. Of course, other blacks do work hard. I think it depends on their upbringing."

Thus, employers recurrently refer to "attitude" as at once characteristic of black workers and exemplifying their deficiencies; in part, this theme embodies contemporary racialized conceptions of African Americans. If, as Bobo and others have argued, Euro-Americans have moved from Jim Crow racism to laissez-faire racism, the employers' complaints about "attitude" and their "underclass" imagery would suggest that they are "in sync" with this drift.

Yet that characterization would overlook other, similar-sounding yet distinct, themes in the employers' discourse, as well as the import of the comparisons the employers drew with immigrants. Employers spoke of "attitude" when describing a variety of objectionable qualities they observed in, or attributed to, black workers and applicants; however, their complaints crystallized around the impression that black workers saw themselves entitled to treatment that other workers, especially immigrants, neither expected nor received. "Of all the ethnic groups, I certainly don't want someone who wants something for nothing," commented the manager of a printing shop. "Lots of blacks feel that way. That's what they have been taught." A hotel manager complained that blacks lacked the qualities looked for in a good worker: "If you're talking about service in the hotel industry you have to have a certain attitude. If you come with a chip on your shoulder, negativeness, 'I've been a victim,' you don't come across as guest-oriented, helpful. You have to smile, use the guest's name, have to be friendly, the attitude shows you want to be friendly in tone and manner. [With blacks] there is an attitude that is there. It's hard to pinpoint, because when you say it you're accused of being a racist."

Happiest with subordinates who quietly accept subordination—a readiness more necessary at the bottom of the labor market, where the demand for subordination is great and rewards are few—employers gave black workers bad marks. "The attitudes [of immigrants and blacks] are different. One's appreciative and one is 'You owe me.'" "They [blacks] complain a lot about work assignments, whereas Asians accept." An Asian-American factory owner, employing two black workers in a crew of twenty-five, described his relationship with them:

> *Field notes:* Talking about the two black workers in the shop, the respondent tells me that, "They're not my two best, they may not be top one-third. Both average. Those [black] individuals have always taken advantage of every situation they could." He then gave an example having to do with vacations. Since he doesn't give any benefits, he lets employees take vacations when they want. . . . So these black employees asked him for vacation before a year had gone by. He concludes by saying: "Both black workers work just as hard as the Latinos in the shop. The difference is that they tend to be more aware of the system and more willing to use it. Other employees will not even ask for two weeks. These people will."

From the employers' standpoint, any group more likely to mouth off was undesirable on this ground alone; making matters worse, as the employers saw it, was the likelihood that friction between themselves and their black workers would be expressed in racial terms. Employers particularly disliked the "black thing," the attitude that, as one manager put it, "you owe me to make up for the past . . . since I'm black." "I just think that the black thing is taken too far. I hate that when it gets thrown in somebody's face, 'It's because I'm black.' It has a lot to do with attitude. With whites, you don't throw in the color. The attitude seems to be better because they don't throw in the color thing."

"There are lots of recriminations of mistreatment, favoritism," noted the manager of a regional fast-food chain. "It's not universal. But I encounter them with too much frequency." "I don't want to sound like I am stereotyping this group," remarked a factory manager, "but they immediately react that they are being discriminated [against] and file a suit against the company." A furniture manufacturer had a similar grievance, charging that black workers "immediately let you know that they are from the 'hood' and that you should not mess with them." A black woman who directed the environmental services department in a hospital noted with some disdain that "some think the job should be given to them because they're black."

Exchanges of this sort were especially distasteful to employers since they felt put on the defensive—as in a furniture factory where management felt "intimidated" by a small group of black workers in the shipping department, who were seen as needing more careful treatment than the average nonblack employee. A printer put it bluntly: "[I]mmigrant men are going to work much harder and take more crap than any black man . . . will take."

It is no surprise that employers should find little relish in having their authority questioned, but the willingness of African Americans to "put you on notice" was related to a further contrast noted by managers between them and immigrants. Blacks, the managers told us, often resisted accepting disciplinary procedures. A hotel manager, for example, argued that immigrants are "more apt to accept what they've done when they break rules," whereas "blacks automatically say, 'You're writing us up because you're racist.' "

Born in the U.S.A.

While employers evinced aversion to hiring blacks because, they said, blacks were too different from immigrants, they were also reluctant to hire blacks, because blacks were too much like native whites. A furniture manufacturer depicted the situation in the following light:

> *Manager:* Like I stated before, it seems like they are not in a hurry to do anything, while the immigrants are more anxious to please.
> *Interviewer:* Why do you think this difference exists?
> *Manager:* I don't think it is a difference between blacks and Hispanics. I think it is the difference between Americans and non-Americans. Between natives and immigrants. I don't think that you can narrow it down to a Hispanic and black thing.

As we noted earlier, similar distinctions emerged when managers compared Latino immigrants with the U.S.-raised children of the foreign-born, seeing the latter as both capable of hewing to the good old ways of the parental generation and susceptible to the siren song of Americanization, with its deleterious effects on work ethos and respect for authority. Put somewhat differently, the employers' complaint was that many workers looking for jobs in the low-wage labor market had caught the "American attitude: they owe me, I'm entitled"—a syndrome afflicting blacks, whites, *and* Latinos, for much the same reasons. In the employers' eyes, blacks thought it legitimate to ask for more because they were native-born, and, in this respect, were just like whites: "Blacks demand more and want more benefits and higher salary," said a hotelier, "because they're Americans." A furniture manufacturer, who maintained that blacks and whites are outperformed by the immigrants, similarly placed the source of the problem at home: "Americans are always crying, they don't want to work hard. They argue that they are not slaves, and are always complaining when they have to work at a fast pace."

Our respondents conceded that the motivation problem stemmed from the disparity between conditions and compensation at the bottom, on the one hand, and the expectations of the native-born on the other:

> *Manager:* Well, I can only hire Hispanics, they are the only ones that apply for these jobs, we had some blacks, but they don't last a week. We try them, but they don't last.
>
> *Interviewer:* Why don't they last? There is a big black community around here.
>
> *Manager:* It is low-pay jobs. They are the worst workers around. We only have one white worker, he is a minimum-wage employee. We have the same problem with them [whites]; they are worst.
>
> *Interviewer:* So the only people that are willing to work are Hispanics?
>
> *Manager:* Yes, they are all Hispanics. We don't have one "legal"—I mean, one American-born worker. Well, except for me.

The owner of a coffee shop depicted black workers as similar to white workers in their reluctance to take the very lowest jobs: "Black men—even American white men—they say, 'I'm not going to wash dishes.' Or, 'I went to high school and I deserve better.'" Well aware that the service sector is "a notoriously low-paying industry," a hotel manager pointed out that "Americans, not just blacks, are not willing to work for a low amount of money." This opinion was seconded by a fast-fooder who thought that without immigrants, "There would be no one working in these stores, because I don't think black people, American people, will work here for four-and-a-quarter."

The Importance of Context

Somewhat higher up in the hierarchy, where the demand for subordination was not so great and the compensation more likely to motivate native-born workers, managers evinced a somewhat different view. An HR manager in one of the city's largest hotels commented, "I don't get a lot of black applicants and, when I do, they are older men who have been laid off or highly articulate, well-dressed younger men." With more schooling came different aspirations. Another hotel manager who "wouldn't say that the black group is any different from whites," noted in this vein that "blacks are also striving. Many are interested in higher positions and promotions. Most of the immigrants are not."

Jobs that required more demanding proficiencies also led managers to see the differences between blacks and Latino immigrants in a different light. For example, a hospital manager, who thought that "Hispanic workers are more content in the lower positions," went on to tell us that, in other jobs, there were "blacks chosen because of the language; they speak English well. These positions have more requirements—writing, reading, computers. These are young guys, providing better services." A retailer similarly noted that between blacks and Hispanic immigrants "are definitely differences. The black workforce for sales, they are better educated than the immigrants and have the necessary communications skills, if they are chosen to perform the job. This makes them far more productive in service, dealing with the customer." A long-established furniture manufacturer gave an example that illustrated just how context could alter preferences in favor of, or against, blacks: "Blacks have been much less stable. That's in the plant. Among the drivers, they've been very good. For shop people, Mexicans have a much better work ethic, in terms of the quality and quantity of work produced and productivity. But not among drivers, truck drivers. The guy working in the shop makes $12,000–$14,000. The driver makes $40,000. There's a difference in the kind of person who takes the job. When he's on the truck, he has $100,000 [of merchandise] with him. More importantly, he is our contact with the customer."

For such jobs, employers were more pleased with the fact that blacks were "like us"; a printer said, "I can talk to them without need of a translator," and a hotelier was pleased that "most can read and write." While employers knew that an American worker came with a greater likelihood of speaking his or her mind, they were also cognizant of disadvantages associated with employing a foreign-born crew (e.g., "You don't want the INS walking in.") In this context, the terms of comparison between blacks and others were changed. As a hospital HR manager said: "I certainly don't put blacks in the same. . . . I wouldn't consider blacks with immigrants; they're not immigrants. Is my experience different with them? I don't have to worry about authorizations and those type of things, but they are also generally hardworking, dedicated. . . . Again, there's differences among people."

CONCLUSION

America may be catapulting toward a postindustrial economy in which we all create, process, and transmit ideas and images without ever dirtying our hands. Regrettably, we are not there yet, not having figured out how to dispense with work of the hard, menial, and unpleasant kind, work still more stigmatized because increasingly removed from the typical job of the postindustrial age. Making matters worse is that the low-skilled worker earns a living in a global economy, competing with similarly situated workers thousands of miles away—which means that the wages paid in Los Angeles are effectively set in Sri Lanka.

It is under these circumstances that we ask the question: whom do employers want? In America's increasingly multi-ethnic, immigrant cities, the answer turns out to be: those least likely to complain about the conditions and compensation of low-level work. The foreign-born comprise the preferred labor force, but not because employers have suddenly developed a soft spot for immigrants, immigration, or the broader cultural or social changes wrought by large-scale immigration. Rather, employers perceive the newcomers as workers who assess their situation relative to the conditions and options encountered "back home." As the employers understand it, the immigrants' dual frame of reference puts America's low-wage sector in a remarkably favorable perspective.

Of course, the employers know that not all immigrants are the same. They look at the immigrant workforce through the stereotypes generated in the world around them—which is why they tend to look down on Mexicans and Central Americans and to have a more favorable, if profoundly ambivalent, view of Asians. But these distinctions have little operational relevance, at least to the jobs we are considering. The employer looking for a dishwasher, janitor, machine operator, or laborer entertains little expectation that Asian applicants will flood through his door.

The same factors that lead employers to prefer immigrants breed an aversion for the native-born. We certainly would not accuse our respondents of lacking patriotism. However, they do seem to have some distaste for American culture and for the "bad habits" and unrealistic expectations it has inculcated in the American worker, who seems to want the American dream—unavailable in the low-wage labor market, at least not with the effort that the American worker deems reasonable. Making the employer's life more difficult, everyone sooner or later falls under the spell of the American dream; as assimilation progresses, the immigrants lose some of their hard-work ethos, and their children have still less.

Employers who think American workers ill-suited for low-level jobs have an even lower opinion of African-American workers. The strength of the employers' antiblack affect, as well as the new and old stereotypes which filter their views, account for much of their aversion toward these workers. But employers are well aware of African *Americans*' dual status, seeing them as in-group members who want and expect more than usually possible at the bottom of the labor market. They also see them as out-group members, whose alienation further increases the likelihood of their making a fuss. Never looking for trouble, employers recognize whom they want—and whom they do not.

CHAPTER 10

Diversity and Its Discontents

Bosses select workers, but not always as they wish. For all the importance of employers' preferences and prejudices, other considerations frequently come into play. The nature of the hiring process may preclude, or at least limit, the ability to act on one's desire for workers of one type, or one's discomfort with workers of another. In small shops or factories, where the lines of authority are clear and influence is tightly controlled by a single boss, preferences can be translated into action with relative ease. In larger organizations, the matter is more complicated, as more players and views require accommodation. True, the sentiments of the highest-ranking relevant boss are likely to be material, but they may not prove decisive, especially for a low-ranking job. Moreover, where the wages are so miserable, the conditions so poor, or the stigma so high that no preferred groups apply, the distaste for hiring an out-group member is unlikely to be as strong as the aversion to spending more money. Thus even a strongly prejudiced employer unburdened by dissenting supervisors may hire workers whom he or she would otherwise avoid.

Employers may also take into account the views of their employees or customers, which, for simplicity's sake, can be characterized as preferences for interactions with like others ("own-preferences") or aversions to dealing with outsiders ("other-aversions"). Economic theories of discrimination suggest that these preferences are exogenous: they originate at home or in the street and are imported to work without change. But this view provides less help today than in the "bad old" *b/w* days, when economists could make reasonable assumptions about whites' tastes, even without knowing how to explain them. Each group of immigrants is likely to arrive with its own set of preferences and aversions, of which the most predictable component is likely to be "own-preferences," although "other-aversions" are likely to be common as well.

African Americans have their "own-preferences" and "other-aversions," and these are no longer as irrelevant as they were in the earlier age of migration (or even when Becker wrote, half a century ago). The greater resources of the expanded African-American middle class make the tastes of African Americans less easy to ignore today, while the changed ideological climate reduces the scope for open displays of any "distaste" for contact with African Americans. Further, as "hyphenated Americans," African Americans are likely to share some of the preferences and aversions of their European American counterparts; the most important of which concerns the linguistic environment of work. And African Americans appear increasingly likely to seek out jobs entailing equal-status contact with whites and increasingly sensitive, if not actually averse, to low-status positions serving whites.

Alternatively, the preferences of workers and customers may be endogenous, embedded in existing practices and in a sense of customary justice that grants priority to transactions with insiders and their associates. As we have seen, the implantation of an ethnic network *may* bear little or no relation to group-specific preferences, as such. Employers often mobilize workers' ethnic connections without quite knowing that they are activating a labor supply of a particular kind. As we have emphasized, efficiency is often the employer's motivation; the network furnishes reliable labor quickly, effectively, and at little cost. Network recruitment also shapes the employment relationship by imparting a set of understandings common to workers and employers, reducing the possibility that informal understandings or implicit contracts will be broken.

The repeated action of network recruitment often produces ethnic concentrations or niches; protecting or expanding these niches provides the motivation for *rational*[1] discrimination against outsiders. Fearful that outsiders might undercut wages, *workers* prefer to train co-ethnic neophytes whom they trust. Anxious about the reliability and performance of job applicants who walk in off the street, *employers* prefer to hire the friends and relatives of key workers. Concerned that a vendor might not deliver on time, or that a customer might delay in paying the bill, *business owners* look for known entities with track records of successful dealings with others. In effect, membership in an ethnic community tells co-ethnic actors that one can be relied on; thus it also provides a ground for excluding outsiders, who lack the traits, histories, and ties conducive to collaboration or trust.[2]

While purely economic motivations can provide the initial impulse for transactions with one's "own kind," the motivational mix may change over time. Frequent interaction in a concentrated niche promotes a sense of group identity; as niche employment grows, the niche itself becomes a group "trait" that helps define who the members are. Consequently, greater attention is paid to the boundaries that define the niche and the characteristics of those who can and cannot cross its boundaries. In the immigrant centers of New York, Los Angeles, and Miami, where ethnic niching is pervasive, the build-up of ethnic specializations provides ample reason for any group to exclude those not members of its own ethnic club.

Motivation is one thing, opportunity another. Whatever the sources of groups' own-preferences and other-aversions, the *potential* to act upon predispositions varies situationally. Workers are always likely to have *some* leverage, but the weight of their preferences is likely to vary with internal organizational features. Organizations depending on informal recruitment and selection mechanisms have less scope to resist the views of incumbent workers, whose influence over recruitment keeps outsiders in the (often small) minority, while also facilitating the expression of hostility toward these same out-groups.[3] In contrast, more bureaucratic recruitment and selection mechanisms are likely to produce work groups characterized by more ethnic diversity, providing a context less conducive to targeted hostility, although conflict may nonetheless occur.

Whatever the organizational structure, the nature of the particular job or set of jobs in question will also affect the degree to which employers prove responsive to workers' views. Work is fundamentally social, and interdependency among workers makes both employers and the outsiders hoping to break into a job dependent on the cooperation of incumbents. Where productivity depends not so much on individual as on group effort, the need to elicit the cooperation of the dominant ethnic group in the workforce may force management's assent to the exclusion of outsiders. On the other hand, interdependencies often span differing occupational layers, with the closure potential of any one network limited to the occupations it effectively controls.

The characteristics, needs, and preferences of the clientele can either reinforce or cut against workers' preferences. But customer preferences do not always come into play; the structure of interaction between customer and provider may hinder their activation. Some contexts effectively hide the workforce from view; restaurant or hotel kitchens make for physical invisibility, and one suspects that social distance between hotel guest and housekeeper has a similar effect. Factory workers are also likely to have a low profile; factories usually sell to other businesses, and these clients interact with owners, managers, salespeople, occasionally a supervisor or skilled worker, but rarely with a rank-and-file employee. Thus, client preferences are likely to be influential only under a limited set of interactional conditions, notably, in settings in which the public has significant direct contact with the workforce. Even in these circumstances, own-preferences may have a strongly functional nature, as when customers desire to communicate, or can only communicate, with employees who speak the same tongue.

Finally, own-preferences need not take a purely invidious form. Clients may not be so much concerned with the ethnicity of any particular employee as with the representation of their own group. Visibility sends a message about the organization and its hiring practices, a message that can either shore up or undermine the organization's legitimacy.

The efforts of workers and customers to realize preferences are the subject of this chapter. In earlier chapters, we frequently noted the lengths to which incumbents would go to ensure that their associates and kin had knowledge of, and were recommended for, job openings; these actions exemplify the actively inclusive, *passively exclusive* side of social closure. We have also pointed out situations in which incumbents withdrew their cooperation to sabotage employers' attempts to introduce other groups into the workforce; circumstances of this sort highlight the *actively exclusive* side of social closure. Situations of diversity involve those where no group has been able to attain effective social closure over a job or set of jobs; our theoretical framework leads us to expect that these are the settings where conflict *among workers* is most likely to arise. However, situations of diversity are more likely to prove satisfactory to a diverse customer base, since the homogeneity resulting from social closure will always, in a heterogeneous environment, mean that *somebody's* own-preferences are ignored. Thus, this chapter sounds the recurring theme of tension between diversity (among both workers and customers) and social closure.[4]

MANAGING DIVERSITY

In our interviews, we principally sought to obtain information about *employers'* preferences. Our questionnaire did not call for scrutiny of the ethnic preferences of incumbent workers or of customers and clients, nor did it direct the interviewer to seek out evidence on the existence of ethnic conflict within the workplace. Nevertheless, managers touched on these subjects frequently, often spontaneously. Managers' comments were commonly provoked by the following query about managing the region's multi-ethnic workforce: "Many people these days say that 'managing diversity' is the human resources challenge of the 1990s. In what way is 'managing diversity' a challenge for you?"

Most respondents initially responded to this innocuous-sounding question with a laugh or a derisive grunt, followed by some equivalent of either "We've always been diverse; there's no change," or "It is a *big* challenge." "Diversity" was not always understood as intended; that a number of respondents used the dubious phrase "people of diversity" or referred to "diverse people" as a category of human beings reveals that "diverse" has become a buzzword and euphemism for "nonwhite." In some cases, respondents who said "We've always been diverse" wanted to tell us that the organization had always employed nonwhite or immigrant employees, *not* that ethnic heterogeneity had persistently been a distinguishing trait. Likewise, the comment that diversity was a "big challenge" might mean only that the company's managers did not speak Spanish very well. Still, asking about "managing diversity" provoked extensive commentary on the challenges presented by a workforce and customer base that were often far more heterogeneous than those that most organizations had known in the not-so-distant past.

Conflict Avoidance

The firms in our sample generally sought to quell conflict between workers. More than one claimed to have a "zero tolerance" policy regarding workplace conflict. These policies meant that squabbling workers were told, as a printer put it, "You're required to get along or you can't stay here." Moreover, conflict management and reduction was often part of our respondents' job description, especially in the case of the human resource managers, with whom we were particularly likely to speak in hotels, department stores, and hospitals. Consequently, respondents who told us that "we have no conflicts" were also telling us that they were doing a good job: "I manage all my workers the same way. We have no conflicts. I'm just a fair person. I give a guy—white, black, Hispanic—give everyone the same opportunity. They adjust to me."

Respondents from the more bureaucratic organizations also framed conflict in ways that reflected a human-resources-management perspective, contending that "there are inevitably culture clashes" but "it all works out, though. There are difficulties understanding each other, but no real conflicts." Because conflict was inconsistent with the prevailing managerial ideology and reports of conflict could in some ways be read as indicators of failure, respondents were probably biased toward underreporting tension among workers.[5]

"Hey, Baby, You Look Fine Today"

Given the diversity of the workforce, it is not surprising that our interviews illuminated conflicts beyond those involved in ethnic tensions. Several respondents, for example, noted conflicts between gay and straight employees. Such conflicts were occasionally informal, but could take a more institutionalized form in organizations like hospitals, where there might be organized gay staff groups. Our respondents were also likely to discuss tensions arising between male and female workers over definitions of appropriate workplace behavior. Consider, for example, the following extract from an interview with a female hospital HR manager:

> Men are used to working in a workplace where they whistle at women, or say "Hey, baby, you look fine today," and now that's causing problems in the workplace . . . [W]omen are going "Hey, wait a minute, that's sexual harassment. . . ." The workplace is changing so quickly, as far as culturally and as far as men and women, that men have to really think about what they say and how they act toward women. And women have to think about what they say and do, because, you know, women, when it was twenty years ago, we sat right in there and told those dirty jokes right along with the guys, you know, we all laughed together. And yet women will do that [among themselves], but if a man turns around and says something [similar], they yell "sexual harassment."

Although the example above speaks to straightforward gender conflict, our interviews often suggested that the nexus between gender and ethnicity could be a flash point for conflict, especially where cultural expectations about gender hierarchy were bent or broken. Gender conflict was often ethnicized at the point of contact across occupations. According to one of our sources, for example, Filipino male immigrant doctors were accustomed to yelling at nurses, a practice that did not sit well with American nurses, who would tell the offenders to "stick it up [their] nose." The female hospital HR manager quoted above high-lighted the problems that arise when "men who come from cultures [where they are told] that they are the superior and women are second-class citizens all of a sudden have a woman supervisor and have a real tough time taking directions from a woman."[6] She continued: "They'll do it, but they do it with a chip on their shoulder, or they'll do it and sabotage the work to make her look bad, or whatever. We have a real problem with that because we have a lot of people coming in from the Middle East that are coming to work for us. And there's a lot of women in middle management. Our administrator is a black female. And half of our administrative assistants are females. And probably most of our division heads are females, and that causes a real problem for men who have a hard time taking directions from a woman." The experiences of a Mexican-American retail manager, however, suggest that respect for authority can trump gender-role expectations. She told us that "I tend to think that Filipino men tend to be more demeaning to the women, but not to me, as a superior."

The gender conflicts reported above, while pivoting around a sense of "group" position, were not typical of the ethnic conflicts among co-workers discussed in this chapter. Organizational size and the elaborate division of labor in health care insured that antagonisms linked to gen-der roles and expectations cropped up most often in the hospital indus-try. The vertical character of these hospital conflicts makes them stand out; our other examples primarily involve horizontal clashes among workers of differing ethnic backgrounds employed in the same or simi-lar occupations.

WORKERS' PREFERENCES AND WORKPLACE CONFLICT

So much of the recent literature on ethnicity and the economy empha-sizes the positive sides of social networks, tending to either downplay or miss processes that give rise to ethnic conflicts at work. By their very na-ture, ethnic networks tend to sort groups into different niches in the la-bor market, as we saw in chapter 6.[7] To the extent that the networks build niches, they decrease workplace heterogeneity and thereby diminish the potential for intergroup conflict. This fact did not escape our respon-dents, one of whom, when asked about the consequences of diversity, replied: "In my store, there's no problem. We're all Latinos." The tacit exclusion produced through network recruitment is always less than perfect, however, and (as we have shown) organizations sometimes actively seek to diversify the workforce; consequently, outsiders leak in, setting the stage for conflict.

The intergroup tensions highlighted by our data arose from many sources (as noted earlier). Managers often invoked conflicting customs, and language or cultural differences, to explain the conflicts that they experienced. One hospital manager told us, "There will always be throwbacks from an age when people believed that they didn't have to work with any other type of employee or any culture or any other language, etc."

Sometimes conflict was neutral, in the sense that it resulted from more or less innocent misunderstandings. Conflicts could also easily be cultural without being a result of intolerance per se, as in the following report from a retail manager, which shows that differing expectations regarding authority relations could generate conflict: "Blacks and Pakistanis never got along at the [discount chain store in the South Bay]—big time. Pakistanis are very direct people but very loyal to their superior and very aggressive to the fact that, if you aren't respectful or loyal to the superior, then they'll let you know. There was trouble with a young black kid, who spoke to me in a manner that I could tolerate, but this middle-age Pakistani woman took him and chastised him."

At other times, however, the apparent basis for strife had to do with prejudice and with notions about appropriate hierarchy specific to the cultural backgrounds of the groups in question. Replying to our question about managing diversity, a hospital dietary services manager suggested that the sources of tension were mixed:

> Semantics is a big problem. Just customs and how people treat each other. I've got people from Thailand, from the Philippines, from Mexico, from, you know, all over, and we've had some very difficult times. How they respect authority, how they don't respect authority, how they respect women, how they don't respect women—.[There's some] difficulty with being a woman in management when you get some of this going on. And it's enough, being in the United States and having people with prejudices against other people. But then I get somebody from Thailand who's prejudiced against someone from the Philippines, and I have no idea what's going on there. So constantly being a mediator for some of those kinds of things. Some people [are] talking their heads off and it seems to be certain ethnic groups, "Excuse me but, be quiet while I talk to you." You know, it goes on like this and some of their—. One's polite in one country is not being polite in another. It's real, real different.

In other cases, hostilities that were manifest in the workplace reflected nonethnic antagonisms that had developed outside—for example, when gang loyalties were brought into the workplace.

Interviewer: What kinds of difficulties or challenges have you faced in dealing with a diverse workforce or diverse customer base?

Manager: You're talking about major stuff here! I mean, like in our [San Gabriel Valley] store, we have the gangs, and we have the Orientals, and they're on our [late-night stocking team]. And, boy, if you want to hold your breath walking through that store at seven o'clock in the morning, oooh!

Interviewer: There's a lot of tension in that store?

Manager: You can feel it, walking through there. In that store, when they do an orientation [for new workers], he's right up front, "Keep your gang-related stuff outside of my store."

Outside events also added something to the brew. For example, the disturbances of 1992 made for work environments where "you could cut the atmosphere with a knife, it was so tense."

These last examples aside, hostility was most evident in situations where one group appeared to try to exclude others. These were the tensions that managers highlighted when they talked, as they often did, about members of two groups "hating" each other. Some of these "realistic group conflicts,"[8] such as those in which U.S.-born workers of any ethnicity became fearful that immigrants "were going to take over," were fueled by those sentiments stirred up when a group's sense of its rightful position vis-à-vis others suddenly was put in play. Fear of displacement was by no means limited to blacks worried about new Latino immigrants. For example, a hospital manager, also answering our question about the challenges of diversity, told us:

The biggest challenge that we have as far as culturally is concerned, is that, here in Southern California, there has been a tremendous influx of Asian persons. From the Philippines, from China, Hong Kong, a tremendous influx of individuals from those countries coming here, where the blacks and Hispanics take offense to the fact that they have immigrated with their skills and taken the jobs. I remember, a year ago, a very vivid conversation that I had with a very angry black lady, who was a phlebotomist [with a] good ten years of experience. She was feeling very frustrated at the time. She talked to me. She wanted to know why she couldn't get a job, why were Filipinos all getting the jobs.

While conflict was not pervasive (although, again, we note the likely *downward* bias in managers' reports), there was much of it. Often, the

antagonisms took the predictable turn of "all against all," as in the furniture factory described by one source: "For example, if you have a
group of white Caucasians working in the shop in whatever capacities,
it seems that the Hispanics feel that these people are given certain projects and are given all of the money and the best jobs. The mix of blacks
and Hispanics tends not to work very well. The Hispanics feel that they
came to this country and are willing to sell oranges at the corner to make
money; they feel like blacks are essentially lazy. That is their view."

In Los Angeles, "all against all" means a potential range of conflicts
that, while possibly impressive to scholars, was frustrating and bewildering to unprepared managers. Among the combinations reported to us
were: Mexicans against Puerto Ricans, Filipinos against blacks, Arme-
nians against Hispanics, Belizeans against Bangladeshis; indeed, just
about any pairing-off seemed a real possibility to these managers. As one
hospital manager observed, "You see that, kind of, not necessarily the
white against the minority, but the minority against the minority, and we
see that more and more happening in our workplace." The unusual pair-
ings meant that circumnavigating a multi-ethnic workplace proved a difficult task for workers and managers alike, with all sorts of unknowns
and anxieties having a potential for trouble: "We tell employees, that's
the workplace now. It isn't all, you know, white Americans, and, you
know, it's very different. We have to be careful of the kind of jokes we
tell and how we conduct ourselves and how we, you know, if we talk
about 'the crazy people in the Middle East,' and [all] that, you know, and
here's an Iranian sitting there. It causes problems." Although this respondent may be correct in her description of how the workplace looks
and functions "now," the on-the-job conflicts reported to us did not
commonly revolve around ethnic jokes. In the following sections, we detail the manifestations of ethnic conflict and illuminate the sources of
these antagonisms.

Black/Latino Conflict

The case for competition between African-American and Latino immigrant workers begins from the assumption that a lack of education leaves
members of both groups with few labor market options, causing them
to contend for the same set of lousy jobs. Even the least-educated black
native typically arrives at the workplace with substantially more schooling than the average Latino immigrant; that the former is also a native
English speaker and the latter may possess little or no English-language

proficiency is hardly irrelevant. These differences, and the network processes described, tend to segregate blacks and Latinos into different lines of work, thus reducing the potential for conflict. Nonetheless, there is still much contact, especially in larger organizations, such as hospitals and department stores, that hire on a large scale and therefore rely on bureaucratic recruitment and selection mechanisms. Even the smaller organizations, more apt to hire from among the friends and relatives of the existing workforce, will accept walks-ins or place "help wanted" ads in the newspaper, opening the door to a heterogeneous workforce.

There is far more black/Latino contact than black/Latino conflict. Twenty-one of our interviews reporting ethnic conflict made note of tension between African Americans and Latinos, but the incidence of these tensions was clearly greater in some industries than in others. Many groups are on edge in department stores and hospitals, but binary conflicts pitting blacks against Latinos seemed relatively rare. Rather, the locus of conflict was in furniture, an industry with many plants in and around the once-black, now increasingly Latino, South Central ghetto. In furniture manufacturing, firm size was relatively small, managerial styles tended toward the nonbureaucratic and even paternalistic, and cooperation was a necessary feature of the job (as discussed in chapter 3). These conditions made conflict more common there than in the other industries, a fact that affected the job opportunities available to African-American workers. As a furniture manufacturer with a lifetime of experience helpfully explained: "The shop has always been 98 percent Latino. I have hired some blacks. You put two men on a machine; the Mexicans won't work with a black. They aggravate him 'til he quits. You can't make it interracially. I'm not going to be a sociologist and tell them, 'You're in the same boat, you ought to work together.' The only place where we have blacks is in the trucks, because they work by themselves. [Although] blacks have been much less stable, that's in the plant. Among the drivers, they've been very good."

In no industry, however, do the interviews suggest that either group is overwhelmed with love for the other. For example, a furniture manufacturer indicated to us, "Blacks aren't happy that there are so many Latinos." A respondent in a large nonprofit hospital on Los Angeles' West Side reported, "We have Latino-and-black conflict. The blacks say that the Latinos have a chip on their shoulder. Latinos say that the black supervisors take sides." A restaurant manager reported, "Blacks and whites think they are better than the Latinos because they speak English." Both Latinos and African Americans entered the work world with antagonisms that often threatened to spill over onto the shop floor. Said a furniture manufacturer: "I think that some of our employees . . . some of our younger employees were probably gang members before they came to work, and so we really discourage graffiti inside of the plant. And the Hispanics outnumber the blacks, and we let them know that if they do it [paint graffiti] in the property, they will be given their checks and be fired."

Any preexisting rivalries are likely to be exacerbated by other differences among the groups. Language, as discussed in chapter 4, is one tension-producing factor: "It's difficult to have a half-Hispanic, half-black housekeeping department, because the Hispanic employees generally speak Spanish to each other and the black employees don't understand it. And because the work ethic and job performance [of the Hispanics] outshine [the blacks], so it creates animosity between them." This hotel manager suggests that blacks and Hispanics have different expectations about what constitutes a reasonable day's work—a matter to which our evidence does not directly speak. However, if blacks adhere to an American standard of a fair workday, while Hispanic immigrants are used to a lower, Third-World norm, then the willingness of Hispanics to put in more work than blacks would raise employers' expectations and make black workers understandably upset.

Most reports of black/Latino conflict came from the furniture industry, as noted, followed by hotels, then by restaurants. In these industries, African American workers tended to be a small minority, working alongside a large and growing population of Latino immigrants, which has expanded largely through reliance on network recruitment. In these situations, the fact of being a quantitative minority has made African Americans more vulnerable to the views and actions of the numerically dominant Latino workforce. A factory manager employing a mostly Latino workforce reported having only bad experiences in hiring blacks. He blamed his failures with black workers on two factors: either "they didn't like working here, or . . . there were overall problems in the shop, and I had to respect other people's problems, too."

When asked why "the people that are not Hispanic don't last very long," another furniture manufacturer arrived at a similar answer.

> *Manager:* Well, because these people don't feel comfortable working
> in a minority situation . . . I believe that could be explained
> to the people doing the hiring. And I think it would be
> racist if we would say that the Hispanics are in there trying
> to get the jobs more so than the blacks. We have hired a
> few blacks and they quit on their own. They don't want to

be a minority. The same could be said of the white population.

Interviewer: And you think they don't feel comfortable because it is a
predominantly Hispanic workforce?

Manager: That is right.

A black manager overseeing operations for a company providing janitorial services to the hospital industry[9] further underlined the difficulties associated with the ethnically tilted situation. Describing the situation of black workers, he told us:

> Working with the Hispanics has become a problem, because they don't
> speak English, and so forth, so it's become a discrimination thing on their
> part . . . I see it in hospitals, like in one hospital we have, you see the blacks
> on one side of the room, the Hispanics are on the other side of the room, at
> one of these general meetings. And you can hear it in some of the questions
> that come up, and some of the answers that come up, the representation
> from the unions. There's a certain amount of animosity because the union
> representative is speaking in Spanish. So it comes up, there's an attitudinal
> thing. I think the blacks feel probably threatened because there's so many
> Hispanics here.

Not only were African Americans likely to be a small minority in these
Latino-dominated contexts, the nature of the work made them highly dependent on their Latino co-workers. Almost all of our respondents rated
"ability to work successfully with co-workers," as a key skill expected of
any applicant. But interethnic conflict often threatened that cooperation,
putting African-American workers at risk precisely because of their small
numbers. A hotel manager explained: "Housekeeping is all Hispanic. You
try to put a black in there, she won't last. They intimidate. We have had
situations where we have different cultures that get put together and we
lose the person. The Hispanic houseman will play pranks and not deliver
linens to the black housekeeper, and then they don't get the beds made.
Blacks mainly work in security, the front office, and transportation."

While some level of antagonism clearly exists between blacks and
Latinos in many workplaces, the degree of tension falls below the level
to be expected had blacks perceived themselves as being displaced. It is
worth pointing out that the black population of Los Angeles County declined over the course of the 1990s, as many moved to outlying counties
or to other parts of the country. This exodus coincided with a continued
flow of Latino immigrants into areas formerly inhabited by blacks. In
both realms, residential and occupational, the amount of conflict de-

tected seems much more consistent with replacement than displacement. We will discuss this topic at greater length in chapter 11.

Conflict among Latino Immigrant Groups

The majority of the managers who participated in our study were Euro-Americans, for many of whom awareness of diversity among Latinos—let alone, of intra-Latino conflict—was a novel acquisition. A representative hotel manager told us, "To me, an Anglo, they're all Hispanic. We tend to see them as all alike." However, experience had taught this manager and his colleagues another lesson: "I know that Mexicans don't like Salvadorans." Or, as a printer put it, "Just because they speak the same language doesn't mean they get along."

Indeed, managers were often surprised by both the intensity of the intra-Latino conflicts and the multiplicity of subethnic groups engulfed by tension. Regional antagonisms transported from the home country were an important basis for struggles that surfaced in Southern California; one furniture manufacturer, referring to three Mexican states from which a large proportion of migrants come, noted that "you have everybody from the Puebla area or Zacatecas area or something like that, and what occurs is that they don't talk to people from Jalisco." Conflict emerged within the multiethnic Central American populations, as well. "We have situations where Ladinos [white Central Americans] are called names and treated as outsiders. The Ladinos are not well-liked." Conflicts among nationalities cropped up along with these subnational rivalries, as noted by a man who had only recently inherited a furniture factory and moved to California. He remarked: "The thing that surprised me was the prejudices that did exist between the various Hispanic groups. You have the Mexicans from Chihuahua over here, and the Mexicans from Guerrero, and then the Colombians. They are very cliquish and nationalistic. There has been conflict, because of the nationalities, and among the Mexicans, the particular state. It's not just blacks. That was a surprise to me." Indeed, "not just blacks" was a common refrain, echoed by a hotelier who told us, "I've noticed that more Spanish people will fight among themselves than [with] black people."

Despite public and scholarly preoccupation with black/Latino conflict, we heard more frequent reports of intra-Latino conflict. These reports were all the more credible as they were often accompanied by positive assessments of the immigrants' performance, as in the case of a factory manager who thought that Latino immigrants "have fairly decent work ethic" but told us that "one of my biggest bitches is intra-group conflict." Although the frequency of these reports may reflect the high levels of Latino representation in both our sample and the Los Angeles workforce—and thus imply a relatively lower probability of conflict than between Latinos and African Americans—the intensity of the intra-Latino conflicts that management reported was impressive:

> There is also conflict between nationalities; it does not matter that they speak the same language, people from El Salvador hate Mexicans, and vice versa. They hate each other's guts. (Furniture factory manager)

> The biggest diversity problem is within Hispanic countries. We have situations where Latinos called each other names, and were treated as outsiders. . . . Fights in garage because of insults, Central American and Mexican conflict. There is outward nontolerance. That's where it is. Call each other names. Set each other up. More diversity problems between Hispanic workforce than cross-culturally. (Hotel manager)

> Within your group you always feel better than others. Mexicans argue with each other over whose state is better than the other. [Say] I'm from Sonora, and there is a worker here from Guantanamo [sic]; he tells me he's better. When someone from El Salvador comes in, then we all get together and are Mexicans. (Fast-food manager)

As the managers saw it, the widespread and intense antipathy between Latino groups often had to do with each group's own-preferences. Showing themselves practical sociologists, managers came to realize that their habitual cognitive frames did not converge with the understandings that the immigrants brought from home. While most "Americans" might be unable to perceive the distinctions that mattered to the migrants before they headed for their new world, these differences, our respondents told us, still counted, at least on the shop floor and selling floor. Workers of the nominally "same" Latino "type" often turned out not to see their "commonality." To be sure, sorting out the source of aversion—as in the fast-food restaurant where "Mexicans say Salvadorans have an attitude and Salvadorans say that Mexicans think they're the best"—is not straightforward; the antagonisms may result from pre-existing conflictual faultlines, or they may have been born in Los Angeles. The manager at a downmarket hotel endorsed the first possibility:

> Within their own subcultures, Mexicans think that Salvadorans are quote unquote below them or vice versa. We have had employee problems with employees from one group or another. We've had employee fights. I don't

want to judge but only because we have more Mexicans, they have proven themselves to be good workers. The others, we find out that the Salvadorans want to work together on the same floor, or the Hondurans. . . . You know, people of the same group always want to be together with people of the same group. It's *natural*. We accommodate them, but we also want them to learn to work with other people. Sometimes we change them and put a Salvadoran in with a Mexican. We don't do it on purpose, but we want to get them experience on another floor. We have terminated employees for constantly bickering among themselves, and it's not work related. They curse each other, "Hey, you slob! You come from El Salvador."

This kind of infighting is perfectly consistent with the tensions we would expect between groups struggling over jobs. Indeed, most reports of intra-Latino conflict appeared to stem from job competition among Latino groups, particularly between Mexicans and Salvadorans. As noted earlier, once a group establishes a niche in an occupation or industry, it may come to see the relevant jobs as group property. Persuading employers to continue hiring through networks helps maintain the niche. But in occupations where there is rapid turnover, or where more formal hiring methods are frequently applied, maintaining the niche may require other measures.

The isolation of black workers, as described in the previous section, represents one technique for maintaining control over a niche. Isolating African Americans proves a viable option both because employers frequently share the antiblack prejudices of their Latino recruits and because black workers will usually have difficulty functioning in a predominantly Spanish-speaking environment, an environment increasingly common in Los Angeles.

However, isolating the out-group seems less likely to prove successful when pursued by one Spanish-speaking immigrant group against another. An alternative strategy entails impugning the reputations of rival groups, in the hope of influencing employers' decision making. A manager in a nationwide motel chain, for example, told us that the immigrants "like to distinguish themselves," with Mexicans telling him that "Guatemalans have a reputation for stealing." Although he felt there might be "some truth to that," he still held that "I cannot tell the difference" between the groups, in regard to their work. Echoing this sentiment, the owner of a furniture factory rejected invidious ethnic claims as "hysterical." She reported that "within the Latinos they'll say, 'Oh, well, the Salvadorans never work.' And then the Salvadorans say, 'Well, the

Guatemalans never work,' " but she saw no difference among the work habits of any of these groups. In any event, since Central American workers were more difficult than blacks to exclude through informal means, and could naturally cope in a monolingual Spanish environment, they were likely to work with each other and alongside Mexicans, creating continuing potential for conflict.

Conflict between Whites and Others

As whites have both moved up occupationally and moved out residentially, they have become relatively scarce in the kinds of entry-level jobs that we studied. Further, given our industry choices in this study, most whites in these jobs were women—sales clerks in department stores, clerical workers in hospitals, or wait staff in restaurants. While we are reluctant to accept stereotyped views that suggest that women are less likely than men to express conflict overtly, our interviews were certainly consistent with this belief. Factory owners and managers, for example, highlighted conflict among African-American and Latino men working on the shop floor, but were also likely to mention that "I've had in the office a couple of black employees at various times, usually a couple of girls in the office who are black," who had apparently had no conflicts with other workers.

In hospitals, few of the menial jobs are held by whites, but whites usually predominate in professional and, especially, managerial posts. While hospitals employ more females than males, doctors and upper managers are mainly men. In contrast to the other industries that we studied, hospitals boast a notable overrepresentation of African-American workers, a pattern particularly true in the public sector. Further, African-American representation in hospitals can be found at all levels, including not only custodial and food service workers but also clerical workers, technicians, nurses, and even some doctors and upper-level administrators. In hospitals, therefore, African- and Euro-American workers enjoy considerable contact both vertically and laterally, and they also see a higher than average incidence of African Americans overseeing Euro-American subordinates. These situations—as this female, Euro-American, public hospital HR official explained—can generate much tension:

> Racism is an ever-present problem, despite the diversity in the workforce. The M.D.s are mainly white. The director [of HR] is a black male; and his decisions are always questioned on ethnic grounds, when he made only fair decisions. Among the staff there are problems, race problems. . . . There's

plenty of name-calling, getting into fistfights. When a chief of a service that employs a lot of blacks does a dance and Buckwheat impressions, that tells you what the mindset is. There's considerable tolerance for racism and sexism. There should be zero tolerance.

Where conflict pits members of socially dominant groups against persons of socially subordinate groups, tensions arise for different reasons. Enforcing discipline is never easy, and is made more difficult when the difference between management and labor is overlaid by the relationship between a dominant and subordinate ethnic group. Under these circumstances, historical understandings and misunderstandings of these relationships shape conflict even while providing a frame for comprehending it. As one experienced manager explained: "When we coach an associate who is of an ethnic background, and myself of course being Caucasian, there is that underlying tone in the associate's voice that we're discriminating." From management's perspective, the situation can unravel all too quickly: "You know, the employee will in a minute yell 'racial discrimination' if the supervisor tells them 'You're not working fast enough,' and the person says, 'He doesn't like me because I'm Iranian.'"

Reports from our respondents suggested that disputes between individual Euro-American managers or workers and African-American workers were especially likely to become racialized and tense. A hotel manager, for example, told us a story about a disagreement between a white and a black worker over job responsibilities. One night, a white desk clerk asked a black security guard to deliver some towels to a guest's room. The security guard refused and, after an argument with the desk clerk, the security guard walked out. According to the manager:

> [the black security guard said] "You know, [the desk clerk] thinks he can boss me around because I'm black." I said, "It doesn't matter whether you're black, white, brown, or yellow. This has always been a part of the job. I know that this was explained to you when you started." He said, "Well, it seems to be getting worse and worse. And I know that it's because I'm black. If I was white, he'd let me watch the desk while he ran up there [to deliver the towels.]" I said, "No, that's his cash drawer. He needs to be there. I've trained him to answer all the phone lines, questions that come in, if a reservation comes in from overseas. You're not trained to handle that position. It's part of the job." "Well I'm not going to do it. I just think that it's because I'm black." Well, I said, "Then you can pick up your check." That's the way it was left. I don't need this attitude, you know.

One need hardly subscribe to the manager's interpretation of this event to see how quickly any incident between black and white workers can be inserted into an interpretive frame shaped by long-term patterns of race relations. Although theoretically suggestive, examples involving black/white conflict at the lateral level, were fairly rare in our survey, reflecting the underrepresentation of white workers among the low-level jobs on which we focused.

CUSTOMERS: OWN-PREFERENCES AND OTHER-AVERSIONS

Thus far, we have emphasized how the "own-preferences" and "other-aversions" of the dominant worker group affect management's hiring decisions. When the preferences and aversions of a *multitude* of groups come to matter, however, taking them into account may induce efforts that yield *greater* ethnic heterogeneity among the workforce. For many organizations providing services or goods in multi-ethnic Los Angeles, the reality is a workplace rather less diverse than the clientele. Such asymmetries do not always prove problematic: because of limited public contact, the region's new demographics are largely irrelevant to the factories, and impinge only mildly on the restaurants, which mainly service a neighborhood clientele and maintain kitchens that are largely hidden; similarly, in the hotels, the immigrant workforce is concentrated in positions with limited guest contact. But retailers and hospitals are in constant contact with the new ethnic Los Angeles, and the own-preferences of the region's new inhabitants compel organizations in these industries to ensure that the workforce mirrors their customer base. These industries furnish the contexts where customer diversity and workplace social closure collide.

As we have seen, department stores and hospitals sought to serve a diverse range of customers, an imperative pushing them toward broad, active worker recruitment and breeding an aversion to reliance on hiring through workers' contacts. To the extent that these larger organizations drew clients from a nearby area, they were sensitive to clients' preferences for others of their "own kind," putting a premium on a workforce mirroring the composition of the neighborhoods served. Thus, department stores bordering the South Central ghetto were in search of black salespersons, whereas, depending on the specifics of location, those in the San Fernando Valley were more likely to want Spanish speakers or Middle Easterners. Often, however, as in the case of the Veterans Administration hospitals or the largest medical facilities, which served a regional base, clients came from a broad geographic expanse. Under these circumstances, customers' own-preferences translated into a search by managers for a workforce that would capture the diversity of the clientele.

LANGUAGE REVISITED

Whether through passive adaptation to the environment or through the deliberate recruitment efforts described, the advent of Los Angeles's large foreign-born labor force has introduced a multiplicity of languages into the workplace. In industries such as hotels and furniture manufacturing, reliance on recruitment through the networks of immigrants has produced a monolingual work world in which Spanish, not English, is the lingua franca. As shown in chapter 4, managers in these immigrant-dominated industries often complained about the linguistic limitations of their workers, but generally chose the path of accommodation. Thus, in industries like furniture manufacturing, hotels, or restaurants, language has surfaced as an axis of conflict *among workers*—but only to a limited extent, as there is a prevalence of Spanish, associated with high immigrant densities.

Department stores and hospitals, by contrast, have secured a more ethnically and linguistically heterogeneous workforce, by recruiting more bureaucratically. Seeking diversity as a goal has produced a consequence that hospitals and department stores surely never anticipated: linguistic differences in these miniature Towers of Babel highlight boundaries, reminding workers and customers alike of their own-preferences and other-aversions.

In these settings of diversity, linguistic differences generate friction under a variety of conditions: when customers and workers do not share a language; when workers do not share a language; when workers do not have the same language as managers. But the most volatile issue, not just entailing practical consequences and inconveniences, but stimulating resentment and anxiety among those who cannot participate in the exchanges they hear, appears to involve the public use of "mother tongues."

CONCLUSION

The multi-ethnic workplace of late-twentieth-century Los Angeles is a conflicted, but far from Hobbesian, world. In this chapter, we have put the spotlight on interethnic tensions at work, but we need to add that little more than a third of the 230 organizations we visited made mention of explicit ethnic conflicts or preferences on the part of customers or workers. It is not entirely clear whether our reports indicate that conflict is notably high, low, or at the level that one would expect—there is no established standard against which to measure.

Immigration, the fundamental transforming factor, is a network-driven process, and the prominent role played by ethnic networks in the labor market makes for ethnic separation, not generally considered an optimal outcome. Detectable levels of interethnic conflict are also organizationally dysfunctional, which is why many organizations we contacted try hard to keep peace, quelling conflict when possible and removing troublemakers when necessary.

Contact is usually thought preferable to separation, but contact is also what makes for conflict. The conditions under which contact occurs vary in ways that structure and crystallize the intergroup tensions that we have reviewed. One axis of variation involves the nature of the recruitment process. Some of the industries we studied—most notably, furniture, restaurants, and hotels—rely heavily on network recruitment, which produces an ethnically tilted situation, in which one group predominates heavily. Outsiders inevitably leak in, but they find themselves highly vulnerable to the views and actions of the numerical dominants. Moreover, the latter are relatively free to act upon their preferences, since the interdependency within the work group is high and management has few incentives to insist otherwise. These situations impinge with particular force on African Americans, who often comprise a small proportion of the workforce, lack the community resources of immigrant groups, and frequently are disliked by employers, as well.

The conditions of conflict are quite different in larger organizations that connect with a mass public. Where bureaucratic mechanisms of recruitment and selection prevail, as in hospitals or department stores, such mechanisms weaken the grip of network-based processes of social reproduction, increasing ethnic heterogeneity. Under these circumstances, tilted groups appear less often. Sales workers are less interdependent than production workers, which in turn means that those in sales are less exposed to the views, and possible coercive actions, of their colleagues. Lower-level hospital employees work more closely together, but since they are also dependent on higher-level workers who are often of a different ethnic origin, they have less leverage to act on own-preferences or other-aversions. Thus, while *mixing* provides the ingredients for conflict, it also diffuses tension and prevents, or forestalls, the emergence of a clear target group.

Before concluding, we must note that we have only looked at ethnic conflict at the bottom, and for that reason probably understate the level and intensity of intergroup tensions at work. After all, this study focuses on the least-skilled jobs, which, as our respondents continually reminded us, "nobody wants." At these lower reaches of the social structure, ethnic succession—the process by which lower-status groups move into niches higher-status groups have abandoned—along with the network-based processes of worker recruitment, keeps insider groups and outsider groups apart. The situation is likely to be different higher up the hierarchy, especially since there seems a perpetual oversupply of workers looking for "good jobs"; insiders have plenty of incentives to hold on to what they have, and ambitious outsiders ample motivation to break in. For these reasons, all is not likely to be quiet on the multi-ethnic labor front.

PART FIVE

Ethnicity at Work

CHAPTER 11

Black/Immigrant Competition

"On the backs of blacks?" asked Toni Morrison in a 1994 essay, contemplating the role of "race talk, the explicit insertion into everyday life of racial signs and symbols that have no meaning other than pressing African Americans to the lowest level of the racial hierarchy"[1] in the assimilation of newcomers into a racially stratified society such as the United States. The question arises naturally in the context of today's immigration debate, after having served as a fulcrum of controversy among scholars and advocates for more than two decades. The reasons for concern are not difficult to discern. Immigrants are achieving a toehold in the American economy, and many are "making it," while progress for many African Americans seems stalled.[2] While the boom of the 1990s reduced poverty, a disturbingly large portion of African Americans, particularly African-American men, did not find their life chances much improved. Under these circumstances, the nation's burgeoning immigrant population emerges as a likely source of the persistent problems affecting less-skilled African Americans.

Or so we thought, when this project began. As the reader now knows, our research took us in a different direction, as we sought to unravel the puzzle of today's immigrant phenomenon—an ever-expanding low-skilled foreign-born labor force in an economy that seems to have no place for poorly skilled workers regardless of national or ethnic background. In the concluding chapter, we will review the lessons learned from our effort to make sense of this paradox and offer thoughts about what prospects it portends, but in this chapter we return to the question with which we commenced, asking how the immigrant advent has affected African Americans.

THE QUESTION OF COMPETITION, REVISITED

One can ground the argument by focusing on African-American employment concentrations, asking whether immigrants have pushed African Americans out of jobs. The logic of inquiry is straightforward. Using census data from 1970 and 1990, we first seek to determine whether immigrants have converged on the same activities toward which African Americans have gravitated. Second, after mapping shifts in the industries in which African Americans have concentrated, we assess whether these changes may be due to displacement or to other factors.

In 1970, just over a quarter of all African-American workers worked in industries that could be characterized as *ethnic niches*—industries in which blacks were overrepresented by 50 percent or more. Two-fifths of these niche jobs were found in the public sector. To some extent, the pattern of concentration reduced exposure to immigrant penetration; most black niches were found in industries in which immigrants not only were underrepresented, but had a very modest presence.

But, as can be seen in Table 11.1, some of the major black employment clusters of the time involved industries toward which immigrants tended to gravitate—not surprisingly, as these were positions that were likely to be occupied by African-American workers with less than a high school degree. In 1970, half of the African-American workers employed in African-American niches were working in industries in which immigrants were also overconcentrated. In particular, private household service had already absorbed a sizeable immigrant workforce, although African Americans were still the more sizeable presence. Immigrants were also overrepresented in laundries, meat packing, auto repair, hospitals, and primary nonferrous industries; in the latter four industries, moreover, immigrants represented a more sizeable presence than did African Americans.

A very different pattern had emerged by 1990, as shown in Table 11.2. For the most part, African-American concentrations in those industries in which immigrants were already overrepresented in 1970 simply disappeared. On the other hand, the level of concentration substantially rose. Much of the increase occurred through greater clustering in industries in which immigrants were likely to be *underrepresented*; this

TABLE 11.1. AFRICAN-AMERICAN NICHES, LOS ANGELES COUNTY, 1970

| | Index of Representation[a] | | All Workers (%) | Characteristics of African Americans Employed in Niches[b] | | |
	African Americans	Immigrants		Number	Managers, Professionals, Technicians (%)	Mean Years of Schooling
Private Sector						
Private households	4.65	1.74	43	9,210	0	9.4
Laundering, cleaning, and dyeing	2.33	1.23	21	5,006	0	8.6
Rubber products	2.02	0.64	18	1,701	0	10.5
Meat products	1.98	1.74	18	1,000	0	10.3
Hospitals	1.50	1.34	14	6,810	26	11.6
Auto repair services and garages	1.54	1.45	14	3,103	3	10.2
Primary nonferrous industries	1.51	1.24	14	1,403	0	11.7
Public Sector						
Welfare and religious services	3.76	0.25	34	4,102	56	13.3
Postal service	3.13	0.29	29	6,608	0	12.7
Hospitals	3.15	0.59	29	6,512	28	12.6
Construction	1.62	0.44	15	1,502	7	11.0

SOURCE: Integrated Public Use Microdata Samples; industries coded on 1950 basis.

[a]Index of representation equals a group's proportion of industry employment divided by a group's proportion of total employment.

[b]Niche is defined as an industry in which a group's representation is 150 percent or more of its share of total employment in the county.

TABLE 11.2. AFRICAN-AMERICAN NICHES, LOS ANGELES COUNTY, 1990

	Index of Representation[a]			Characteristics of African Americans Employed in Niches[b]		
	African Americans	Immigrants	All Workers (%)	Number	Managers, Professionals, Technicians (%)	Mean Years of Schooling
Private Sector						
Gas and steam supply systems	2.95	0.35	27	1,404	0	14.0
Street railways and bus lines	2.79	0.65	25	2,314	0	12.5
Crude petroleum/natural gas extraction	2.65	0.43	24	1,118	12	13.1
Telephone	2.50	0.43	23	7,904	16	13.3
Warehousing and storage	1.94	1.28	18	1,092	0	11.7
Primary nonferrous industries	1.80	1.49	16	1,261	0	11.8
Aircraft and parts	1.56	0.41	14	19,838	39	13.6
Petroleum refining	1.56	0.50	14	1,391	29	12.9
Hospitals	1.53	0.93	14	16,510	33	13.2
Public Sector						
Street railways and bus lines	5.79	0.29	52	1,261	21	14.3
Welfare and religious services	3.78	0.70	34	4,875	61	14.7
Aircraft and parts	3.65	0.31	33	1,586	35	12.6
Postal service	3.61	0.60	33	8,788	7	13.0
Hospitals	3.19	0.58	29	9,477	41	13.6
Medical/other health services, except hospitals	2.94	0.81	27	2,314	62	14.8
Federal public administration	2.58	0.56	23	13,481	34	12.9
Electric-gas utilities	2.49	0.66	23	2,262	16	13.1
State and local public administration	1.69	0.25	15	6,188	25	13.8
Educational services	1.67	0.44	15	24,037	66	14.6

SOURCE: Integrated Public Use Microdata Samples; industries coded on 1950 basis.

[a]Index of representation equals a group's proportion of industry employment divided by a group's proportion of total employment.

[b]Niche is defined as an industry in which a group's representation is 150 percent or more of its share of total employment in the county.

reduced exposure to immigrant-over-represented industries was largely achieved by yet greater concentration in the public sector. Unlike 1970, when the niches were likely to attract less-skilled African Americans, in 1990 the situation had been reversed: the average education of African Americans in the niches of 1990 stood above the high school degree in *every case*. Moreover, of the industries that qualified as African-American niches in 1990, only two also served as immigrant niches, and in both cases, African-American employment was relatively slight.

Thus, the historical pattern in Los Angeles seems consistent with a story that has African Americans being "pulled" rather than "pushed" out of their employment concentrations. Indeed, this is the outcome one would expect, confirming the argument advanced in this book: since informal networks channel job seekers into industries or occupations where other like persons are already concentrated, categorically different groups of workers end up sorted into distinctive places in the labor market.

But, as also noted, the scope of network penetration is limited by the characteristics of the organizations with which those networks connect and by the employment practices that these organizations deploy. Not only is the exclusion produced through network recruitment often less than perfect, it also has an asymmetric impact, affecting small groups far more than large. Thus, by 1990, low *relative* exposure to immigrant employment nonetheless meant that African Americans were likely to encounter a sizeable foreign-born presence, even in black niches. Black niches were also sites of extensive contact with categorically *different* workers; in such cases, the tendencies generating ethnic conflict, discussed in the previous chapter, are commonly found.

Further, if the chief African-American concentrations have also shifted to higher-skill sectors in which organizations recruit, screen, and select in a more bureaucratic fashion, then the less-skilled members of the group who cannot pass the employers' tests may be left out in the cold. This means that the most poorly schooled members of the group may be in more trouble than before, kept out of the new African-American concentrations with relatively high skill thresholds and, instead, having to look for work in organizations where an unwelcoming, or even hostile, immigrant presence predominates. Put somewhat differently, immigration may harm the most vulnerable African Americans and yet yield no *net* negative effect on Los Angeles's African Americans as a whole. Immigration may even bring a net *positive* effect, if we consider its role in swelling demand for the types of public services in the provision of which African Americans have specialized.

Even if the net effects are positive, the impact on the African Americans most at risk is a matter of which the social, as opposed to statistical, significance cannot be overstated. To be sure, the options for even the least skilled African-American workers might look better were it not for the additional obstacles they confront, including the residential and transportation barriers that keep them from taking advantage of job-rich areas in the outlying suburbs, and the hostility they encounter from white and sometimes from Latino or Asian employers. But these obstacles are real, no matter how unpleasant or dismaying. More importantly, they leave less-skilled African-American workers reliant on that segment of the labor market where immigrant densities are likely to be highest.

IMMIGRANTS AS SUBSTITUTES
OR COMPLEMENTS FOR NATIVE WORKERS

Although the fact is usually overlooked, the emergence of Los Angeles as an immigrant mecca involved a massive turnover in the ranks of its working class. In 1970, whites comprised the majority of workers in *each* of the industries we studied; twenty years later, this dominance still held in only one case, printing—and the slim majority held there by whites as of 1990 was surely gone by the turn of the twenty-first century. Clearly, immigrants converged on those sectors of the Los Angeles economy where skill requirements were low enough to permit the entry of newcomers possessing little formal schooling, English language skills, or familiarity with American patterns of work and on-the-job behavior. Yet the availability of nominally low-skilled jobs does not in itself account for immigrant penetration, as we have already seen. Neither can we say simply that immigrants converge on jobs so unpleasant or low in status that natives simply do not apply.

Details are all-important; industry structure, organization type, and the specific requirements entailed in a job can either facilitate immigrant entry or make access harder. There are plenty of difficult, dead-end, menial, and inherently unsatisfying jobs in hospitals, for example, and yet immigrants do not garner low-level hospital positions with the same success registered in some other sectors examined. In part, as we noted in chapter 3, the jobs at the very bottom of the hospital hierarchy demand cognitive skills beyond those in comparable slots in a hotel or restaurant, making it harder for the least-schooled immigrants to function at the levels required. To some extent, the skill difference derives from the nature of the job: a janitor in a hospital has to know how to read a variety of signs and instructions, an ability not as crucial for a housekeeper in a hotel.

But it is also the case that the hospital janitor and the hotel house-keeper maintain work relationships of very different kinds, the former in contact with the full panoply of hospital personnel, the latter largely iso-lated within an occupational group, and usually working on her own. Thus, differences in the division of labor condition the potential for im-migrant entry; interdependency across hospital ranks increases the im-portance of English, whereas occupational isolation in hotels makes En-glish practically irrelevant.

Moreover, the social processes that work so well for immigrants in ho-tels or restaurants are not quite so effective in the bureaucratic environ-ment that the hospital represents. Networks among hospital workers still perform the usual function of passing the word about job openings from incumbents to job seekers, and an applicant for a job in the industry still enjoys a somewhat better chance when armed with a referral from an es-tablished worker. To the extent that network hiring simply reproduces the current labor force, the tendency to hire insiders' associates works to the advantage of African Americans, at least in those institutions where they have reached a critical mass. On the other hand, many hospitals are actively shaping the labor pool by recruiting workers with no connection to the established workforce, causing inside information and insider con-nections to lose value. Further, the hospitals sift applicants with care, us-ing extensive screening and standardized efforts at selection. With these efforts, they stand guard against the homogenizing consequences that inattentive reliance on network hiring may yield. It may be true that the hotel housekeeper is socially invisible, from the viewpoint of the guest in an upscale establishment—who in any case expects stigmatized outsiders to fill stigmatized jobs. But hospitals' environmental services technicians, dietary aides, admitting clerks, and the like interact with a diverse pub-lic that expects the workforce to bear some resemblance to the clientele. Thus, large organizations servicing a broad market, as do hospitals and department stores, cannot allow networks to influence the hiring process to the extent true in the back of the house in restaurants and hotels, or on the factory floor.

Changes in the broader social and economic environment have rami-fications that narrow employment options for African Americans, and nowhere is this more true than in those segments of the hospital indus-try where large African-American clusters are found. As one might ex-pect, African Americans enjoy a particularly strong presence in medical institutions adjacent to, or within, the traditional areas of black residential settlement. In prior years, the institutional interest in securing a labor force mirroring the local patient base worked in favor of less-educated African Americans. Now that these neighborhoods are undergoing a demographic transition, with immigrants from Mexico and Central America moving in and established African-American residents moving out, the same policy works to African Americans' detriment. Furthermore, the linguistic and, to some extent, cultural requirements needed for adequately serving the new patient base yield a preference for workers who possess the appropriate skills—that is, those immigrants or children of immigrants who can effectively become bridges between the institution and the ethnic communities it serves. Ironically, the pressures to produce a workforce more representative of Los Angeles's new demography are likely to be most intense in the public sector, precisely that segment of the industry where African Americans have been most secure.

Moreover, if changing demographics breed a preference for immigrant workers, other factors push employers in the same direction. Even in hospitals, the managers we interviewed tended to prefer immigrant to African-American labor. As noted in chapter 10, employers often complained about the skill levels of African-American applicants. However, one is hard-pressed to take these complaints seriously, given that among hospital housekeepers, for example, black employees have on average four more years of schooling than their Latino immigrant co-workers—11.7 vs. 7.7 years. It seems unlikely that the Mexican, Salvadoran, and Guatemalan school systems are so much better than American schools at imparting basic literacy and numeracy that immigrant workers, with so much less education than their American peers, can boast superior or even comparable levels of cognitive skill. Rather, managers in the Los Angeles hospital industry, like their counterparts in the other industries studied, perceive immigrants as more tractable—hence preferable when making assignments to difficult, menial, unpleasant jobs that U.S.-born workers of any ethnic background find undesirable. As managers' views are also informed by specific biases about African Americans, and the nature of the hiring process leaves ample scope for inherently subjective judgments, we suspect that the ethnic preferences of hiring agents further narrow, *regardless of institutional features,* the options for African-American workers.

BUT IS THERE COMPETITION?

The word "competition" connotes an equal, head-to-head contest for control over some desired good or outcome. In our effort to detect labor market competition between less-educated African Americans and immigrants, we have focused on the contest. But we also need to ask about the outcome: would the African Americans who are now underemployed, unemployed, or out of the labor market—in short, doing poorly—be holding jobs if the new immigrant labor force were not available? For the answer to be "yes," employers would need to be willing to hire disadvantaged African Americans, and African Americans would need to be willing to take the jobs that the employers offered. Our answer is a qualified "no." It is true that some instances were identified in which immigrants did appear to be displacing black workers. In most instances, however, even among the most discriminatory employers or in situations where hiring more black workers would have powerfully skewed the demographics of the workforce away from those of the clientele, there was little reason to believe that the absence of immigrants would have yielded significant gains for African Americans.

We commonly heard from our respondents that, without immigrants, as one hotel manager put it, "We'd be in serious trouble. We wouldn't have anybody to work." Certainly, this generalization could not have been made by all of the employers we interviewed. Organizations recruiting for more attractive positions, such as some clerical positions in hospitals or the most skilled jobs in printing, still drew heavily on a Euro-American, native-born labor pool. The bad times of the early 1990s were good for those organizations able to withstand the pressures of recession, bringing in a bumper crop of job-seekers. True, this development was viewed with ambivalence, since many entities were loath to hire workers whom they perceived to be overqualified. But lower down in the hierarchy, especially in hotels, restaurants, and furniture manufacturing, our interviews provided much evidence that hard, menial, entry-level jobs no longer attracted native workers—not at the going wage, not even during the period of high unemployment that Southern California was then experiencing:

> Those [immigrants] are the people applying for those jobs. . . . Other ethnic
> groups don't apply for them. That flap about immigrants taking jobs from
> natives, I don't buy. We only see Hispanics applying for those jobs. Very
> few blacks apply for those jobs or any jobs. I don't think they're displacing
> anyone. Other groups have chosen not to do those jobs. It's not like they're

in line for those jobs and being turned away. They're simply not in line.
(Manager in large hotel)

The Mexican presence [in furniture] is historical. I don't agree with the
media about immigrants. It's a two-edged sword. There's a very great
demand for immigrants. I started in the industry in 1957. It was fifty-fifty
white and Hispanic, not many blacks. . . . I would say that in the '60s it
started to change. A lot of it was the pay structure. A greater influx of
Hispanics. You couldn't get a [native] kid out of high school; they wouldn't
start a low-wage job. I think we're too low-paid for blacks. There are very,
very few who come in [to apply] for anything. Usually [they apply] for
warehouse or forklift, which I don't have. I *have* had a few nice black girls
in the office. (Manager in furniture factory)

What was striking about these interviews was the sense that it was not
only white but also black native workers who had dropped out of the labor supply feeding into the low-level labor market. "I can't remember the
last time a black man came looking for a job," remarked one restaurant
owner (with twenty-five years in the business), expressing a sentiment that
we often heard. The manager of a hotel in West Los Angeles told us, "I
don't remember ever getting an application from a black female since I've
been here." The plant manager of a furniture factory said, "We have never
had a young black man apply for a job." "Blacks don't apply," observed
the manager of a very high-tech printing plant; "I don't think I've had a
single black applicant. That's true when I put an ad in a paper." Although
our respondents in these industries reported relatively few attempts to recruit blacks, the efforts they did make seemed to produce meager results.
"When I have advertised, I get very low turnout, even though I targeted,"
recounted a hotel manager who ran ads in two black newspapers. "I've
had very few applicants, almost none of whom qualify."

Of course, experiences varied greatly across, and within, the industries we studied. The furniture manufacturers were particularly likely to
report a paucity of black applicants. Hotels, with a very different personnel system and larger organizational size, fared only somewhat better. While printers enjoyed a more sizable black applicant flow, only a minority reported that African-American workers regularly applied for
bottom-level jobs. Hospitals and department stores were far more likely
to receive applications from black job-seekers.

Geography made some difference. Location in neighborhoods of high
Latino density significantly reduced the likelihood of black applications;
by contrast, a high black density in the surrounding area neither boosted

nor depressed the application rate. Hotels near the airport, located in close proximity to a substantial black population, were more likely to receive a steady stream of black recruits; printers in this core area also reported a somewhat heavier black applicant flow. But it was striking to visit a furniture plant in the middle of heavily black Compton and hear that blacks "don't apply, very few do. And there is a black area 'round here." Similar reports were made by: fast-fooders with outlets near a black concentration in Venice, a coastal section of Los Angeles; printers in Pasadena, an eastern-style city with a large black population; hotels in downtown Los Angeles, an area in close proximity to the South Central ghetto. As one downtown hotelier observed: "Oh, it is a known factor, and we have records to prove that. Our applicant flow has little to no blacks. I'm astonished that [there are so many blacks] in the downtown area, and still you see our numbers—it's 33 people out of 320, much fewer than Asians. But definitely they do not apply. Little to no blacks or whites for the hospitality jobs."

The Squeeze

There is ample evidence that employers often prefer immigrants to African-American workers, but, as we have emphasized, this finding must be taken in context. As we argued in chapter 10, there is a deeply racialized component to employers' views, as evidenced by the underclass lens through which they tend to perceive African-American workers. But as we interpret our material, it is the *American* component to which employers proved most averse, not wanting native workers for positions that have evolved into *immigrant* jobs. African Americans have the temerity to expect good wages for hard work, when employers have no difficulty finding immigrants who are happy (as far as the employer can tell) to work hard at an unpleasant job for low wages.

There is also evidence that hiring preferences are contextual. African-American workers have advantages over most less-educated immigrants in regard to occupations not yet tagged as immigrant jobs, even if the openings occur in a firm that looks down on hiring African Americans for its dirtiest work. Skill factors circumscribe the scope for the activation of bias. When the job is somewhat removed from the bottom, the match between the skills of African-American workers and the requirements of employers is likely to be better than for the least-skilled jobs. For the more-skilled jobs, requirements for English-language facility and literacy curb the flow of immigrant applicants. At such intermediate points in the job hierarchy, the reward/effort equation is also more consistent with the expectations of native-born workers, and this is another reason why the situational preference for immigrants is stilled.

Finally, whites continue to dominate the shrinking pool of "good jobs" that do not require large amounts of formal education but provide attractive rewards, in dollars or in social standing. Blacks have made only limited progress in the construction industry, for instance, despite the decreasing number of whites in the county. (Latino immigrants have made inroads in construction, however, by skirting the Anglo establishment, doing "odd jobs," and forming or working for small, nonunion firms.) In manufacturing, the remaining craft jobs continue to be dominated by whites. Low-level managerial positions are, like those at higher levels, still disproportionately held by whites.

In effect, less-educated blacks find themselves squeezed into a narrow and shrinking segment of the labor market where competence in basic skills—literacy, numeracy, and communication—is a must, and the rewards of the work are consistent with the expectations entertained by most native workers. Further up the job ladder, where demand for schooling is greater, the concentrations of white workers grow more dense; further down, immigrant densities grow; thus (as unemployment and labor force participation statistics continue to attest), many African Americans are being squeezed out.

THE FINAL WORD

What we have observed is a process of cumulative causation in which a set of mutually reinforcing changes raise barriers to the hiring of blacks. Network hiring has a dual function, bringing immigrant communities into the workplace and, at the same time, detaching vacancies from the open market (thus diminishing opportunities for African Americans). If blacks are less likely than immigrants to have inside information, they are also less likely to meet the criteria employers use when making hiring decisions. To some extent, this second disparity flows from black exclusion from recruitment networks. But blacks are not helped by the intangible qualities that managers seek in applicants: since employers are not looking for measurable general skills (like reading or writing) but for the unmeasurables of attitude and "people skills," they have considerable motivation to use ethnic markers as crude, if effective, proxies for these traits. Moreover, employers perceive immigrants as far more desirable employees than blacks, largely because they see the immigrants as "different" from Americans, hence more likely to accept managerial authority without question. Any managerial propensity to favor immigrants is likely to be reinforced by the attitudes of the predominantly Latino workforce, as inserting a black worker in a predominantly Latino crew is not likely to increase productivity, given the hostility between the two groups. And African Americans seem to play their own role in this process, apparently opting out of the low-level labor market in response to rising expectations, on the one hand, and in anticipation of conflict on the job, on the other.

CHAPTER 12

Conclusion

America entered the twentieth century in the throes of a mass migration; it began the twenty-first century in much the same way. Like their predecessors, today's new arrivals cluster at the bottom of the skill spectrum, many arriving with few of the proficiencies that the native-born enjoy. Like the immigrants of old, most of today's less-educated newcomers hail from countries where the industrial structure has not caught up to that of the United States, limiting the degree to which skills can be transferred from back home.[1] As before, the racial status of the newcomers is in question—although the transformation of the "swarthy" immigrants from southern and eastern Europe into white "ethnics" and then white Americans is a reminder that a group's "racial status" is a characteristic of the host society, not something inherent in the group. In the end, the key difference between then and now involves the economy and the role it affords the newcomers: America's booming industries once hungered for any worker with two arms and two legs, but today the immigrant-dominated industries of old are all but gone.

So, since the industries that fed on past waves of immigration have themselves passed on, why do less-educated immigrants continue to arrive? Of course, life in the United States is better than in the places from which the immigrants came; even at the bottom of the U.S. labor market, wages rank high when compared to those in nearby countries—sufficiently so, that would-be movers are persuaded that migration is well worth its not inconsiderable costs. What is less clear is how the U.S.

economy can actually accommodate so many unskilled newcomers, especially when the market for poorly educated natives of any ethnicity appears to be collapsing.

As we have argued, processes of labor market segmentation do much to explain the immigrant paradox. From the viewpoint of the economist's stylized model, the labor market resembles an open bazaar, in which buyers and sellers of labor power encounter each other freely and, after a bit of squeezing the merchandise and kicking the tires, haggle out a deal. But a more sociological view suggests much greater compartmentalization. The actual extent of negotiation between buyers and sellers tends to be negligible, especially in the usual buyer's market for less-educated workers. Further, the market exchange tends to be structured by networks that link a particular set of jobs with a distinctive component of the labor supply—for example, when employers recruit women to fill slots defined as "women's jobs." Segmentation arguments, such as these, emphasize recurrent patterns of labor recruitment: that employers keep going back to the same well is why a labor force organized around some particular social category (gender, nativity, ethnicity, geographic origin) tends to be reproduced time and again.

At the bottom of the labor market, however, the workforce is likely to prove unstable, a problem that employers must either solve or work around. Natives tend to spurn the least desirable jobs; the pay is bad, the hours odd, and the working conditions poor. Often, the positions are filled by outsider groups, whose stigmatized status spills over onto these positions.[2] As it turns out, employers find immigrants a perfect match for positions that natives decline. As long as newcomers remain attached to the communities they left behind, whether planning to return or simply remembering the impoverished conditions there, the terms of remuneration even at the bottom of the U.S. labor market provide ample motivation to work hard and well.

So there are bad jobs and people willing to take them. But just how much space is there at the bottom of our postindustrial economy for less-skilled workers to find or carve out? Clearly, the past half century has seen significant upgrading of job requirements, even if the image of a labor market in which only college graduates need apply bears little relationship to a more complex reality in which old proficiencies are degraded even as new skills are created. On the one hand, the typical secretary needs to be proficient in a constantly changing set of skills, applied to technologies that were not imagined thirty years ago; however, the same technological revolution has turned the operation of a cash register at McDonald's or Wal-Mart into a "no-brainer." On the other hand, progress in rates of high-school graduation, college attendance, and college graduation among younger U.S.-born workers show that the newest domestic cohorts possess skills lacked by their predecessors thirty years ago.[3]

Still, actual job-skill requirements bear only a tenuous relationship to level of schooling, let alone to educational credentials. Many jobs require relatively little in the way of cognitive skills obtained through extensive education. Instead, job requirements emphasize either personal qualities—friendliness, enthusiasm, smiling, subservience—not obtained in school, or small or moderate amounts of skill that can be picked up on the job in cooperation with other workers.

Networks and Social Closure

In the continuing importance of these two factors—job-specific skills and personality traits—we find the pressures that open the door of the U.S. economy. But there is something else that allows the immigrant flow to *first* take hold and widen: the social ties linking veterans in the United States with friends and relatives back home, and connecting newcomers to the entry portals of domestic industries.

As the scholarly literature tells us, immigration can be best understood as a social-network activity, with pioneer immigrants establishing themselves and then providing a path for the newest arrivals. In some respects, today's newcomers may burden the established immigrants, taxing the limited resources that the settlers possess. But the obligation need not be overwhelming, as employers who operate on the "birds-of-a-feather" postulate may see great promise in adding more workers like the hardworking immigrant incumbents, and at practically no cost. Thus, in search of a convenient supply of reliable hired hands, the employer installs a regime of network hiring—only later to discover a workplace in which most, if not all, of the help share an ethnic, national, or even hometown connection.

Of course, we do not mean that only migrants possess social networks, or that they are the only group to use networks instrumentally, as tools to gain employment. Far from it. As demonstrated by studies dating back almost four decades,[4] most job seekers utilize social connections, with positive results. If this were the whole story, however, this would be a very short book; no one should be surprised to learn that immigrants, like everybody else, use their networks to find jobs. By focusing our analysis at the level of the individual organization, however, we add something to the usual tale. It is not only that employers find virtue in recruiting through connections, concluding that hiring networks handle informational problems that reliance on normal labor-market processes does not resolve, nor that network recruitment is appreciated for securing dependable workers at remarkably low costs. Rather, the novelty of our argument is that these advantages, so emphasized in the literature, count most in the *short* run; over the long term, hiring known commodities is often too much of a good thing. Hard to control and difficult to monitor, network recruitment can backfire on employers, yielding a power shift that redounds to the benefit of job-hungry immigrant groups, and giving personnel policies a nepotistic cast that is hard for the most vigilant organization to uproot.

In a sense, our analysis echoes the story told earlier by proponents of the segmented-labor-market hypothesis. In their view, workers in the so-called primary sector gained job security and access to a well-defined job ladder as a result of large employers' efforts to smooth out bumps in the production process. On the one hand, the workers, through their unions, offered employers labor peace; on the other, the employers provided high wages and good benefits, along with an agreed-upon framework for regulating access to jobs. As long as the price was not too steep, the desire for labor peace promoted accommodation; when incumbents sought exclusion of out-group members, employers were often ready to comply with such low-cost preferences of their established workers.[5]

But the segmented labor market theorists neglected to scrutinize the actual processes through which specific groups of workers were consistently matched to distinctive sets of jobs. Consequently, as one researcher has argued, they did not notice that in a labor-surplus environment, workers could only be "moved from secondary to primary jobs with the assistance of customary social linkages between their . . . social groups and particular groups of primary jobs."[6] Nor did they conceptualize the matching process as one circumscribed by social closure, with the structures that allow a specific category of workers to secure jobs also generating resources allowing them to exclude outsiders and constrain managerial authority. Moreover, earlier researchers conceptualized the secondary sector in largely undifferentiated terms, but its salient attributes take quite defined form. The jobs often demand a real proficiency specific to a particular task; the workforce is interconnected, through the linkages that we have repeatedly described. Consequently, the secondary labor market is home to a set of quasi communities, nested in particular occupations or industries, and these characteristics structure the patterns whereby workers move from one job to the next.

The Social Dimension of Skill

The advocates of dual labor market theory made it clear that the skills required by the primary-sector factory jobs around which their analysis revolved were largely learned on the job. Beyond basic reading and mathematics, the proficiencies learned in school were not especially relevant.

As we have seen, much the same holds true for the jobs we studied. Some cognitive skills were relevant, but generally *not* those imparted by schooling through or beyond the high-school degree. Yet performing the jobs did require proficiencies that the man or woman on the street would be unlikely to possess. Some skills could be learned quickly by the typical applicant. At the low end of the low-skill spectrum, restaurant managers thought that their entry-level jobs could be mastered in eight days; according to hotel managers, entry-level applicants needed a little more time—eleven days—before they could execute required tasks acceptably. In other industries, bottom-level jobs generally required a bit more initial training. Hospitals had more exacting expectations of entry-level help, yet inserted the new hires into an organization where movement upward from bottom-level jobs was difficult, if not impossible, without additional schooling or formal training. In printing, a female factory worker was almost sure to be stuck where she started—in the bindery— but a man could begin there, become a jogger, and eventually move up into the pressmen's ranks. In furniture, a worker might be deployed on easy-to-learn upholstering tasks and subsequently move up through various machine-handling positions and, eventually, into carpentry, the pinnacle of the furniture manufacturing shop-floor hierarchy.

But the key to acquiring skills on the job involves the cooperation of established workers, who already possess the needed know-how and can train new arrivals by showing them how the job gets done. As emphasized throughout this book, work is a fundamentally social process, lubricated by successful interaction, whether on the factory floor or across the shop and service counters. Since social ties and social similarity facilitate integration, skill transfer depends on membership in the group. Sometimes, the more skilled workers are innocently unable to train those who do not share their language; sometimes, the incumbents are just unwilling to train newcomers who do not belong to their group. In either event, trouble awaits the workers lacking the connections to get started. Employers can try to force the skilled worker to cooperate, but the effort rarely seems to them worth the cost; the goodwill of the experienced worker simply counts for more.

Yet it is important not to focus solely on skills and on the process by which proficiencies are acquired, since very little know-how, whether practical or theoretical, matters in performing the jobs of interactive service. It is true that department stores may expect salespersons to read, write, add, subtract, and even speak English with at least minimal proficiency. Learning to do these jobs may also take time—thirty days for the acquisition of full competence, according to our respondents. Nonetheless, the attributes essential for success on the selling floor have to do with personality and the presentation of self—not with "skills" in the everyday, or even dictionary, sense of the word. Put differently, the most important traits in the service interaction are qualities that workers bring to the workplace, not skills that they pick up on the job.

In sum, interaction with helpful co-workers almost always mattered, whether or not task performance fundamentally entailed working with or working "on" people. Even when employers wanted the "hard skills" required to make or transform a thing, the ability to successfully interact with co-workers was valued as a means to an end. Elsewhere, employers were more concerned with the personal qualities deemed appropriate for the setting, and that would signal an ability to fit in happily, both with one's co-workers and at the bottom of the organizational chart. Thus, the factors that smoothed the transition from the external labor market into the organization had little to do with the know-how possessed by an applicant. The person possessing the most skills, the superior educational background, or the most convincing employment history might seem the most attractive candidate, from an abstract point of view, but not when evaluated in light of the particular job and organization.[7] In jobs that involved working on things, who one was *relative to co-workers* mattered more than what one knew. By contrast, in jobs that involved working with people, who one was *relative to customers* also counted more heavily than the knowledge one possessed. In either case, "getting along" was of utmost importance, although getting along with co-workers tended to be paramount on the more egalitarian shop floor, whereas getting along with customers, to whom deference was often expected, took on primary importance in the service interaction. As the employers told us, enthusiasm, friendliness, and an outgoing disposition made it easier to "get along"; even so, getting along involved a good deal more than "people skills."

Attitude: "Good" and "Bad"

For all these reasons, "attitude," *not* "skills," ranks at or near the top of the list of "what employers want." From the employers' perspective, attitude basically comes in two forms—"good" and "bad." Needless to say, employers are looking for applicants equipped with attitudes of the first type. As we've emphasized, the importance of attitude derives, in part, from the inherently social nature of work. Most tasks involve some interdependency, and thus require at least the propensity to cooperate flexibly with the co-workers whose aid is required to get the job done. Where the job involves ongoing contact with customers, as in the service industries studied, employers' expectations about interaction are higher still. Since the quality of the service received can only be partially detached from the quality of the interaction with the service provider, employers want workers who can present customers with a pleasant, friendly face. And while customers' expectations for friendliness is an acquired taste, obtained under the tutelage of American mass merchandisers, today's customers have been well educated. The stylized routine of the cashier who asks "How may I serve you?" renders change, and then says "Have a good day" may represent no more than false friendliness—but it is what the consumer wants.

Yet organizations' interest in securing workers with appropriate personality traits goes beyond what these employers see as necessary for task completion. The firm, after all, has a political structure, within which the interests of management and labor are frequently in conflict. Bosses are concerned with profit maximization, a matter of only limited import to workers, who tend to be more interested in performing less work for more pay. Of course, modern management is well versed in the techniques of keeping recalcitrant workers in line, and possesses a huge arsenal of techniques to monitor productivity, deter slacking, and increase output. But few control structures work perfectly, and in any case the conditions of work at the bottom of the labor market do not inspire happy compliance. By definition, bottom-level jobs provide few rewards, material or intrinsic; more often than not, the work is punishing to the body, the spirit, or both. Under these circumstances, employers of low-skilled help find it particularly preferable to hire those applicants most likely to accept subordination, and to do so with the fewest complaints. Thus, employers' recurrent invocation of "attitude" serves as shorthand for deference or its absence. What bosses call "bad attitude" implies a tendency to mouth off. The preferred worker, by contrast, has come with a "good attitude," the managerial euphemism for the proclivity to say "yes" with no questions asked.

Bureaucracy

But "you can't always get what you want," as the famous song reminds us. At the bottom of the labor market, employers lack the profitability needed to outbid competitors and offer the wage rates that could attract "quality" help, especially since additional monetary compensation is probably needed to offset the psychic costs associated with the low-status, stigmatized jobs involved. At the time of our interviews, in the early 1990s, recession simultaneously made for a relatively favorable supply situation—lots of workers looking for too few jobs—and constrained employers' ability to offer much in the way of wages, benefits, or working conditions.

Having few tools to actively stir the labor market, many employers fell back on hiring networks, which meant that they did not necessarily hire the workers they sought, but instead got the recruits their established workers wanted. As noted above, network reliance often met employers' ends. Probabilistic factors increased the likelihood that referrals brought in by "good" workers would share their sponsors' favorable traits. Sponsors also had a vested interest in assuring that everything worked out as the employer wanted: screening out their less trustworthy friends or kin; helping their newly recruited associates learn the job; and pressuring the newcomers if the latter did not conform.

Nonetheless, reliance on network hiring represents the lazy manager's out; one will never see the best "goods" on the market if all one does is ask established workers to "spread the word." Of course, this is just why such an unlikely alliance occurs: managers often prefer not to make *too* many choices. However, the influence of the established workers' networks may be such that choices narrow far more than management would like. Not only does network recruitment keep information from leaking out; it makes it hard for outsiders to start and to establish the competencies needed to retain a job. The greater the reliance on networks, the greater the probability of exclusion, whether of a tacit sort, due to linguistic factors or informational monopolies, or an active sort, as when categorically distinctive workers engage in exclusionary closure.

For the reasons already catalogued, larger organizations found that their quantitative needs for labor could only be partially met by established hiring networks—which had the additional disadvantage of furnishing a workforce of a quality often not deemed adequate. The imperatives of shaping and sifting the labor force involved bureaucratic techniques, which tended to substitute one principle of exclusion for another. Eligibility for network hiring hinged on whom one knew; therefore, applicants without contacts to insiders were largely out of luck. By contrast, bureaucratic systems screened and selected on the basis of some predetermined set of qualities, usually a combination of skills, personality traits, and various ethnic characteristics. Under these circumstances, applicants with contacts to insiders still enjoyed an edge, but rarely one that proved decisive; by the same token, being an outsider carried few disadvantages.

On the other hand, bureaucratic hiring mechanisms turned out to be less formal and impersonal than the typical human resources management textbook would suggest. At the end of the process, one human being would select another,[8] ultimately drawing on an idiosyncratically developed body of knowledge and on the arbitrary, subjective preferences on which everyone relies. While bureaucratic mechanisms reduced the influence of any single person, they also increased the number of persons who could effectively dash an applicant's chances. Thus, the formalities of the process were often short-circuited, as when low-level bureaucrats put applications in the "dead letter box" on the basis of an intuitive judgment, without any formal screening. And, in all cases, the manifold intangibles of the interaction between applicant and hiring agents played heavily in the decision-making process.

Subjectivity and Its Consequences

The social organization of labor sometimes expands and sometimes limits the potential immigrant employment base of a firm. Networks do not simply connect newcomers to a tier of low-level jobs; they also provide a mechanism for extending their base well beyond an initial set of entry-level positions, with the potential for expansion largely a function of the efficiencies generated by hiring through social connections. But networks can only reach so far. Organizational characteristics affect the potential payoff of those connections on which immigrants are so dependent; where bureaucracy prevails, low-skilled immigrants with few advantages other than their ethnic ties find the going tougher. But, as noted above, the scope for subjectivity remains, whether in the smallest of shops, or the largest, most rule-ridden of organizations. The personal idiosyncrasies and tastes of hiring agents provide the window through which ethnic preferences enter into the hiring process.

Recall that employers decide whom they will hire based on a series of distinctions, discriminating between workers with "good" attitudes and bad, between faces that appear sullen and those that seem friendly, between job-seekers who project enthusiasm and those exhibiting "negativity." Making these distinctions from a brief individual encounter with any certainty almost always proves difficult; as our interviewees reminded us, it is hard to test for personality. One can, however, turn to alternative sources of information, such as one's own views about the social categories to which particular workers belong.

Employers' views structure their hiring preferences, although in a notably ironic way. The relevant scholarly literature primarily tells a story about actions based on preferences for one's own kind. This perspective may explain one's choice of neighbor, friend, or mate, but it does not shed much light on the discriminations under consideration; bosses do not generally think of workers as their "own kind," especially with regard to the relatively unpleasant and unrewarding jobs examined in this book. Under these circumstances, employers look for, and find, ethnic differences along a dimension of crucial importance to the maintenance of an ongoing work routine: the likelihood of accepting subordination. They see outsiders as the optimal candidates, perceiving virtue in the immigrants' difference and dual frame of reference.

At the bottom of the labor market, therefore, social insiders are not wanted. Employers evince considerable disdain for the work effort and ethos of the Euro-American labor force remaining at the bottom of the labor market, but those views yield limited impact, given the relatively high skills and correspondingly greater options of the region's Euro-American workers. The losers turn out to be African Americans, who are disqualified on two counts. First, employers of less-skilled labor exhibit an aversion to, *all* "American" workers, preferring foreigners not for their difference as such, but for what this difference implies. Second, employers show a strong dislike for American workers of African descent, blending traditional antiblack stereotypes with new views disseminated in the discourse surrounding the "black underclass."

Immigrants are wanted because they aspire to employment standards that do not match U.S.-born expectations; however, no good thing lasts forever. Americanization renders immigrants less desirable; it also makes their U.S.-raised children unlikely candidates for labor at the very bottom. In the short run, immigration solves the problem it was designed to handle—the procurement of workers willing to fill the jobs no one else wants. But in the long run, it reproduces the original dilemma in intensified form—as the second generation may have to start where the first generation began, but will surely aspire to much more.

The Puzzle of Assimilation

In this book, we have sought to unlock the riddle of the contemporary immigration puzzle: how has America managed to accommodate such a large flow of unskilled newcomers when the American economy is proceeding rapidly toward a new, knowledge-intensive, and skill-intensive world of work? But it is now time to go beyond the past and to look to the future, examining the prospects for this particular immigrant working class and the trajectories likely for the immigrants' descendants.

Scholars, policymakers, and the man and woman in the street think about the immigrant future in much the same way: the appropriate immigrant future involves entrance into the American mainstream. The concept of assimilation stands as a shorthand for this point of view.

Although the point of departure from which almost all scholarly examination begins, this particular perspective deserves a skeptical reassessment. "Assimilation" is surely a peculiar scholarly concept, resonating with a normative vision of national life that envisions a direct relationship, unmediated by ethnic ties, between the individual and the nation. While the dictionary provides a number of core meanings for the term, one idea occupies the place of honor in scholarly and policy discussions alike: the notion that assimilation entails a reduction in ethnic difference.[9]

But this definition begs the root question—difference from whom? How can any particular other be judged distinct, if the "self" to which it is contrasted is hardly of one piece? Although the literature offers any number of phrases attempting to identify the bedrock against which the *un*-American can be compared—the "majority," the "core cultural group," or "the mainstream"—there was, when last we looked, no such thing. In effect, the discussion of assimilation simply sets up an artificial contrast between immigrants, depicted as distinctive from the start, and a national self, imagined as homogeneous. It takes only a few moments of reflection to realize that what passes for "mainstream" is riven by divisions—cultural, political, class, religious, and so on—making it a very problematic, if not irrelevant, benchmark. Indeed, the national "self" is mostly a result of a contrastive process: without outsiders (aliens abroad, foreigners at home, or domestic minorities deprived of full membership), neither "mainstream" nor "majority" would *be*.

While scholarly and public understandings of assimilation tell a story of ways "outsiders" become similar to this poorly defined "self," the sociology of assimilation has not bothered to ask how such similarity might develop. An obvious answer involves one of the other, usually forgotten meanings of assimilation—similar treatment. Acceptance, however, is a condition that implies change on the part of dominants, not only of newcomers. Understood in this light, assimilation becomes a process of which the subjects are insiders as well as outsiders. Together, both groups make "assimilation" through an interactive process, drawing and redrawing the lines that determine who is "in" and who is "out."

Where the Story Begins

From this perspective, the story begins with *insiders,* who create "otherness" by deploying the newcomers in ways that define them as *outsiders.* As employers repeatedly told us, immigrants are useful precisely *because* they are different: their dual frame of reference and less-entitled status make them the ideal candidates to fill jobs that others do not want. From the employers' standpoint, immigrants' suitability for society's dirty work is one of the newcomers' salient traits, and their greatest virtue. As shown in this book, employers may not particularly like immigrants, but they cannot do without them. American society may be hurtling toward a computerized age, in which unpleasant, menial jobs are either exported overseas or accomplished through automatic means—but it is not there yet. Bottom-level jobs still have to be filled—preferably, in this era of intensified competition, at bargain-basement rates.

A habit like this is hard to break. Take away immigrant cooks and hotel housekeepers, and room and restaurant and prices go up. One might want a larger number of better-educated, English-speaking workers, but improving the "quality" of workers assigned to low-status, unpalatable jobs would require a hike in wages and benefits that this new age of inequality seems not to allow. The immigrant phenomenon, providing outsiders who furnish economic contributions yet can be excluded from civic membership and all that it entails with little effort, proves difficult to stop.

As emphasized throughout this volume, the networks between veterans and newcomers fuel migration's persistence, making for an immigrant economic base that expands steadily and has its own dynamic. Consequently, immigrants pile up at the bottom, filling low-status economic functions. In deploying immigrants to perform the tasks that natives find dishonoring, dominants structure interaction in ways that enhance, rather than diminish, difference. The stigma associated with the immigrants' jobs comes to define the newcomers, adding disrepute to the liabilities that derive from foreign origins. In the conventional approach, such differences denote a lag, or even failure, in the progress of assimilation—but such a view mistakes effect for cause. Immigrants' otherness is not an inherent attribute; its meaning derives from the newcomers' relationship to the natives who want their labor but not their social presence. Thus, the most crucial differences are those created, first, through the processes of migration and, second, through the encounter between the immigrant outsiders and those lucky enough to take membership in the civic nation for granted.

Bringing Politics Back In: California's Immigrant Quandary

In this book, we have focused on the processes that allow immigrants to establish and expand on beachheads in particular occupations and industries, as well as on the factors that retard their progress. This concern has led us to zero in on a particular slice of the immigrant reality—the interaction between workers of different ethnicities and the managers who select them and coordinate their work. But we have done so at the expense of the broader context; we have allowed ourselves to understand immigration as a fundamentally social phenomenon, its politics those of the relatively small-scale world of the organization and the workplace. Immigration is, however, a euphemism for inter*national* migration, a phenomenon that is fundamentally a matter of state. Thus, as we turn to consideration of the future, the politics of immigration become salient, moving us to a macrosociological scale.

Immigrants are most useful when both hidden and silent, as suggested by the experience of California's largest immigrant group. For many years, the nature of the migration process cloaked the import and scale of Mexican immigration to California. This migration long bore the imprint of its origin as a source of temporary agricultural labor, with the migrants heading back and forth across the border in response to seasonal labor demands—and moving, for the most part, as single adults. But over time, sojourners left the circular migration streams, putting down roots, and sending for spouses and children. This development was greatly accelerated by the amnesty provided undocumented immigrants by the Immigration Reform and Control Act of 1986.

In a sense, Mexican immigrants were neither seen nor heard. Anglo Californians have long indulged in their fantasies of the "Spanish" past, a pursuit made all the more enjoyable by the invented nature of a history that hid the continuity of the Mexican presence in Los Angeles and its environs. The jobs that the immigrants held also contributed to their obscurity. It is not just that the Anglo suburbanite lives miles from the grimy factories in which the immigrants labor; the very division of labor—between front of the house and back of the house, for example—keeps the foreigners conveniently out of sight. The rituals of interaction further cloud this human presence; as we have argued, so many interactive services furnished by immigrants are enjoyably consumed precisely because they are provided by subordinates, not equals.

Not fully seen, Mexican immigrants were also not fully heard. The heavily illegal component to their migration made for substantial quiescence. Proximity to the host country, the immigrants' continued belief in the "dream of return," a political system that discouraged participation, a union movement that until recently had lost the ability to stir the immigrant masses—these factors allowed the immigrant population to build up without noise, and therefore without much notice from the region's dominant group.

Matters drastically changed in the early 1990s, just as we went into the field, when the optimism that had long characterized Southern California seemed to have vanished. The long tide of postwar, Cold War–induced prosperity had just come to a crashing halt. Factories closed, retailers and banks dropped not only clerks but managers, property values plummeted. Gradually it became clear that Angelenos were witnessing not the end of a boom but the cessation of the region's history of near-continuous growth. With good times gone, the region's hospitality to outsiders disappeared.

The mood induced by recession produced the 1994 "Save Our State" initiative, which in due course became Proposition 187. The proposed law was of dubious legality, promising to shut illegal immigrant children out of schools when the constitutional right to education for all resident children, legal or otherwise, had been reaffirmed by the Supreme Court just ten years before. And, setting aside legality and ethics, the proposed law was of little dollar-saving value, since enforcing exclusion carried a significant monetary cost. But voters had little patience for such niceties, and the state's political leadership saw no capital in educating them otherwise.

Proposition 187 won handily, receiving over 59 percent of the vote. Although the bill did best among Anglos, it had broad appeal; one-half of the black and Asian voters and more than one-fourth of the Latino voters also voted yes. Legal action stopped enforcement within a week of the proposition's passage; five years and several losing court battles later, California's new Democratic governor declared the law a "dead letter." Anti-immigration fever subsequently subsided, but not before Washington responded with hasty passage of bills that had a far-reaching impact on legal immigrants' entitlement to welfare and on a panoply of issues related to immigrant rights. Even though professional Republican politicians quickly realized that an anti-immigrant stance would soon consign them to oblivion in a state where the Latino electorate could only grow, they proved unable to put the genie back in the bottle. In 1996, California's voters had another go at the specter of immigration, voting to end bilingual education; the issue, although of very great complexity, was one on which Anglo opinion was less influenced by the latest scholarship than by the view that immigrants should start adapting to American ways, and fast.

So, in spite of much talk, scholarly or popular, about assimilation, California's voters opted for a *dis*-assimilating mode. The anti-immigrant "allergy" stimulated nativist sentiment, further excluding and marking the foreign-born as outsiders whose very presence was a threat. But this backlash sent a message to the immigrants and to the native-born ethnic host groups of which they were gradually becoming a part: one could no longer stand silent. Rather, it was time to make oneself heard. The nativist reaction boomeranged, producing an ethnic reaction of equal or greater force. Evidence for this came in the form of surging rates of naturalization and electoral participation, and of growing militancy among the immigrant workers on whose quiescence many employers, such as those we interviewed, had long counted. The conflict over immigrants' access to full membership in the American nation has now become engaged.

What the Future Brings

Thus, we stand at a very different pass than conventional approaches allow. It is well and good to debate the pros and cons of immigration policy, asking, for example, whom we shall admit, but that discussion has an academic flavor when more than 10 percent of the population consists of immigrants and another 10 percent is made up of the immigrants' descendants. For the most part, the newcomers are here to stay; the question at hand concerns their participation in the broader civic nation. Will we engage in programs, policies, and public behaviors that explicitly or implicitly serve to exclude? Or will we find the wherewithal to redraw boundaries, granting newcomers full membership in the society they have already joined?

The assimilationist biases of scholarly and popular thought answer that, to gain membership, the immigrants need to change, abandoning their distinctive traits and relationships, and opting out of a preference for their ethnic group and its ways. But, as we have argued, immigrants are different because difference is what was wanted. Once in place, original differences get accentuated, in part through the stigmatized role that immigrants fill, in part through the reactions that occur when the native-born population sees the Faustian bargain it made in recruiting and employing immigrant labor, and decides to renege on the deal.

So, the route to full civic membership will not be easy. Complicating matters are the low levels of education of many immigrants, who are penalized in an economy where low-skilled workers of any sort are in trouble and public efforts to upgrade the earnings and capacities of the less-skilled have gone by the boards. The immigrants' children are likely to do better, but their aspirations will also exceed their parents', having forgotten about the home country and having set their sights on the lifestyle and living standard that the average American enjoys. While this goal may be in reach, it will not be attained without complications. After all, we are talking about "who gets what," and the distribution of resources has always been a matter of strife. The immigrant laborers may comprise a group of willing helots for now, but not forever. And their children will certainly be ready to fight for their piece of the American dream—not to speak of the particular good life to which Californians have long aspired. Thus, unless the nation takes steps to speed the course of immigrant integration, a future of ethnic conflict awaits. And while academics will be largely irrelevant to any such outcome, we should prepare ourselves for its study—a very different intellectual project than the program laid out by the American sociology of immigration and ethnicity as it exists today.

The Local Context

Angelenos have never been shy of boosting the charms of their artificial Eden on the West Coast, but the newfound status of Los Angeles as capital of Immigrant America is one boast to which Southern California can legitimately lay claim. Los Angeles now has the nation's largest immigrant concentration, having surpassed that of New York well before the twentieth century passed into the twenty-first.

The size of its foreign-born population notwithstanding, Los Angeles does not receive a cross-section of America's international migrants; instead, it disproportionately attracts the most poorly educated immigrants. Not only do these poorly schooled immigrants quickly find themselves at the bottom of the economic hierarchy in Los Angeles, they also find that the distance between themselves and their native-born counterparts is larger than elsewhere in the United States.

Immigrant Los Angeles has been widely touted by scholars, journalists, and publicists as the exemplar of multi-ethnic America. While there are immigrants from all over the world living in Los Angeles, the great majority come from a handful of places. As of the mid-1990s, a single source country—Mexico—accounted for almost half of the region's foreign-born residents, with El Salvador and Guatemala collectively contributing another 10 percent. Add in the seven next most important sending countries (all but one located in Asia), the top ten places of origin account for 78 percent of all foreign-born Angelenos. In the rest of the country, by contrast, newcomers from Mexico, El Salvador, and

Guatemala make up only a quarter of the foreign-born population. In fact, fewer than half of all foreign-born U.S. residents hail from the ten countries that nearly eight in ten Angelenos left behind.

National origins matter, partly as a result of the skill differences among migration streams. Low-skilled persons greatly overshadow highly educated persons among immigrant Angelenos, even if the latter represent a nontrivial number. In the late 1990s, Los Angeles had two immigrants lacking a high-school degree for every one immigrant who had completed college. In New York, in contrast, high- and low-skilled immigrants were roughly equal in number.[1] Not surprisingly, the educational deficits of immigrant Los Angeles yield disproportionately high levels of poverty. In the late 1990s, 27 percent of all immigrants in Los Angeles were living in poverty, as opposed to only 8 percent of the area's native whites. By comparison, only a fifth of foreign-born New Yorkers were living in poverty.[2]

Los Angeles's status as capital of Immigrant America may be uncontested, but it is recently acquired. For most of its modern existence, the city predominantly attracted migrants who were white and native-born. In 1920, just before the close of the *last* great immigration wave, only 17 percent of Angelenos had been born abroad—compared to 35 percent of their contemporaries in New York.[3] The next decade saw the arrival of a substantial Mexican inflow, but the movement northward stopped with the onset of the Depression. The politics of those times led to the deportation of Mexicans, natives as well as migrants, throughout the Southwest, further diminishing the Mexican presence. Immigrants were soon replaced by internal migrants in search of the California Dream, made all the more attractive by the prosperity that developed during World War II and in the early postwar years. The native-born newcomers were not identical, ethnically. Most important, the 1940–1970 period saw a large-scale arrival of African Americans, attracted by the region's relatively hospitable race relations and by its burgeoning economy. With the arrival of domestic migrants en masse, and the replacement of earlier Mexican and Asian migrants by their second- and third-generation descendants, the immigrant experience became consigned to the region's past.[4]

Or so it seemed in 1960, when the foreign-born numbered a mere 617,000 of the nearly 7 million inhabitants of Los Angeles County, and the Mexican-born constituted less than two percent of the total population. Although the region's Mexican-origin population was sizable, it was primarily a second- or third-generation group, with the foreign-born making up a relatively small and aging mass. *The Mexican-American People*, an encyclopedic landmark study published in 1970 and based on research conducted during the mid-1960s, observed that the situation seemed destined to continue. Even the experts—let alone the average Angeleno—could hardly imagine how quickly the tables would turn and how far-reaching the changes would be.[5]

However, the face of the future was already taking shape. The *Bracero* program, begun during World War II, had rekindled the outflow of migrants from Mexico's central plateau. Abolition of the program in 1964 changed only the legal status of the migrants, leaving in place the factors that pushed them out of Mexico and pulled them to California. As time went on, agricultural workers left farm labor for better-paid pursuits in the city. By 1970, Los Angeles was registering an uptick in its foreign-born population—even as, nationwide, Immigrant America fell to its nadir.

For the next two decades, the movement of newcomers to Los Angeles ratcheted upwards in a far more radical way, with the Los Angeles–bound immigration rate growing steadily more out of line with that of the rest of the nation. The area's immigration simultaneously diversified, with Los Angeles attracting large numbers of newcomers from East Asia and the Middle East. Refugees, especially those fleeing the aftermath of the U.S. war effort in Southeast Asia, numbered significantly among the arrivals from these two source areas. For the most part, however, Asian and Middle Eastern newcomers were successful professionals and entrepreneurs who, despite difficulties with language and professional credentials, moved directly into the middle class.[6] Quite a different fate awaited the immigrants who flocked to Los Angeles from Central America. Like the Southeast Asians, the Central Americans were escaping political unrest, but unlike their Asian counterparts, the Central Americans had the bad fortune to be fleeing right-wing regimes propped up by the U.S. government. Whereas the Southeast Asians received resettlement assistance from the government, most Central Americans crossed the border as unauthorized migrants. Although the Southeast Asians did not uniformly prosper, the legal status of the Central Americans, combined with their low skills, gave them a more unenviable starting position.[7]

The recent immigrant advent occurred in the context of a rapidly changing regional economy. For most of the twentieth century, the Los Angeles region had been home to a fabulous job machine. To be sure, the 1910s and 1920s did not see the region's economy diversify as quickly or as extensively as its real-estate and commercial kingpins had wished. But the heavy industrial base that developers and business interests so strongly desired arrived in the 1930s, in the form of branch plants exported by the Midwestern tire, steel, and auto giants of the time. World War II unleashed a growth spurt, fueled in part by the region's acquisition of the nascent aerospace industry from the East Coast. The onset and continuation of the Cold War did the rest; thanks for the robust growth of Southern California's high technology complex belonged almost entirely to the Department of Defense.[8] Although natural resources, tourism, and Hollywood—"the industry" in local parlance—helped, the region's stupendous population growth can be traced to its quiet emergence as the nation's premier concentration of manufacturing.

The steel-glass-auto complex that sprang up before the war shriveled in the 1970s and early 1980s, as the globalization of production took its toll, but success in other areas allowed locals to remain proud of the city's "recession-proof" economy. In particular, the Reagan-era military buildup kept the aerospace/high technology complex alive and well through the late 1980s. A regime of easy money, and the region's attraction to foreign capital (especially from Japan), made for a burst of downtown office development. As in other metropolitan areas, the service and finance sectors grew rapidly during the 1980s. For a while, Los Angeles seemed poised to emerge as the home to a new international finance complex that would surpass that of San Francisco and perhaps even rival that of New York.

In the early 1990s, with the end of the Cold War, the flow of military contracts virtually ended. This triggered the most severe economic downturn that Southern California had experienced since World War II. Thousands of jobs disappeared in the ensuing mergers, many with out-of-town firms, and downsizing. Engineers and skilled aerospace workers were laid off in droves; major banks were absorbed by outsiders; the negative spillovers were felt far and wide.

The recession hit hard and lingered long; still, by the late 1990s, the region had turned around. Its resurgence was based on the strengths of a greatly expanded and diversified entertainment industry, a revived high technology sector, a re-engineered defense economy that had found new markets and products, and a buoyant low-wage sector that had largely survived the recession unscathed. While job gains were disproportionately concentrated near the top of the totem pole between 1970 and 1990, Los Angeles, in contrast to the paradigmatic postindustrial centers of New York and San Francisco, also generated new jobs for the low-skilled.[9]

Los Angeles's restructured economy provides ample room for less-educated immigrants, setting it apart from other major metropolitan areas. Of no small importance is the continued strength of its manufacturing sector. There is loose talk about Southern California's "rust belt," but visits to a few industrial parks can confirm what the statistics reveal: while some industries may have gone, the goods production sector remains a colossus—alive, reasonably well, and providing employment. Moreover, the distress at the high end of the Los Angeles manufacturing complex has hastened the outflow of native workers, creating a game of musical chairs, in which immigrants can pick up jobs by taking the place of natives who have left.

Thus, the structure of the Los Angeles economy has created a place for low-skilled newcomers. While the region's established residents are at best ambivalent about the immigrants, its employers know a good deal when they see one; why complain about an incessant stream of job-seekers willing to do any job at bargain basement rates? The Los Angeles economy has adapted to the availability of low-skilled help by expanding the range of occupations open to workers with few, if any, formal skills. The newcomers have become thoroughly integrated into the production systems of the region: of the eighty-three manufacturing industries with one thousand or more employees identified by the census in 1990, fifty-three had an overrepresentation of Mexican immigrants employed.[10] Predictions about the factory or office of the future notwithstanding, the reality of the Los Angeles economy remains close to the work world of the past, with abundant jobs for poorly educated but manually proficient workers.

Of course, the focus on the modal group—Los Angeles's less-educated immigrant masses—pushes the experience of the high-skilled newcomers out of view. As noted in chapter 1, the story of middle-class newcomers, whose numbers are substantial, is often overlooked. In contemporary Los Angeles, such coveted occupations as medicine, dentistry, and various engineering and computer specialties have become immigrant niches. And business, small and large, also contains a very noticeable immigrant presence. Chinese immigrants, particularly those from Taiwan, have established an extraordinary "ethnoburb" in the San Gabriel Valley, west of downtown Los Angeles, complete with up-market retail complexes and a vast array of ethnic export-import firms, high-tech establishments, and producer service organizations—each employing a mainly foreign-born workforce.[11]

A survey of the recent past of ethnic Los Angeles would not be complete without mention of the 1992 disturbances, the largest and costliest urban uprisings in the postwar United States. Triggered by the acquittal of the police officers who viciously—and visibly, thanks to a bystander's videotape—beat a speeding black motorist, Rodney King, the violence, looting, and burning spread throughout Los Angeles County. African-American anger over continued police brutality provided the spark, but the fuel came also from other sources: blacks' resentment of immigrant, especially Korean, businesses in their neighborhoods; Central-American and Mexican immigrant workers' rancor toward their mostly immigrant employers; and the desire of the deprived to enrich themselves in the midst of chaos. Subsequent efforts to revitalize local neighborhoods and local economies proved meager. Despite the abundant hype that surrounded the 1993 launch of "Rebuild LA," only a handful of inner-city projects of any significance were begun, much less completed.

April 1992 marked a turning point of sorts for Los Angeles, but not toward better times. Instead, it turned out to be the prelude to two more years of disasters, including widespread brush fires and floods in 1993 and a major earthquake in 1994. An economic downturn that had begun in 1991 sent unemployment shooting up toward 10 percent in 1992 and remaining there into 1995. All of these events conspired to knock the floor out of housing prices—a boon to some, but a major blow to many new homeowners who had arrived during the height of the 1980s real estate speculation boom. It was during this time of turmoil, in the early 1990s, that we conducted our field research.

THE SIX INDUSTRIES

As noted in chapter 1, our initial purpose was to learn how and to what extent the arrival of less-educated immigrants had an impact on native workers. Our intuition told us that the effects would be greatest in jobs with low skill requirements, and would be felt most strongly by African Americans. We carefully selected industries to ensure that our sample included cases with both high and low immigrant representation, and both high and low African-American representation (see Table 1.1). These considerations led us to choose the six industries studied in this book: hotels, restaurants, hospitals, department stores, printing, and furniture manufacturing.

Restaurants and hotels are prototypical service industries, featuring a large proportion of menial, poorly compensated jobs. Like these industries, the health care sector provides services; however, hospitals have an elaborate division of labor, employing significant numbers of workers with both far more and somewhat less education than has the average American. Department stores are more "people-oriented" than any of the three other service industries we studied, with a large proportion of department store workers dedicated principally to dealing with customers. Furniture manufacturing and printing represent the "small-batch" end of manufacturing industries, requiring more skills than old-style "Fordist" mass production industries, but less than older craft industries.

Of our selected industries, only two, furniture manufacturing and hotels, were primarily *export* industries, each serving a clientele from outside the Los Angeles region. Both were, however, partially dependent on the state of the local economy. The high cost of production in Los Angeles impinged most heavily on furniture manufacturers, vulnerable to direct competition from domestic manufacturers in the U.S. southeastern seaboard and from international manufacturers as close as northern Mexico. Insofar as the hotel industry competed for clients—for example, convention visitors—on a nationwide scale, the higher costs of doing business in Los Angeles impinged on it as well.

For the other industries in our study, competition mainly occurred at the regional or local level. While Los Angeles does boast UCLA, Cedars-Sinai, Daniel Freeman, and other nationally known hospitals possibly competing for patients beyond the scale of the Los Angeles region, local hospitals serve the local market for health care, and do not face much outside competition. Local department stores, printers, and restaurants also have a "captive audience." To be sure, department stores compete with other retail outlets, and increasingly have to worry about the internet, and print jobs can be shipped out of town, but in general these industries live or die on local demand for their products, not on their ability to compete with outside producers of goods and providers of services.

Dependent on the then-weak local market, many firms we surveyed were doing badly at the time we visited them. Many had not hired for some time, even to replace lost workers. In fact, nearly half (48 percent) of our respondents told us that their business were doing poorly or were suffering a decline (see Table A1). This was true of two-thirds of the furniture manufacturing concerns, and of just over one-half of the hospitals and hotels. Still, 46 percent of the department stores and 37 percent of the restaurants saw their current business performance as good or improving. U.S. Bureau of the Census data for the 1992–94 time frame[12] are generally consistent with what respondents told us. Restaurant employment was on the upswing at this point; furniture employment was flat, after a pronounced decline; all other industries studied showed small decreases in employment. Aside from restaurants, and health services,[13]

TABLE A1. STATUS OF SAMPLED FIRMS (%)

	Poor/Worsening	No Change	Good/Improving	Total
Department Stores	38	17	46	100
Furniture Manufacturing	67	15	18	100
Hospitals	52	35	13	100
Hotels	55	28	18	100
Printing	40	33	28	100
Restaurants	35	28	37	100
All Industries	48	26	26	100

SOURCE: Skills Study (N = 220)

which showed an employment increase between 1989 and 1992, the industries showed employment declines relative to 1988.

The industries were moving along differing longer-term trajectories, as seen in the twenty-year snapshots we present in the following pages. For reasons having to do with differences in market segmentation, management style, and corporate strategies, the impact of the business cycle and of industry trends was often experienced by *individual* organizations in distinctive ways.

Department Stores

By our definition, the department store industry includes chains selling to the masses as well as to the most affluent of the elite. Over the past two decades, traditional department stores have seen customers defect in droves to discount stores, on the low end, and specialty stores, on the high end. Along with payroll cost-cutting, competition led to a small absolute decline in department store employment over the 1970–1990 period (see Table A2). Although the ethnic composition of the workforce also changed significantly during these years, the content of the jobs and the predominantly female composition of the workforce remained much the same.

In 1970, nearly three-quarters of department store workers were white, compared to less than one-half in 1990. Since the ranks of black workers increased hardly at all, most of the difference was made up by Latinos; by 1990, one-third of department store workers were Latinos, divided evenly between the native-born and immigrants. Since, as we have argued, stores often hire workers to serve specific ethnic clienteles, it appears that native-born Latinos, overrepresented relative to their proportion in the overall population, are often hired to serve the foreign-

TABLE A2. DEPARTMENT STORE WORKER
RACIAL/ETHNIC AND SEX COMPOSITION, LOS
ANGELES COUNTY, 1970–90 (%)

	1970	1980	1990	Growth 1970–90
White	73	60	43	−41
Latino Native-Born	10	15	17	68
Latino Foreign-Born	5	7	16	261
Black	10	12	13	27
Asian/Other	3	6	11	306
Female	67	67	65	−3
Lower Nonmanual	71	69	71	0
Lower Manual	12	12	13	8
N	57,100	67,820	53,312	−7

SOURCE: U.S. Census, 1970, 1980, 1990
NOTE: Because the census made significant changes in its occupational classification system, we have, following a suggestion from Donald Treiman, grouped occupations into broad categories that are roughly comparable. In the categories of the 1980 census, lower nonmanual are sales occupations and administrative support occupations, including clerical. Lower manual occupations include machine operators, assemblers, and inspectors; transportation and material moving occupations; handlers, equipment cleaners, helpers, and laborers; protective service occupations; service, occupations, except protective and household; and private household occupations.

born—who remain underrepresented. In spite of large percentage gains for nonwhite groups, however, nonwhites and immigrants remain generally underrepresented in this industry.

The makeup of the department store workforce reflects the industry's needs. Roughly 70 percent of department store workers (the lower nonmanual workers in Table A2) have customer contact as a primary part of their job. Although many customers who shop in Los Angeles department stores do not have English as their native language, department store management expects all customer contact personnel to be able to serve customers in English (even if facility in languages other than English is considered a plus). Less clearly articulated is the requirement that all workers be able to make a white, middle-class customer comfortable—a capacity judged by the officials doing the hiring. Department stores, along with hospitals, are one of the two industries in our sample where establishment size typically is large. With an average of 209 employees per site, and with only 2 percent of all establishments employing under 20 workers (see Table A3), department stores require, on the whole, a more developed personnel or human relations bureaucracy than do establishments in most other industries we studied.

TABLE A3. ESTABLISHMENT AND INDUSTRY CHARACTERISTICS, 1994

| SIC | Industry | Number of Employees | Annual Payroll per Employee($) | Establishments | | Establishments with < 20 Employees (%) |
				Total	Employees per Establishment	
2500	Furniture and fixtures	24,203	22,148	760	32	64
2700	Printing and publishing	50,053	32,965	2,448	20	82
5310	Department stores	40,374	13,877	193	209	2
5800	Eating and drinking places	209,741	10,036	13,393	16	74
7010	Hotels and motels	36,682	15,503	935	39	75
8060	Hospitals	141,974	31,406	167	850	8

SOURCE: County Business Patterns, 1994

NOTE: Numbers of employees and other industry characteristics may differ from other statistics cited in this chapter, due to different sources of information and differing industry categories.

Hospitals

Like department stores, the hospital industry is a large-firm industry, with an average of 850 employees per establishment and less than 10 percent of establishments employing under 20 workers in 1994 (see Table A3). The industry grew rapidly over the 1970–90 period, adding 77,000 jobs, almost all in the private sector (see Table A4). Because of the high private-sector growth, by 1990 only one in five hospital jobs was in the public sector. Private-sector construction and the increasing clout of insurance companies led to excess capacity and a shakeout in the industry during the early 1990s. The recession of the early 1990s exacerbated the problem by leaving many workers—including those formerly employed in hospitals—without medical insurance.

Although over two-thirds of hospital employees were white in 1970, by 1990 this held true for fewer than four in ten. Blacks were overrepresented in the industry in 1970; their representation remained constant over this period. Latino natives increased their numbers significantly, but it was foreign-born Latinos who grew most rapidly, from just 4 percent in 1970 to 15 percent of all workers in 1990. Asians grew next most rapidly; there were more Asians than blacks in hospital jobs by 1990.

Still, Latinos, and immigrant Latinos in particular, remained underrepresented in hospitals in 1990. If, however, we restricted Table A4 to the "lower manual" category of jobs, we would see that Latino immigrants made significant inroads to the least-skilled jobs in this industry during the 1970–90 period. Latino immigrants in these positions faced the same difficulty confronted by less-skilled African Americans before them: only a minority of hospital jobs fell in the lower-non-manual and lower-manual categories. Hospital service positions declined in importance during these years, although they still represented a large pool of jobs. Clerical positions increased after 1970, but took a downward trend after 1980. As of 1990, however, these two categories still accounted for 40 percent of hospital positions. Many of the clerical jobs, and most of the other 60 percent of jobs, however, simply were out of reach of most less-skilled persons, immigrant or native.

Hospitals are fascinating organizations, with a high degree of complexity and high interdependence among classes of workers. In addition to the pressures that drove down hospital stays, innovations in medical and organizational technology led to significant changes in how hospital work was organized.

Hospitals, like department stores, deliver services to "customers"

TABLE A4. HOSPITAL INDUSTRY
RACIAL/ETHNIC AND SEX COMPOSITION, LOS
ANGELES COUNTY, 1970–90 (%)

	1970	1980	1990	Growth 1970–90
White	68	51	39	−43
Latino Native-Born	5	9	9	88
Latino Foreign-Born	4	9	15	278
Black	17	20	17	−1
Asian/Other	6	11	20	249
Female	75	72	71	−5
Lower Nonmanual	17	19	17	−1
Lower Manual	37	28	23	−36
Public Sector	29	25	21	−29
N	90,900	165,500	168,277	85

SOURCE: U.S. Census, 1970, 1980, 1990
NOTES: See Table A2.

whose backgrounds represent the whole Los Angeles community. Cultural understanding is even more critical in hospitals than in the retail
arena, since clear communication may be a matter of life or death.

Furniture Manufacturing

Relatively small in comparison to the other industries studied in this
book, but still of significance for the region, furniture manufacturing
grew by over one-third between 1970 and 1990. More than any other in
our sample, this industry's growth can be attributed to immigration. The
previous generation of furniture workers had been, to a large extent,
European immigrants rather than white natives. As in the other industries, white employment in furniture fell precipitously after 1970.
Foreign-born Latinos, already one-fifth of all furniture workers in 1970,
more than took up the slack, apparently displacing both blacks and
native-born Latinos. Since the proportion of jobs fitting into the "lower
manual" category dropped from 75 percent in 1970 to 45 percent in
1990, it is clear that Latino immigrants moved into other occupations
within furniture manufacturing, including into some of the most highly
skilled jobs the industry has to offer.

Nearly two-thirds of furniture manufacturing establishments in Los
Angeles County employed less than twenty workers as of 1994 (see Table
A5), which implies that small-firm hiring and promotion practices pre-
vailed. Skill levels ranked relatively low (even if gently rising); although the

TABLE A5. FURNITURE MANUFACTURING
RACIAL/ETHNIC AND SEX COMPOSITION, LOS
ANGELES COUNTY, 1970–90 (%)

	1970	1980	1990	Growth 1970–90
White	54	27	17	−68
Latino Native-Born	17	12	9	−51
Latino Foreign-Born	22	53	67	211
Black	5	5	2	−46
Asian/Other	2	2	5	91
Female	20	20	21	5
Lower Manual	75	49	45	−40
N	24,100	34,900	32,826	36

SOURCE: U.S. Census, 1970, 1980, 1990
NOTE: See Table A2.

industry saw a substantial decline in the number of "lower manual" jobs, it still employed a higher proportion of less-skilled manual workers than did, for example, hospitals. For the most part, these workers had no need to interact with customers; they did, however, have to work as a team to manufacture products. Despite the great distance in earning power and respect between top-level craftsman and entry-level laborer in this industry, official credentials were relatively unimportant. Whereas a janitor in a hospital, for example, would realistically have no opportunity to become a doctor, a new furniture "gofer" could reasonably expect to eventually work *his* (or even, occasionally, her) way up into the skilled ranks.[14]

Hotels

Tourism has long been a mainstay of the Los Angeles regional economy, and it remains so, providing the grease on which the region's hotel industry runs. But the region's hotels do more than cater to tourists; some primarily serve businesspeople passing through, and some thrive on convention trade. In spite of the image of hotels as the behemoths that populate parts of downtown Los Angeles and its airport's periphery, three-quarters employ less than twenty people.

For our purposes, the industry has changed in one decisive way: the takeover of its workforce by Latinos from abroad. True, by 1990 Latinos still had not captured a majority of hotel jobs (49 percent were held by Latinos, including the native-born, as seen in Table A6), but their pres-

TABLE A6. HOTEL RACIAL/ETHNIC AND SEX
COMPOSITION, LOS ANGELES COUNTY,
1970–90 (%)

	1970	1980	1990	Growth 1970–90
White	68	44	30	−56
Latino Native-Born	9	6	6	−31
Latino Foreign-Born	12	31	43	264
Black	10	9	7	−29
Asian/Other	1	10	13	1280
Female	56	50	44	−22
Lower Manual	56	61	56	1
N	21,000	27,000	38,889	85

SOURCE: U.S. Census, 1970, 1980, 1990
NOTE: See Table A2.

ence had grown significantly since 1970, when only one in five workers in the industry had been Latino. In 1970, blacks had been underrepresented in hotels, and in 1990 they were even more poorly represented.

If this massive inpouring represented a success story for Latino immigrants, it was a dubious one; in spite of the efforts of union activists, the local hotel industry hardly qualified as one of the most desirable niches in the region. Wages were low, and career ladders were short. About 23 percent of the hotels we visited were unionized, a percentage less than in hospitals (47 percent) and furniture manufacturers (28 percent). The industry did appear vulnerable to further unionization and wage upgrading, but the prevalence of small establishments should prove limiting.

Printing

If hotels represent the ultimate success story for immigrant networks, printing presents a more complicated picture. Printing boomed during the 1970–90 period, reflecting both the expansion of the region and the increasing importance of printed communications of all sorts. Of our target industries, printing was the only one in which a majority of workers were still white as of 1990 (see Table A7). After hospitals, it was also the industry in which native-born Latinos showed the largest gain. There were only two industries in which African Americans showed employment gains during this period, printing and department stores, and their gains in printing were the more substantial. Even amid the concurrent growth of immigrant employment, printing, by its structure and characteristics, somehow favored the employment of natives.

TABLE A7. PRINTING RACIAL/ETHNIC AND SEX
COMPOSITION, LOS ANGELES COUNTY,
1970–90 (%)

	1970	1980	1990	Growth 1970–90
White	83	66	53	−36
Latino Native-Born	6	12	11	85
Latino Foreign-Born	6	11	21	265
Black	3	5	5	85
Asian/Other	3	6	11	228
Female	28	37	37	31
Lower Manual	51	39	36	−30
N	28,100	44,940	55,659	98

SOURCE: U.S. Census, 1970, 1980, 1990
NOTE: See Table A2.

The earnings of printing workers may provide one clue; the wages for entry-level workers and the earnings potential for these workers were near the top in our sample. While not necessarily regarded as craft jobs, the work on and around a printing press generally required skills. Most of these skills could be learned on the job, but one proficiency—the ability to read and write English—involved an ability that most workers had to possess when they applied. Even among delivery drivers, the ability to communicate in English with customers was likely to be a requirement. Thus, the higher-wage jobs would attract natives, while English requirements screened out many immigrants.

Restaurants

If printing favors natives, restaurants present the starkest contrast of the industries surveyed. By 1990, over half of all restaurant workers in Los Angeles were Latino, and most of these were immigrants (see Table A8). The story looks much like that in hotels, with the proportion of whites shrinking from nearly three-quarters to just under one-third. As in hotels, the proportion of jobs held by women dropped from over one-half to four-tenths, as Latino men replaced women of other groups.

As our interviews revealed, the kitchen and storage sections of the restaurant were a Spanish-speaking domain, not to be invaded by others. In some upscale restaurants, there was one exception to the rule—the French or German chef. Even in Chinese and other ethnic restaurants, kitchen help below the rank of head cook often rested on Latino

TABLE A8. EATING AND DRINKING PLACES
RACIAL/ETHNIC AND SEX COMPOSITION, LOS
ANGELES COUNTY, 1970–90 (%)

	1970	1980	1990	Growth 1970–90
White	73	53	31	–57
Latino Native-Born	7	9	9	22
Latino Foreign-Born	7	23	42	509
Black	5	6	4	–21
Asian/Other	7	10	14	86
Female	52	48	40	–23
Lower Manual	78	73	69	–12
N	96,000	146,840	191,935	100

SOURCE: U.S. Census, 1970, 1980, 1990
NOTE: See Table A2.

ranks. The "front of the house"—the public-contact portion of the restaurant—involved a different story. Actors, largely white, were often the preferred labor force in the middle range of restaurants.

Firms and Jobs

Workers are not employed by an industry, they labor for a specific entity. Yet, although employment characteristics vary significantly across organizations, industry averages can be meaningful. In Table A3, we reported some industry-wide and establishment-level statistics for our sample industries based on data collected by the U.S. Bureau of the Census. In Table A9, we present some firm and job characteristics from our own research. Printers, averaging 60 workers per plant, comprise the smallest firms in our sample; hospitals, with an average of 2,865, comprise the largest. A comparison with the patterns reported in Table A3 suggests a slight bias in our sample toward larger establishments, an outcome probably resulting from a variety of factors. First, managers at larger firms were more likely to make themselves available to us than were those at smaller establishments. Second, larger, more established firms were more likely to have disseminated information about themselves, and were less likely to have gone out of business since the directories we used had been printed. Third, we purposely excluded the smallest firms, seeking to arrange interviews in establishments with a minimum of five workers (and, in the hospital industry, setting the minimum at fifty employees). While we may have missed some of the

TABLE A9. AVERAGE FIRM AND SAMPLE JOB CHARACTERISTICS,
BY INDUSTRY

	Firm			Sample Job				
	Number of Employees	Annual Turnover	Years in Business	Entry Wage	High Wage	Health Plan	Unionized	Low Mobility
Department Stores	194	22%	23	$4.97	$9.75	100%	0%	8%
	106.3	*0.2*	*17.5*	*0.5*	*2.5*	*0.0*	*0.0*	*0.3*
	(25)	(22)	(24)	(25)	(24)	(25)	(25)	(25)
Furniture Manufacturing	97	17%	35	$6.40	$10.55	72%	28%	28%
	103.9	*0.5*	*22.9*	*2.5*	*4.5*	*0.5*	*0.5*	*0.5*
	(39)	(34)	(39)	(39)	(37)	(39)	(39)	(39)
Hospitals	2865	4%	42	$7.88	$11.26	94%	47%	31%
	5570.1	*0.1*	*28.4*	*2.0*	*3.2*	*0.2*	*0.5*	*0.5*
	(31)	(22)	(24)	(30)	(30)	(32)	(32)	(36)
Hotels	270	6%	24	$5.46	$7.32	90%	23%	20%
	252.2	*0.1*	*18.0*	*1.0*	*3.3*	*0.3*	*0.4*	*0.4*
	(40)	(29)	(40)	(32)	(31)	(30)	(30)	(40)
Printing	60	10%	40	$7.13	$12.04	89%	5%	20%
	65.3	*0.2*	*25.2*	*2.5*	*5.3*	*0.3*	*0.2*	*0.4*
	(44)	(41)	(44)	(43)	(43)	(44)	(44)	(44)
Restaurants	94	—	16	$4.40	$8.53	—	—	9%
	262.5	—	*11.8*	*0.4*	*6.4*	—	—	*0.3*
	(44)	—	(44)	(42)	(30)	—	—	(44)

SOURCE: Skills Study
NOTE: Early surveys did not include the items on turnover, health plan, or union membership. The "Low Mobility" item is the proportion who answered that the chances of a person in the sample job moving up into a better job were lower than 4 on a scale of 1–7. Standard deviations in italics, *N*'s in parentheses.

dynamics that characterize smaller firms, we believe that we did capture most of the range of practices in each industry.

As for wages, restaurants paid the lowest starting salary ($4.40), while department stores paid little more ($4.97). Department stores, perhaps not coincidentally, boasted the highest reported turnover rates among these industries (22 percent annually). Printers paid the highest wage for an experienced worker who started in an entry-level job ($12.04), while hotels seemed to offer the fewest chances for improved earnings. Surprisingly, the majority of firms appeared to offer health plans to their entry-level workers; even in furniture, the least supportive industry, 72 percent qualified for health benefits (although the firm may have contributed little to the payments). Unionization ranged from 47 percent among hospital workers to none at all among department store workers.

CONCLUSIONS

The modern history of Los Angeles has been one of constant growth and change. The last three decades have been a period of ongoing transformation, combining enormous population growth, unprecedented levels of immigrant influx, and rapid and far-reaching economic shifts. Our research project sought to zero in on one part of this social and economic picture, in an effort to understand the dynamics of the low-wage labor markets into which immigrants have deeply, if unevenly, penetrated in recent decades.

The period during which we collected our data, stretching from late 1992 into early 1994, was somewhat different from the one that exists as we complete this book, in the year 2002. At the time of our interviews, the disturbances of 1992 were still fresh in people's memories, and the uncomfortable tensions that surfaced then may well have made respondents more circumspect—and at the same time more philosophically inclined—than would likely have been the case later. Finances were tight and labor markets were slack. For these reasons, hiring was low, voluntary turnover was reduced, and pressures on workers and wages were high. It is probably the case that, in this "buyer's market," we were able to obtain a clearer picture of employers' preferences than had we been watching employers when they had a more restrictive set of alternatives. Employers were bound to complain about the quality of workers available, but, at that time of high unemployment, they probably had more choices available than they would later in the decade.

Notes

1. As pointed out by Michael Walzer in *What it means to be an American* (New York: Marsilio, 1992), p. 24, building on an earlier observation by Horace Kallen, "The United States . . . has a peculiar anonymity." (cited in Walzer, p. 23).

2. See Roger Waldinger and Mehdi Bozorgmehr, eds., *Ethnic Los Angeles* (New York: Russell Sage Foundation, 1996), especially chapters 11, 12, 15; and Barry Edmonston and James P. Smith, *The new Americans: economic, demographic, and fiscal effects of immigration* (Washington, D.C.: National Academy Press, 1997). The diversity of today's immigrant flows is a central theme sounded in Alejandro and Rubén G. Rumbaut Portes, *Immigrant America*, 2d ed. (Berkeley and Los Angeles: University of California Press, 1996).

3. Immigrants make up 13 percent of all persons 25–64 years old, but over half of those possessing no more than an eighth-grade education, and 17 percent of those with some high school education (calculations from a merged sample of the 1994–97 Current Population Survey). For further background, see Roger Waldinger and Jennifer Lee, "New immigrants in urban America," in *Strangers at the gates: new immigrants in urban America*, ed. Roger Waldinger (Berkeley and Los Angeles: University of California Press, 2001).

4. One of the most systematic formulations of this approach can be found in George Borjas, "Economic theory and international migration," *International Migration Review* 23, no. 3 (1989): 457–85.

5. Scholars advanced two distinct, though related, "mismatch" hypotheses. One emphasized skills, underscoring the lack of fit between urban employers and the proficiencies, as measured by years of education, of minority urban residents. The second, focusing on geography, underscored the dislocation that occurred as low-skilled jobs, once located in inner cities, gravitated to suburbs, which

inner-city residents could not easily travel to nor, given the more expensive hous-ing, live in. For a recent exposition of this view, see William Julius Wilson, *When work disappears: the world of the new urban poor* (New York: Alfred A. Knopf, 1996) and the references therein. For a reiteration of the "skills mismatch" view, based on data from a recent employer survey, see Harry J. Holzer, *What em-ployers want: job prospects for less-educated workers* (New York: Russell Sage Foundation, 1996). The classic statement of the spatial mismatch hypothesis ap-peared in John Kain's seminal article "Housing segregation, Negro employment, and metropolitan decentralization," *Quarterly Journal of Economics* 82 (1968): 175–97. A critique of the skills mismatch hypothesis appears in Roger Waldinger, *Still the promised city? African-Americans and new immigrants in postindustrial New York* (Cambridge, Mass.: Harvard University Press, 1996).

6. See Roger Waldinger, "Up from poverty? 'race,' immigration, and the prospects of low-skilled workers," in *Strangers at the gates*, ed. Waldinger.

7. The theory of labor market segmentation was first developed in Peter B. Doeringer and Michael J. Piore's pathbreaking book, *Internal labor markets and manpower analysis* (Lexington, Mass.: Heath Lexington Books, 1971); for an up-to-date reformulation and defense of the approach, see Chris Tilly and Charles Tilly, *Work under capitalism, new perspectives in sociology* (Boulder, Colo.: Westview Press, 1998).

8. The queue theory of the labor market was developed by Lester Thurow in his books *Income and opportunity* (Washington, D.C.: Brookings Institution, 1968) and *Generating inequality: mechanisms of distribution in the U.S. econ-omy* (New York, Basic Books: 1975). In *A piece of the pie: blacks and white im-migrants since 1880* (Berkeley and Los Angeles: University of California Press, 1980), Stanley Lieberson applied queue theory to examine the effect of compo-sitional differences in black and immigrant employment, across a sample of U.S. cities in 1900. Although the concepts of queue order and shape and of "workers' rankings" were implicit in these earlier writings, they were first made explicit in the editors' chapters of *Job queues, gender queues,* ed. Barbara Reskin and Pa-tricia Roos (Philadelphia: Temple University Press, 1990). Our application of queue theory has its roots in the work of both Thurow and Lieberson and draws on the arguments developed in Waldinger, *Still the promised city?* chapters 1, 9, and *passim.*

9. Cf. Michael Piore, *Birds of passage* (Cambridge: Cambridge University Press, 1979), chapter 3.

10. See, for example, Paul Attewell, "Skill and occupational changes in U.S. manufacturing," in *Technology and the future of work*, ed. Paul Adler (New York: Oxford University Press, 1992).

11. Saskia Sassen is a well-known proponent of this view. See, for example, *The mobility of labor and capital* (Cambridge: Cambridge University Press, 1988).

12. This view is maintained by Michael Piore in "An economic approach," in *Dualism and discontinuity in industrial societies,* ed. Suzanne Berger and Michael J. Piore (Cambridge: Cambridge University Press, 1980), especially p. 18.

13. "The informal side of socialization," as Gary Alan Fine noted in a study that focused on some of the same occupations with which we are concerned, "is crucial in many occupations, but seems particularly salient in locales ... in

which formal models of education are weak and where some assume that the job can be mastered by anyone with sufficient provision. If socialization is assumed routine and painless, little provision is made for acquiring knowledge . . ." Gary Alan Fine, *Kitchens: the culture of restaurant work* (Berkeley and Los Angeles: University of California Press, 1996), p. 51.

14. The references are to Oscar Handlin's classic immigration history, *The uprooted* (Boston: Little Brown, 1952); and John Bodnar's revisionist work, *The transplanted* (Bloomington: Indiana University Press, 1985).

15. These two paragraphs do no more than present a stylized summary of a vast literature; for a lucid discussion of network theory, with ample references, see Douglas Massey et al., "Theories of international migration: a review and appraisal," *Population and Development Review* 19, no. 3 (1993): 431–66; "Continuities in transnational migration: an analysis of 19 Mexican communities," *American Journal of Sociology* (May 1994): 1492–533.

16. For a review of the concept of social capital, with numerous references to the immigration literature, see Alejandro Portes, "Social capital: its origins and applications in modern sociology," *Annual Review of Sociology* 24 (1998): 1–24.

17. Thomas Bailey and Roger Waldinger, "Primary, secondary, and enclave labor markets: a training systems approach," *American Sociological Review* (August 1991): 432–45.

18. Alejandro Portes and Julia Sensenbrenner, "Embeddedness and immigration: notes on the social determinants of economic action," *American Journal of Sociology* 98 (1993): 1320–50.

19. On the ethnic economy, see Ivan Light and Stavros Karageorgis, "The ethnic economy" in Neil Smelser and Richard Swedberg, eds., *The handbook of economic sociology* (Princeton: Princeton University Press, and New York: Russell Sage Foundation, 1994); on the ethnic enclave, see Alejandro Portes and Robert Bach, *Latin journey* (Berkeley and Los Angeles: University of California Press, 1985); on the ethnic niche, see Waldinger, *Still the promised city?*

20. As argued by Douglas Massey and his collaborators (Rafael Alarcón, Jorge Durand, and Humberto González) in *Return to Aztlan* (Berkeley and Los Angeles: University of California Press, 1987).

21. On the role of networks in matching workers with jobs, Mark Granovetter's *Getting a job*, 2d ed. (Chicago: University of Chicago Press, 1995) is a basic source. Other useful sources include Mark Granovetter and Charles Tilly, "Inequality and labor processes," in *Handbook of sociology*, ed. Neil J. Smelser (Berkeley and Los Angeles: University of California Press, 1991), 175–221; David Stevens, "A reexamination of what is known about jobseeking behavior in the United States," in *Labor market intermediaries*, Report no. 22 (Washington, D.C.: National Commission for Manpower Policy, 1978), 55–104; Margaret Grieco, *Keeping it in the family: social networks and employment chance* (London and New York: Tavistock Publications, 1987); Walter W. Powell and Laurel Smith-Doerr, "Networks and economic life," in *Handbook of economic sociology*, pp. 368–402.

22. See Waldinger, *Still the promised city?* especially chapters 7 and 8; and "The 'other side' of embeddedness: a case-study of the interplay of economy and ethnicity," *Ethnic and Racial Studies* 18, no. 3 (1995): 555–80.

23. As noted by Peter Capelli, a broad array of sources indicate that "employers see the most important consideration in hiring and the biggest deficit among new workforce entrants as being the attitudes that they bring with them to their jobs." Personality—"one's basic dispositions toward the outside world"—ranks as the work-attitude axis most frequently emphasized by employers. Peter Capelli, "Is the 'skills gap' really about attitudes?" *California Management Review* 37, no. 4 (summer 1995): 110, 112. Similarly, Philip Moss and Chris Tilly's study of low-skilled employers found that "majorities of respondents . . . pointed to soft skills" (the authors' term for motivation and interaction) "as the most important qualities they sought." Drawing from the evidence for their study, as well as material from the broader literature, they conclude that "the United States has seen a rising tide of skill requirements, but nothing like a tidal wave." See Philip Moss and Chris Tilly, *Stories employers tell: race, skill, and hiring in America* (New York: Russell Sage Foundation, 2001), p. 83.

24. For a review of this literature, see John Duckitt, *The social psychology of prejudice* (New York: Prager, 1992).

25. The preference is not a direct result of the distaste, however. Let us say that a particular employer highly values ambition in others; if, however, he is hiring for a dead-end job and wants a stable workforce, he will probably hire from a group he considers unambitious.

26. On the experiences of the earlier groups, the now exploding literature on "whiteness" and "whitening" is instructive. See Noel Ignatiev, *How the Irish became white* (New York: Routledge, 1995), for a particularly insightful example.

27. For a review, see Nelson Lim, " 'On the back of blacks'? immigrants and the fortunes of African-Americans," in Waldinger, ed., *Strangers at the gates*.

28. George Borjas, "The economics of immigration," *Journal of Economic Literature* (1994): 1667–717.

29. For evidence of this sort, see Joleen Kirschenman and Kathryn Neckerman, "We'd love to hire them, but . . . : the meaning of race for employers," in *The urban underclass*, ed. Christopher Jencks and Paul E. Peterson (Washington, D.C.: Brookings Institution, 1991), pp. 203–32; Katherine Newman, *No shame in my game: the working poor in the inner city* (New York: Knopf, 1999), chapter 8.

30. As this book returns to the concerns of Waldinger's *Still the promised city?* a few words on the relationship between the two works seem in order. *Still the promised city?* told a story of historical change, focusing on the interplay of ethnicity and economy in New York during the twentieth century, with an emphasis on that century's second fifty years. It argued that the opportunities and obstacles confronted by immigrants and African Americans resulted from America's serial incorporation of outsider groups and from those groups' attempts to create protective economic shelters. The history of continuous recourse to migration made ethnicity the crucial and enduring mechanism whereby categorically distinctive workers were sorted into an identifiably distinct set of jobs. The path up from the bottom involved finding a good niche and dominating it, which meant that an earlier group's search for labor-market shelters eventuated in barriers confronting the next round of arrivals. Under certain conditions, established groups moved up the queue, creating opportunities for newcomers. Under other circumstances—as when the preferences of low-ranked groups changed

quickly while older groups remained attached to their customary niches—ethnic competition, as opposed to ethnic succession, ensued, with newcomers seeking to alter hiring and promotion rules, and incumbents trying to maintain the structures protecting their group's jobs. *Still the promised city?* sought to elaborate this argument using a range of methodologies, including analysis of census data and historical as well as contemporary case studies. For the most part, however, the book emphasized the importance of exclusionary efforts, whether informal or concerted, directed by one group of ethnic workers against some distinctive other.

How the other half works lacks the historical dimension of the earlier volume. But it sheds light, we believe, on a set of dynamics largely unexplored there. In part, the dividends stem from a difference in methodology, as we use a richer set of indepth interviews, allowing more careful investigation of the interplay between the "structures" of organization and technology, on the one hand, and the active efforts by workers and managers to shape their environment, on the other. We develop the concept of "exclusionary" and "usurpationary" closure to show how immigrant networks expand beyond the economic functions emphasized in earlier work; at the same time, we show how organizational features constrain the reach of immigrant networks (a theme not at all anticipated in *Still the promised city?*). Similarly, the chapters on employer preferences present a framework entirely different from the approach offered in the earlier book, which had relatively little to say either about the nature of employer preferences or the ways those preferences might be implemented and why.

31. For overviews of the contemporary demographic and economic transformation of Los Angeles, see Waldinger and Bozorgmehr, *Ethnic Los Angeles,* chapters 1–3; for an update of immigration trends based on data from the mid-1990s, see Roger Waldinger, "Not the promised city? Los Angeles and its immigrants," *Pacific Historical Review* (May 1999).

32. For an elaboration of this argument, with application to a very different type of immigrant place, see Waldinger, *Still the promised city?*

33. All employers are single-counted, even if owners or managers of multiunit operations. Three of the hospital interviews involved persons not directly employed by hospitals; these were with the vice-president of a company supplying contract housekeeping services to hospitals, an official in a large public sector hospital workers' union, and two personnel officials in a local government department responsible for general health-care services.

34. The interviews with restaurants, and, to a much more limited extent, with hotels, served as our pilot interviews; we completed these first, using a version of the survey instrument that underwent subsequent modifications, almost entirely without the aid of a tape recorder. In most cases, subsequent interviews were recorded and later transcribed; otherwise, detailed notes were made of interviewees' responses. We did the least interviewing in the department store sector, as most stores were part of larger chains with centralized personnel departments; finding the person in charge of hiring for a specific store was difficult, and the companies were generally quite shy about giving interviews. Overall, however, we came close to our goal of forty firms per industry.

2. WHAT EMPLOYERS WANT

1. Frank Levy and Richard Murnane, "U.S. earnings levels and earnings inequality: a review of recent trends and proposed explanations," *Journal of Economic Literature* 30 (1992): 1333–81; Richard Murnane and Frank Levy, *Teaching the new basic skills: principles for educating children to thrive in a changing economy* (New York: Free Press, 1996).

2. Roger Waldinger, "Up from poverty? 'Race,' immigration, and the prospects of low-skilled workers," in Roger Waldinger, ed., *Strangers at the gates: new immigrants in urban America* (Berkeley and Los Angeles: University of California Press, 2001).

3. Clark Kerr et al., *Industrialism and industrial man: the problems of jobs and management in economic growth* (Cambridge, Mass.: Harvard University Press, 1960).

4. Robert Blauner, *Alienation and freedom* (Chicago: University of Chicago Press, 1964). Thus, Blauner emphasized the uncertain effect of automation. While continuous-process work substituted mechanical for human labor, the process was highly subject to instability; since automated systems inevitably crashed, workers had the opportunity to act together creatively to bring the process back on line.

5. Daniel Bell, *The coming of post-industrial society* (New York: Basic Books, 1974).

6. Tolnay says that "Originally, 'The Great Migration' was a term used to describe the sharp increase in the northward migration of southern blacks during and after World War I. In its more general application, it also includes the subsequent surge in South-to-North migration that occurred during and after World War II." We use the second, broader sense. Stewart E. Tolnay, "The great migration and changes in the northern black family, 1940 to 1990," *Social Forces* 75 (1997): 1213–38.

7. Harry Braverman, *Labor and monopoly capital* (New York: Monthly Review Press, 1974).

8. Michael Spence, *Job market signaling* (Cambridge: Harvard University Press, 1974).

9. Footnote to Randall Collins, *The credential society: an historical sociology of education and stratification* (New York: Academic Press, 1979).

10. *Case studies on the labor process*, ed. Andrew Zimbalist (New York: Monthly Review, 1978), provided an early celebration. Reassessments of a more critical sort were soon forthcoming, although Braverman's influence lingered. For a selection of reconsiderations, see Paul Attewell, "The deskilling controversy," *Work and Occupations* 14, no. 3, (1987): 323–34, and Vicki Smith, "Braverman's legacy: the labor process turns 20," *Work and Occupations* 21, no. 4 (1994): 403–21.

11. David Howell and Edward N. Wolff, "Trends in the growth and distribution of skills in the U.S. workplace, 1960–1985," *Industrial and Labor Relations Review*, 44, no. 3 (1991); Sue E. Berryman and Thomas Bailey, *The double helix of education and the economy* (New York: Institute on Education and the Economy, Teachers College, Columbia University, 1992).

12. Paul Adler, "Introduction," in Adler, ed., *Technology and the future of work* (New York: Oxford, 1992).

13. Beverly Burris, "Computerization of the workplace," *Annual Review of Sociology* 24 (1998): 141–57.

14. John Heritage, *Garfinkel and ethnomethodology* (Cambridge, England: Policy, 1986).

15. As shown in the classic studies of Christy Mathewson, *Restriction of output among unorganized workers* (New York: Viking, 1931), and the famous articles by Donald Roy, e.g., "Efficiency and 'the fix': informal group relations in a piece work machine shop," *American Journal of Sociology* 60 (1955): 255–66.

16. Ken Kusterer, *Know-how on the job: the important working knowledge of 'unskilled' workers* (Boulder, Colo.: Westview, 1978).

17. Michael Burawoy, *Manufacturing consent* (Chicago: University of Chicago Press, 1979).

18. For the variety of segmentationist views, see Peter Doeringer and Michael Piore, *Internal labor markets and manpower analysis* (Lexington, Mass.: Heath, 1971); Richard Edwards et al., ed., *Labor market segmentation* (Lexington, Mass.: Lexington Books, 1975); David Gordon et al., *Segmented work, divided workers* (Cambridge: Cambridge University Press, 1982).

19. As implied by Michael Piore and Charles Sabel in *The second industrial divide* (New York: Basic Books, 1984).

20. Tilly and Tilly, *Work under capitalism* (Boulder, Colo.: Westview, 1997); Christopher Jencks, Lauri Perman, and Lee Rainwater, "What is a good job? a new measure of labor-market success," *American Journal of Sociology* 93 (1988): 1322–57; Neal Rosenthal, "More than wages at issue in job quality debate," *Monthly Labor Review* (December 1988): 4–8.

21. As hypothesized by Doeringer and Piore in *Internal labor markets*, workers attached to a particular labor market segment tend to adopt (or already exhibit) segment-appropriate behavior. Behaviors that mirror the instability of the secondary sector (or segment) are unlikely to win approval in the primary sector. This is another possible barrier to mobility from the secondary to the primary sector.

22. As argued by Michael Piore, *Birds of passage* (New York: Cambridge University Press, 1979).

23. The phrase is Arthur Stinchcombe's, although invoked in a discussion of a different occupational setting; see Stinchcombe, "Work institutions and the sociology of everyday life," in Kai Erikson and Steven Peter Vallas, eds., *The nature of work: sociological perspectives* (New Haven: Yale University Press, 1990).

24. Studies of the archetypically deskilled job, fast-food work, illustrate this point in great detail. See Katherine Newman, *No shame for my game: the working poor in the inner city* (New York: Knopf, 1999), chapters 4 and 5; and Robin Leidner, *Fast food, fast talk: service work and the routinization of everyday life* (Berkeley and Los Angeles: University of California Press, 1993), chapter 3. Leidner first notes (p. 72), in her ethnography of a McDonald's, that "McDonald's had routinized the work of its crews so thoroughly that decision making had practically been eliminated from the jobs." But she later (p. 77) points out that "McDonald's work may be considered unskilled, but it was by no means easy to

do well. Window workers had to be able to keep many things in mind at once, to keep calm under fire, and to exhibit considerable physical and emotional stamina." Reminiscing on his own experience as a young McDonald's worker, historian Robin Kelley provides another view of "employees at the central Pasadena McDonald's . . . constantly inventing new ways to rebel," which implies some considerable scope for freedom from management's imposition of routines. See Robin Kelley, *Race rebels* (New York: Free Press, 1994), pp. 1–3.

25. Supporting evidence for this view comes from two books, both written from a standpoint of considerable sympathy, if not alignment, with a segmentationist perspective: Roger Waldinger, *Through the eye of the needle: immigrants and enterprise in New York's garment trades* (New York: New York University Press, 1986); Thomas R. Bailey, *Immigrant and native workers: contrasts and competition* (Boulder, Colo.: Westview, 1987).

26. Michael Piore, *Birds of passage* (Cambridge: Cambridge University Press, 1979), p. 55.

27. Arlie Hochschild, *The managed heart* (Berkeley and Los Angeles: University of California Press, 1983). Hochschild's work was anticipated by many years in C. Wright Mills's discussion of the "personality market." See C. Wright Mills, *White collar: the American middle classes* (New York: Oxford University Press, 1951).

28. See also: Leidner, *Fast food, fast talk*; Ester Reiter, *Making fast food: from the frying pan into the fryer* (Montreal: McGill-Queen's University Press, 1991), especially pp. 85–91.

29. Greta Foff Paules, *Dishing it out: power and resistance among waitresses in a New Jersey restaurant* (Philadelphia: Temple University Press, 1991).

30. Stanley Hollander, "A historical perspective on the service encounter," in *The service encounter: managing employee/customer interaction in service businesses,* J. Czepiel et al., eds. (Lexington, Mass.: Lexington Books, 1985).

31. Erving Goffman, *Interaction ritual* (New York: Pantheon, 1967), especially pp. 81–85 and pp. 90–95; Erving Goffman, *The presentation of self in everyday life* (New York: Doubleday, 1959), pp. 151–152.

32. Gender interacts with nativity so that, as Betsy Aron noted in a study of labor conflict in Boston's hotel industry, women "who come from societies without a tradition of egalitarian underpinnings to the class structure are even more attractive to employers, who value their apparent willingness to display docile and subservient behavior." See her *Defeat from the jaws of victory: the rise and fall of Local 26, Hotel Employees, and Restaurant Employees (HERE) in Boston* (unpublished manuscript, 1999), p. 19.

33. As suggested by various studies of domestic workers. For the second generation Japanese-American women studied by Evelyn Nakano Glenn, U.S. conditions furnished the principal frame of reference, the main reason why the U.S.-born Nisei experienced greater "status degradation" than did their foreign-born, or Issei, counterparts. See her *Issei, Nisei, war bride* (Philadelphia: Temple University Press, 1986), pp. 177–82. The women interviewed by Judith Rollins in her study of domestics in Boston came from a variety of ethnic and national backgrounds, but most were either from small towns, the countryside, or foreign countries. "Now urban themselves," Rollins notes in describing her respondents,

"none of them would want their daughters to become domestics." See *Between women: domestics and their employers* (Philadelphia: Temple University Press, 1985), p. 113.

3. DOING THE JOB

1. As defined by Philip Moss and Chris Tilly, *Stories employers tell: race, skill, and hiring in America* (New York: Russell Sage Foundation, 2001), p. 44. Moss and Tilly distinguish two clusters of "soft skills," one entailing *interaction*, the second *motivation*. Even as they advance the concept of "soft skills," the authors note that the concept "is a misnomer," precisely because the bundle of attributes referred to as "soft skills" is culturally defined, confounded by employer/worker differences in cultural norms, and viewed by employers as immutable. They found, as did we, that "employers genuinely view interaction and motivation as skills"; thus they use the concept in their analysis. In utilizing "soft skills" as an analytic category, however, they seem to lend it face validity. But as we argue in this chapter, what employers *say* and what they *mean* are two different things. In the employers' discourse, the qualities denoted by "motivation" or "attitude" refer to the traits relevant to relationships with co-workers, customers, or bosses. Insofar as these relationships involve authority relations they take a political form—which is precisely what the everyday talk about "soft skills" is designed to obscure.

2. As argued by George Sternlieb and James Hughes, "The uncertain future of the central city," *Urban Affairs Quarterly* 18, no. 4 (1983): 455–72, or any of the other proponents of the skills mismatch hypotheses, a literature review in Waldinger, *Still the promised city? African Americans and new immigrants in postindustrial New York* (Cambridge, Mass.: Harvard University Press, 1996), chapter 1.

3. The literature on the two manufacturing industries that we studied remains scant. When they could still be classified as highly skilled members of the blue-collar élite, workers in the printing trades received a good deal of scholarly attention; although this interest persisted as long as the impact of computerization was still uncertain, academic attention disappeared once it became clear that the new technology would sweep aside the old craft skills. Bob Blauner's book *Alienation and freedom: the factory worker and his industry* (Chicago: University of Chicago Press, 1967), with a chapter on printers and the printing trade, remains a classic reference. A more recent overview of technological trends, with an assessment of their implications for training, can be found in Thomas Bailey, Ross Koppel, Roger Waldinger, *Education for all aspects of the industry: overcoming barriers to broad-based training* (Berkeley: National Center for Research in Vocational Education, Graduate School of Education, University of California, Berkeley; Washington, D.C.: U.S. Dept. of Education, Office of Educational Research and Improvement, Educational Resources Information Center, 1994). Further information can be found in Karen Chapple, "The transformation of traditional industries in San Francisco: the cases of printing and apparel manufacturing," Working Paper 701 (Berkeley: University of California, Institute of Urban and Regional Development, 1998). Scholarly studies of the furniture

industry are rarer still. Mark Drayse, "The development and structure of labor markets in the Los Angeles furniture industry" (Ph.D. dissertation, UCLA, 1997), provides an overview of trends in the industry, with conclusions, regarding the role of immigrant labor, quite similar to those that we report in this book.

4. Peter B. Doeringer and Michael J. Piore, *Internal labor markets and manpower analysis* (Lexington, Mass.: Heath Lexington Books, 1971).

5. Thomas Bailey's study of immigrants in the restaurant industry, *Immigrant and native workers: contrasts and competition* (Boulder, Colo.: Westview Press, 1987) provides background on the structure of the industry and its occupational demands; for a similar discussion of the hotel industry, see Waldinger, *Still the promised city?* chapter 5, and Dorothy Sue Cobble and Michael Merrill, "Collective bargaining in the hospitality industry," in *Collective bargaining in the private sector*, ed. Paula Voos (Madison, Wisc.: Industrial Relations Research Association, 1999).

6. William Whyte's classic article, "The social structure of the restaurant," *American Journal of Sociology* 54, no. 4 (1949), first underscored the interdependencies and uncertainties of restaurant work and the complexities that ensued, a point that subsequent research has confirmed. Nonetheless, the long-term trend is one toward deskilling, propelled largely, but not exclusively, by the explosion of fast food restaurants. While job demands increase with prices printed on the menu, the decline of occupational unionism in the restaurant has certainly diminished servers' ability to exercise craftlike control over the way in which the work gets done. See Dorothy Sue Cobble, "Organizing the postindustrial workforce: lessons from the history of waitress unionism," *Industrial and Labor Relations Review* 44, no. 3 (1991): 419–36.

7. Gary Alan Fine's recent study, *Kitchens: The culture of restaurant work* (Berkeley and Los Angeles: University of California Press, 1996), repeatedly underscores the complexity of the impression-management techniques used by servers as they respond to the unpredictable flow of food and traffic in a constant effort to "manipulate customers" (pp. 98–110).

8. Moss and Tilly similarly report that "as clichéd as it may seem, numerous managers in retail and service establishments boiled down the requisite interaction skills to 'a smile.' " Moss and Tilly, *Stories*, p. 59.

9. Mandating impression-management policies seems a widespread practice. For example, Burger King's training manual includes the following instruction: "Smile with a greeting and make a positive first impression. Show them you are GLAD TO SEE THEM. Include eye contact with the cheerful greeting." Cited by Sarah Reiter, *Making fast food: from the frying pan into the fire* (Montreal: McGill-Queen's University Press, 1991), p. 85; (capitals in the original).

10. The fast-fooders studied by Katherine Newman similarly expected workers to "servic[e] customers with a smile." Although hardly a skill, smiling involved an impression-management requirement of a non-trivial nature, since, as Newman wrote, "Customers can be unreasonably rude, even insulting, and workers must count backwards from a hundred in order to stifle their outrage." In *No shame in my game: The working poor in the inner city* (New York: Knopf, 1999), p. 89.

11. In recent years, the literature on clerical work has been dominated by accounts that are largely consistent with Braverman's emphasis on deskilling:

Rosemary Crompton and Gareth Jones, *White collar proletariat: deskilling and gender in clerical work* (London: Macmillan, 1984); Evelyn Nakano Glenn and Roslyn Feldberg, "Proletarianizing clerical work: technology and organizational control in the office," in Andrew Zimbalist, *Case studies on the labor process* (New York: Monthly Review, 1978).

12. The offset press is a very commonly used printing technology.

13. In underscoring the contingent, contested nature of managerial authority, we build on the fundamental Marxist insight, exemplified by Harry Braverman and his radical critics. As James Rebitzer argues, the social relationships within a firm can be understood as *political*, insofar as "they involve conflicts of interests between parties that are resolved by the exercise of power." "Radical political economy and labor markets," *Journal of Economic Literature* 31 (1993): 1396.

4. THE LANGUAGE OF WORK

1. The sentence is paraphrased from Douglas Massey, Rafael Alarcón, Jorge Durand, and Humberto González, *Return to Aztlan: the social process of migration from western Mexico* (Berkeley and Los Angeles: University of California Press, 1987), where the authors write that "landless Mexican *campesinos* may be *poor in financial resources,* but they are wealthy in social capital, which they can readily convert into jobs and earnings in the United States"; (italics added).

2. William Form, "On the degradation of skills," *Annual Review of Sociology* 13 (1987): 30.

3. Stephen R. Barley, "Technology, power, and the social organization of work: towards a pragmatic theory of skilling and deskilling," *Research in the Sociology of Work* 6 (1988): 33–80.

4. See Everett C. Hughes, "The linguistic division of labor in industrial and urban societies," in *Advances in the sociology of language*, vol. 2., ed. Joshua Fishman (The Hague: Mouton, 1972), p. 309. And see Joshua Fishman, *The sociology of language* (Rowley, Mass.: Newbury House, 1972); Calvin Veltman, *Language shift in the United States* (Berlin: Mouton, 1983); David Lopez, "Social and linguistic aspects of assimilation today," in *The handbook of international migration*, ed. Charles Hirschman, Philip Kasinitz, and Josh Dewind (New York: Russell Sage Foundation, 1999).

5. As noted in Ralph Fasold, *The sociolinguistics of society* (Oxford: Blackwell, 1984).

6. Joshua Fishman, *Sociology of language*, p. 45.

7. Joshua Fishman, *The rise and fall of the ethnic revival* (The Hague: Mouton, 1985), p. 61.

8. Alejandro Portes and Ruben Rumbaut, *Immigrant America* (Berkeley and Los Angeles: University of California Press, 1990) p. 217.

9. One can identify still a third alternative, made possible when immigrant entrepreneurs from one group employ immigrant workers from another. In this case, the workers adapt to the linguistic practices of the entrepreneurs, as the literature suggests, which means learning not English but a second "foreign" tongue. For an example, see Stuart Silverstein, "Crossing language barriers," *Los Angeles Times*, Wednesday, 8 December 1999, p. A-1.

10. We refer, for example, to contact that Ralph Grillo has described as "ethnic enclavement," a notion apparently invoked by him without reference to or awareness of the U.S. literature on "ethnic enclaves." As Grillo concedes, "enclavement" is the exception, not the rule, in immigrant situations. See R.D. Grillo, *Dominant languages: language and hierarchy in Britain and France* (Cambridge and New York: Cambridge University Press, 1989).

11. Howard Giles, R.Y. Bourhis, D.M. Taylor, "Towards a theory of language in ethnic group relations," *Language, ethnicity, and intergroup relations,* ed. Howard Giles (London and New York: Academic Press, 1977).

12. Everett C. Hughes, "The linguistic division of labor in industrial and urban societies," pp. 296–305 in Joshua Fishman, ed., *Advances in the sociology of language,* vol. 2 (The Hague: Mouton, 1972).

13. Raymond Breton, Gail Grant, and the Institute for Research on Public Policy, *La langue de travail au Québec: synthèse de la recherche sur la rencontre de deux langues* (Montréal: Institut de recherches politiques, 1981), p. 42.

14. This borrows from Stanley Lieberson, who argues that the demand for bilingualism in the workplace varies based on the "(1) linguistic composition of co-workers; (2) importance of communication with co-workers; (3) linguistic composition of customers and relevant outsiders; and (4) importance of communication with customers and outsiders." Stanley Lieberson, *Language diversity and language contact* (Stanford: Stanford University Press, 1981), p. 174.

15. Richard V. Teschner, "Beachheads, islands, and conduits: Spanish monolingualism and bilingualism in El Paso, Texas," *The International Journal of Sociological Language,* no. 114 (1995): 97.

16. June A. Jaramillo, "The passive legitimization of Spanish. A macrosociolinguistic study of a quasi-border: Tucson, Arizona," *The International Journal of Sociological Language,* no. 114 (1995): 82.

17. Roger Waldinger, *Still the promised city? African Americans and new immigrants in postindustrial New York* (Cambridge, Mass.: Harvard University Press, 1996).

18. Joshua Fishman, "Language maintenance," in *Harvard encyclopedia of American ethnic groups,* ed. Stephan Thernstrom (Cambridge, Mass.: Belknap Press of Harvard University, 1980), pp. 629–38.

19. Similarly, other researchers have found that Korean immigrant owners learn Spanish phrases in order to give direction to the Latino workers whom they mainly employ. (Personal communication from Jennifer Lee.)

20. Baldwin Hills is an area at the boundary between the largely Anglo west side and beach communities, and the middle-class, African-American enclave of the larger south central area.

21. The manager in question noted that this consideration went both ways— English-speaking patients interacting with non-English-speaking staff, and vice versa.

22. The story that we have told reports both on language change at the workplace and on employers' views of this process. Only the former issue connects directly with the analytic question—how organizational characteristics, internal and external, affect language choices at work. The information on employers' at-

titudes needs to be treated with care, as the forces affecting these attitudes derive from factors exogenous, not endogenous, to the workplace. But employers' attitudes are nonetheless illuminating, as they highlight the deep embedding of Spanish and other foreign languages within the workplace, notwithstanding employers' wishes to the contrary.

23. The respondent is referring to *La Opinión*, Los Angeles's largest and oldest Spanish-language daily.

5. NETWORK, BUREAUCRACY, AND EXCLUSION

1. This is no more than a stylized, partial summary of a vast literature; for a lucid discussion of network theory, with ample references, see Douglas Massey et al., "Theories of international migration: a review and appraisal," *Population and Development Review* 19 (1993): 3, 431–66.

2. See J. Edward Taylor, "Differential migration, networks, information, and risk," in *Research in human capital and development*, vol. 4: *Migration, human capital, and development*, ed. Oded Stark (Greenwich, Conn.: JAI Press, 1986), pp. 147–71.

3. On page 169 in Douglas Massey, Rafael Alarcón, Jorge Durand, and Humberto González, *Return to Aztlan: the social process of migration from western Mexico* (Berkeley and Los Angeles: University of California Press, 1987).

4. On pages 1501 and 1528 in Douglas Massey et al., "Continuities in transnational migration: an analysis of 19 Mexican communities," *American Journal of Sociology* (May 1994): 1492–1533.

5. See for instance, Massey et al., *Return to Aztlan*, p. 171.

6. See page 17 in Leslie Moch Page, *Moving Europeans: migration in western Europe since 1650* (Bloomington: University of Indiana Press, 1992).

7. See also page 84 in Charles Tilly, "Transplanted networks," in Virginia Yans McLaughlin, *Immigration reconsidered* (New York: Oxford University Press, 1990).

8. See Mark Granovetter, "The strength of weak ties: a network theory revisited," *Sociological Theory* 1 (1983), especially pp. 209–13.

9. See page 12 in Alejandro Portes, "Introduction," in Alejandro Portes, ed., *The economic sociology of immigration* (New York: Russell Sage Foundation, 1995).

10. Mark Granovetter, "The strength of weak ties," *American Journal of Sociology* 78 (May 1973): 1360–80.

11. Ronald S. Burt, *Structural holes: the social structure of competition* (Cambridge, Mass.: Harvard University Press, 1992).

12. See Walter Powell and Laurel Smith-Doerr, "Networks and economic life," in Neil Smelser and Richard Swedberg, eds., *The handbook of economic sociology* (Princeton: Princeton University Press; New York: Russell Sage Foundation, 1994).

13. Emphasis added, page 14 in Alejandro Portes, "Economic sociology and the sociology of immigration: a conceptual overview." in *The economic sociology of immigration: essays on networks, ethnicity, and entrepreneurship*, ed. Alejandro Portes (New York: Russell Sage Foundation, 1994).

14. Max Weber, *Economy and society*, ed. Guenther Roth and Claus Wittich (Berkeley and Los Angeles: University of California Press, 1978), p. 343.

15. Rogers Brubaker, *Citizenship and nationhood in France and Germany* (Cambridge, Mass.: Harvard University Press, 1992), p. 23.

16. Frank Parkin, *Marxism: a bourgeois critique* (New York: Columbia University Press, 1979).

17. Chris Tilly and Charles Tilly, "Capitalist work and labor markets," in Smelser and Swedberg, eds., *Handbook of economic sociology*.

18. We would say the same if we were talking about the actions of a labor union. A labor union can only be effective when it exercises social closure, and when it does exercise social closure, it can potentially usurp the prerogatives of management.

19. See Rosabeth Kanter, *Men and women of the corporation* (New York: Basic Books, 1976).

20. Harry Holzer, "Why do small establishments hire fewer blacks than large ones?" PSC Research Report Series 96–374 (Ann Arbor: Population Studies Center, University of Michigan, 1996).

21. Holzer might be unconvinced, however. In a study of job searching among young white and African-American males, he found that African Americans received fewer job offers from employers regardless of what method of search was used. See Harry Holzer, "Informal job search and black youth employment," *American Economic Review* 77 (1987): 446–52.

22. "Newspaper ads and informed referrals are the most frequent means of recruitment. Exclusive network hiring is used mainly by small, less formal establishments," notes Peter V. Marsden in "The hiring process: recruitment methods," *American Behavioral Scientist* 37 (1994): 979–91.

23. We say "non-network," because it appears that in many cases walk-ins are what we might call "weakly sponsored" or "non-sponsored" referrals. The applicant has knowledge of the workplace and the job opening through an incumbent or former worker, but the applicant's sponsor is not taking an active role in the hiring process.

24. See Richard D. Arvey and James E. Campion, "The employment interview: a summary and review of recent research," *Personnel Psychology* 35 (1982): 314. There is little evidence that this message has gotten through to managers who hire. In a survey of human resources professionals in the Dallas–Fort Worth metropolitan area, 90 percent said that the interview was the first or second most important selection tool they used, and 87 percent rated it as no less reliable than alternative methods. See Renee Ruhnow, Robert M. Noe, Randall Odom, and Stanley Adamson, "Interviews: a look at their value and reliability," *HR Focus* 69 (1992): 13.

25. " 'Is this test valid?': a guide for determining the validity of a pre-employment test," *Personnel Journal* 71 (1992): A05.

26. Elaine D. Pulakos and Neal Schmitt, "Experience-based and situational interview questions: studies of validity," *Personnel Psychology* 48 (1995): 289–308.

27. Harry Holzer's large-scale employer survey found that 90 percent of the organizations that he contacted interview applicants; from this finding, he con-

cluded that "most employers want an opportunity to judge their applicants personally in a format in which they can go beyond the information obtained from more objective measures." Harry Holzer, *What employers want: job prospects for less-educated workers* (New York: Russell Sage Foundation, 1996), p. 57.

28. John F. Kain, "Housing segregation, Negro employment and metropolitan decentralization," *Quarterly Journal of Economics* 82 (1968): 175–97; Harry Holzer and Keith R. Ihlanfeldt, "Customer discrimination and employment outcomes for minority workers," *Quarterly Journal of Economics* 113, no. 3 (1998): 835–67.

29. Page S97 in James Coleman, "Social capital in the creation of human capital," *American Journal of Sociology* 94, Supplement (1988): S95–S120.

30. Powell and Smith-Doerr, "Networks and economic life," p. 374.

31. As noted by Granovetter, who found that job-seekers needing employment badly were more likely to rely on strong ties. See Mark Granovetter, *Getting a job* (Cambridge, Mass.: Harvard University Press, 1974).

32. Paul DiMaggio and Walter Powell, "The iron case revisited: institutional isomorphism and collective rationality in organizational fields," *American Sociological Review* 48 (1983): 147–60.

33. See Brian Uzzi, "The sources and consequences of embeddedness for the economic performance of organizations," *American Sociological Review* 61, no. 4 (1996): 674–99.

34. See page 491 in Mark Granovetter, "Economic action and social structure: the problem of embeddedness," *American Journal of Sociology* 91 (1985): 481–510.

6. SOCIAL CAPITAL AND SOCIAL CLOSURE

1. Ivan Light and Edna Bonacich, *Ethnic entrepreneurs: Koreans in Los Angeles, 1965–1983* (Berkeley and Los Angeles: University of California Press, 1988).

2. Thomas Bailey and Roger Waldinger, "Primary, secondary, and enclave labor markets: a training systems approach," *American Sociological Review* 56, no. 4 (August 1991): 432–45.

3. Alejandro Portes and Julia Sensenbrenner, "Embeddedness and immigration: notes on the social determination of embeddedness," *American Journal of Sociology* 98, no. 6 (1993): 1320–1350.

4. Alejandro Portes, "Introduction," in Alejandro Portes, ed., *The economic sociology of immigration: essays in networks, ethnicity, and entrepreneurship* (New York: Russell Sage Foundation, 1994).

5. James Coleman, "Social capital in the creation of human capital," *American Journal of Sociology* 94, Supplement (1988): S95–S120.

6. Portes, "Introduction."

7. J. Miller McPherson and Lynn Smith-Lovin, "Homophily in voluntary organizations: status distance and the composition of face-to-face groups," *American Sociological Review* 52, no. 3 (June 1987), pp. 370–79.

8. The Private Industry Councils were created in 1983 under the now-

defunct Job Training Partnership Act to help steer targeted workers toward employment opportunities.

9. The historical literature is replete with examples that provide support for this point of view. In *Dark sweat, white gold: California farm workers, cotton, and the New Deal* (Berkeley and Los Angeles: University of California Press, 1994), Devra Weber shows how the same networks that growers used to recruit farm laborers provided the linchpin for unionizing efforts, during the 1930s. Daniel Soyer tells a similar story in *Jewish immigrant associations and American identity in New York, 1880–1939* (Cambridge, Mass.: Harvard University Press, 1997), although in this case the rupture pitted Jewish immigrant workers against bosses with whom they shared not only a common ethnic tie but the very connection, to a common hometown, around which the nexus at the work site had been built. A more recent chapter in labor history, the Justice for Janitors campaign in Los Angeles, similarly shows how immigrant networks were used for recruitment purposes but then provided "the chain" by which union organizers could "turn things around." See Roger Waldinger et al., "Helots no more—a case study of the Justice for Janitors campaign," in Kate Bronfenbrenner et al., eds., *Organizing to win* (Ithaca: Cornell University Press, 1997).

7. BRINGING THE BOSS BACK IN

1. These patterns are consistent with the conclusions drawn by other scholars. Harry Holzer, for example, found that referrals from current employees generated 25 percent of hirings; taking into account other informal sources, Holzer concluded that informal mechanisms accounted for 35 percent to 40 percent of new hires. See Harry Holzer, *What employers want: job prospects for less-educated workers* (New York: Russell Sage Foundation, 1996), p. 51.

2. A brief discussion is warranted of the "other methods" of recruitment used by printers. In most cases, such recruitment involves referrals from the local Printing Industry Association (PIA), an industry (employers') association, which also serves as an informal hiring hall for experienced workers. Seventeen of forty-five printers mentioned using referrals from the PIA. (Employers were not specifically asked about the use of referrals from other employers or from industry associations. It is possible that, if they had been, the PIA would have been mentioned even more frequently.) The PIA also acts as a training organization, as several respondents mentioned. In fact, the PIA plays a fairly important labor-market role, in this industry of primarily small and medium-size firms—both brokering employment and providing training opportunities that few of the firms could afford to handle on their own, especially given the need to keep expensive equipment busy and the potential costs associated with training errors. Thus, it is possible for labor-market institutions like the PIA to play a role that is networklike but does not compromise the authority of managers.

3. The federal government runs military-related hospitals, including the extensive chain of Veterans Administration hospitals and the hospitals that belong to each branch of the military services. There are no state-run hospitals per se in Los Angeles County, and the county's public hospital system is the largest and most important in the area.

4. For a similar discussion, see Philip Moss and Chris Tilly, *Stories employers tell: race, skill, and hiring in America* (New York: Russell Sage Foundation, 2001), chapter 6.

5. Moss and Tilly similarly conclude that "formality in screening does not eliminate subjectivity altogether," in *Stories*, p. 234.

6. For example, one tabulation of the Los Angeles Survey of Urban Inequality revealed that 37 percent of African-American men with a high-school education or less reported some experience in reform school, detention center, jail, or prison, compared to 10 percent of their foreign-born Latino counterparts. Based on the authors' tabulation from the Los Angeles Sample of *Multicity Studies of Urban Inequality*. Lawrence Bobo et al., *Multicity Study of Urban Inequality, 1992–1994;* Atlanta, Boston, Detroit, and Los Angeles household survey data; computer file; 3rd ICPSR version (Atlanta, Ga.: Mathematica; Boston: University of Massachusetts, Survey Research Laboratory; Ann Arbor: University of Michigan, Detroit Area Study and Institute for Social Research, Survey Research Center; Los Angeles: University of California, Survey Research Program [producers], 1998; Inter-university Consortium for Political and Social Research [distributor], 2000).

8. WHOM EMPLOYERS WANT

1. Gary Becker, *The economics of discrimination* (Chicago: University of Chicago Press, 1957).

2. Ray Marshall, "The economics of discrimination: a survey," *Journal of Economic Literature* 12, no. 3 (1974): 849–71.

3. Joleen Kirschenman and Kathryn Neckerman, " 'We'd love to hire them, but . . . ' The meaning of race for employers," in Christopher Jencks and Paul Peterson, *The urban underclass* (Washington, D.C.: Brookings Institution, 1991); Kathryn Neckerman and Joleen Kirschenman, "Hiring strategies, racial bias, and inner-city workers," *Social Problems* 38, no. 4: 801–15.

4. William J. Wilson, *When Work Disappears* (New York: Knopf, 1996).

5. The classic reference is Kurt Lewin, "Self-hatred among Jews," reprinted in his *Resolving social conflicts* (New York: Harper Brothers, 1948), pp. 186–200. Lewin's view that a positive relationship to the category to which one belongs (or to which one has been assigned) is a prerequisite for mental health was picked up by Kenneth and Mamie Clark. The Clarks' landmark article, "Emotional factors in racial identification and preference in Negro children," *Journal of Negro Education* 19 (1950): 341–50, documenting the psychological damage experienced by black schoolchildren in segregated school settings, affected the 1954 Supreme Court decision *Brown v. Board of Education*.

6. Harry Braverman, *Labor and monopoly capital* (New York: Monthly Review Press, 1974), pp. 67–68.

7. For an exhaustive summary of the literature, see John Duckitt, *The social psychology of prejudice* (New York: Prager, 1992). Thomas Pettigrew's "Theories of prejudice," *Harvard encyclopedia of American ethnic groups* (Cambridge, Mass.: Harvard University Press, 1980), is also useful.

8. The concern with equality is implicit in the continued centrality of the

concept "social distance," which denotes the ways antipathies or preferences for certain groups prescribe or proscribe interaction at varying levels of intimacy.

9. R. M. Blackburn and Michael Mann, in a British study of unskilled workers in the early 1970s, found that "recruiters relied on their subjective impressions of the likely cooperativeness of the applicant," supplemented by likely indicators of this desired trait. For example, "the ideal worker was considered to be married with small children," on the grounds that "the worker with dependents will do as he is told, not risk losing his job, be keen to do overtime, and show himself capable of promotion to a higher-paid job." In general, Blackburn and Mann concluded that " 'Willingness to work' seems to be the crucial variable . . . . [m]en who will work on their own, who do not need to be pushed, who are responsible." See Blackburn and Mann, *The working class in the labor market* (London: Macmillan, 1979), p. 105.

10. Or, as Richard Jenkins argues, managers try to predict whether workers will "integrate smoothly into the managerial procedures and social routines of the employing organization." "Acceptability," as Jenkins calls it, is "a function of the general problems inherent in the capitalist labour process when viewed from a managerial perspective." See Richard Jenkins, *Racism and recruitment* (Cambridge: Cambridge University Press, 1986), p. 47.

11. Although these "traits" can be seen as individual characteristics, what they have in common is that they are also markers of general—that is, not work-related—categorical distinctions within the population. Marking a trait off-limits represents a decision that a social category (e.g., sex) is not relevant to the employment decision, whether or not individual employers may agree. While "people who don't know how to work an offset press" is a category, it classifies according to a proficiency that is at once context-specific and independent of all characteristics (such as gender or nativity) not directly relevant to the context. Such a category, therefore, is unlikely to be a basis for unfair discrimination.

12. In most cases, the basis for discrimination is citizenship status rather than nativity. Recall, however, that discrimination against immigrants is built into the Constitution: the president of the United States of America must be native-born.

13. Robert K. Merton, "Discrimination and the American creed," in Robert K. Merton, *Sociological ambivalence and other essays* (New York: The Free Press, 1976), pp. 189–216.

14. In our investigation, this formulation may have been complicated by the fact that the employers with whom we spoke may have been thinking of a job of type X as if it were the entire universe of jobs, and thus did not pinpoint the limits of the jobs for which group A would be suited.

15. Justice Thomas is a *token* in the sense that, as an African American at the top of the U.S. judiciary, he is *very* much in the minority. This is the sense used by Rosabeth Moss Kanter in her groundbreaking 1977 work, *Men and women of the corporation* (New York: Basic Books).

16. Karen Hossfeld, "Their logic against them: contradictions in sex, race, and class in Silicon Valley," in Kathryn Ward, ed., *Women workers and global restructuring* (Ithaca: New York State School of Industrial and Labor Relations, Cornell University Press, 1990), pp. 149–78.

17. Herbert Blumer, "Race prejudice as a sense of group position," *Pacific Sociological Review* 1 (1958): 3–7.

18. This discussion draws on the pioneering work of Gordon W. Allport in *The nature of prejudice*, and on its reflections in the work of other authors. We use "attitude," however, to mean what Allport called "prejudice." To Allport, the attitudinal portion of prejudice was simply the emotion for or against the object of the attitude, not the cognitive component, or rationalization. See Gordon W. Allport, *The nature of prejudice* (Reading, Mass.: Addison-Wesley, 1979).

19. For an exhaustive, up-to-date discussion of the literature, see Susan Fiske, "Stereotyping, prejudice, and discrimination," in Daniel T. Gilbert et al., eds., *The handbook of social psychology*, 4th edition, vol. 2. (Boston: McGraw-Hill, 1999). This discussion draws heavily on Thomas F. Pettigrew's work in *Harvard encyclopedia of American ethnic groups*, ed. Stephan Thernstrom (Cambridge, Mass.: Belknap Press, 1980).

20. See Thomas Pettigrew, *Harvard encyclopedia*.

21. Edmund Phelps, "The statistical theory of racism and sexism," *American Economic Review* 62: 659–61; Kenneth Arrow, "The theory of discrimination," in O.A. Ashenfelter and A. Rees, eds., *Discrimination in labor markets* (Princeton: Princeton University Press, 1973).

22. See Lester Thurow, *Generating inequality* (New York, Basic: 1975).

23. Of course, the ability to move between groups is more important, in distinguishing caste from class relationships, than are the outward differences in perquisites and appearances between the groups. Still, substantial movement within a firm is not very likely.

24. W.E.B. Du Bois, *The souls of black folk: authoritative texts, contexts, criticism*, ed. Henry Louis Gates Jr. and Terri Hume Oliver (New York: W.W. Norton, 1999), p. 17.

25. Lawrence Bobo and Vincent Hutchings, "Perceptions of racial group competition: extending Blumer's theory of group position to a multiracial social context," *American Sociological Review* 61 (1996): 951–72.

9. "US" AND "THEM"

1. Benjamin Disraeli, *Sybil; or, The two nations*, reprinted. (Oxford: Oxford University Press, 1981).

2. James Matles and James Higgins, *Them and us: struggles of a rank-and-file union* (Englewood Cliffs, N.J.: Prentice-Hall, 1974).

3. We note that some respondents, having worked up from the shop floor or service setting, had social backgrounds very similar to those of the workers they employed or supervised. At the time of our interviews, however, the respondents occupied managerial positions, which, in their implications for status, earnings, demeanor, and presentation of self, entailed considerable difference from the positions of the entry-level workers about whom we asked.

4. It is also the case that many of the managers earned less than the twenty-dollars-per-hour wage enjoyed by the ex-aerospace workers. On the other hand, restaurant and department store managers generally wanted persons from middle-class backgrounds for front-of-the house positions, although here the

halo effect produced by interactions with high-status patrons compensated for the relatively low wage. Revealingly, the omnipresent actors bore significant similarity to the immigrants, in that the actors' sense of self-worth derived from achievement accomplished outside of work. (And waiting tables not only paid the bills, it allowed for the flexibility needed for auditions.)

5. This refers to teenagers from the San Fernando Valley, assumed to come from the affluent families in its more select areas. The reputed "spoiled" manner of these teens was lampooned in the movie "Valley Girl," starring Nicholas Cage, and in the Frank Zappa song of the same name.

6. As argued by Kenneth Arrow, "What has economics to say about racial discrimination," *Journal of Economic Perspectives* 12, no. 2 (1998): 91–100.

7. Here, we echo the critique of the Beckerian approach made by Ray Marshall in "The economics of discrimination: a survey," *Journal of Economic Literature* 12, no. 3 (1974): 849–71.

8. As argued by Edna Bonacich in her works on the "split labor market": "A theory of ethnic antagonism: the split labor market," *American Sociological Review* 37 (1972): 547–59, and "Advanced capitalism and black/white relations in the United States: a split labor market analysis," *American Sociological Review* 41 (1976): 34–51.

9. Lawrence Bobo, James R. Kluegel, and Ryan A. Smith, "Laissez-faire racism: the crystallization of a 'kinder, gentler' ideology," in *Racial attitudes in the 1990s: continuity and change*, ed. S. A. Tuch and J. K. Martin (Westport, Conn.: Praeger, 1997).

10. Donald R. Kinder and David O. Sears, "Prejudice and politics: symbolic racism versus racial threats to the good life," *Journal of Personality and Social Psychology* 40 (1981): 416.

11. There are a variety of views about the origins of the "urban underclass" and about its most salient features, and we have neither room nor reason to delve deeply into the topic here. William Julius Wilson's version of the concept has been one of the most influential, even though Wilson plays down the importance of "welfare dependency," emphasizes the importance of black middle-class migration, and reworks the "culture of poverty" notion. Conservative views, like those of Lawrence Mead, still remain salient. See Lawrence Mead, *The new politics of poverty* (New York: Basic Books, 1992); William Julius Wilson, *The declining significance of race* (Chicago: University of Chicago Press, 1978); William Julius Wilson, *The truly disadvantaged: the inner city, the underclass, and public policy* (Chicago: University of Chicago Press, 1987).

10. DIVERSITY AND ITS DISCONTENTS

1. Here, "rational" is used in the economists' sense, meaning "maximizing material gain."

2. For an elaboration of this argument, see Roger Waldinger, *Still the promised city? African Americans and new immigrants in postindustrial New York* (Cambridge, Mass.: Harvard University Press, 1996), ch. 1.

3. Rosabeth Moss Kanter, *Men and women of the corporation* (New York: Basic Books, 1976).

4. To state this another way: members of a group will often strive, as workers, to attain social closure over a job or set of jobs; workers from other groups, in striving to enter and themselves attain, perhaps, social closure, are in effect struggling for diversity. The situation with customers is similar, with the key difference being that customers from a particular group are more likely to be concerned that their group be represented than that their group be dominant.

As emphasized later in the chapter, employers typically desire diversity only when it serves an instrumental function, e.g., creating a workforce with the linguistic skills to serve a given customer base. Diversity causes friction, and may increase training and other costs. Employers recognize that there are risks in "putting all of their eggs in one basket," yet this has not stopped many from doing so, in positions that require little customer contact.

5. See Corwin P. King, "When people bite: how to handle conflicts," *HR Focus* 70, no. 1 (1993): 19, for a "human resources" handling of this issue.

6. This is not an isolated example. Concerns about men, especially immigrant men, not taking direction from women were common.

7. As emphasized in Waldinger, *Still the promised city?* see especially chapter 4.

8. Realistic group-conflict theory holds that intergroup conflict is the result of contradictory interests or competition over resources, rather than of, for instance, innate dispositions. Robert A. LeVine and Donald T. Campbell, *Ethnocentrism: theories of conflict, ethnic attitudes, and group behavior* (New York: Wiley, 1971).

9. Because private contractors in this industry typically hire nonunion Latino immigrants, and because many of the incumbent hospital workers the immigrants replace are African-American, this is an instance in which outsourcing has led to the substitution of Latino for African-American workers.

11. BLACK/IMMIGRANT COMPETITION

1. Toni Morrison, "On the backs of blacks," in *Arguing immigration: the debate over the changing face of America*, ed. Nicolaus Mills (New York: Simon & Schuster, 1994), pp. 97–100. See also Jack Miles, "Blacks vs. browns," *Atlantic Monthly*, October 1992, 41–68.

2. For a recent summary of studies on racial inequality, see Marcus Alexis, "Assessing 50 years of African-American economic status, 1940–1990," *American Economic Review* 88, no. 2 (1998): 368–75. To be sure, researchers disagree regarding the state of racial inequality and the socioeconomic condition of African Americans. For example, William A. Darity Jr. and Patrick L. Mason, in "Evidence on discrimination in employment: codes of color, codes of gender," *Journal of Economic Perspectives* 12, no. 2 (1998): 63–90, document the continuing significance of race in the labor market. James J. Heckman, in contrast, contends in "Detecting discrimination," *Journal of Economic Perspectives* 12, no. 2 (1998): 101–16, that it is not race but the limited skills of African Americans that sustain the apparent racial gap in the labor market.

12. CONCLUSION

1. Since most contemporary migrants come from urban centers, not from rural villages and farms, likely the discontinuity is less. In addition, skills learned elsewhere may need augmenting and updating, but the skills needed by a carpenter in Mexico, for instance, are likely to be similar to those needed in the United States. Still, the average Mexican or Central American immigrant—or the average Southeast Asian refugee—does not arrive with the competencies that America's Brave New Economy is supposed to require.

2. As we pointed out earlier, the status of more highly esteemed jobs also enhances the status of groups that hold them.

3. At least, we hope that greater educational attainment means greater acquisition of skills and knowledge, and not simply credential inflation.

4. Albert Rees, "Information networks in labor markets," *American Economic Review* 56, no. 2 (1966): 559–66.

5. Virtually without cost to the employer, of course, not to the passed-over workers. If we believe Becker's *Economics of discrimination* (Chicago: University of Chicago Press, 1957), however, that costlessness may be illusory. Becker argues that employers pay in wages and efficiency, when indulging their own or their workers' taste for discrimination. That cost may have been so invisibly integrated into the "contract" underlying labor-market segmentation, however, that it was invisible to the participants.

6. On page 413 in Howard Wial, "Getting a good job: mobility in a segmented labor market," *Industrial Relations* 30, no. 3 (1991): 396–416.

7. In fact, several employers told us that they preferred candidates without a history in their industry, since they did not want to have to try to break "bad habits" inculcated by other employers.

8. Although many persons may be involved in the hiring process, we found that the final choice to hire a specific person is almost always the responsibility of a single manager. This is true even where candidates are interviewed and ranked by committee, or where multiple managers—and sometimes workers—sit in on the process.

9. Richard Alba and Victor Nee, "Rethinking assimilation theory for a new era of immigration," *International Migration Review* 31, no. 4 (1997): 826–74.

APPENDIX: THE LOCAL AND ECONOMIC CONTEXT

1. Roger Waldinger and Jennifer Lee, "New immigrants in urban America," in Roger Waldinger, ed., *Strangers at the gates: new immigrants in urban America* (Berkeley and Los Angeles: University of California Press, 2001), pp. 51–52.

2. William A. V. Clark, "The geography of immigrant poverty: selective evidence of an immigrant underclass," in Waldinger, *Strangers at the gates*, p. 167; data are for the New York and Los Angeles Consolidated Metropolitan Statistical Areas.

3. The data for Los Angeles apply to the larger region; in Los Angeles County itself, the foreign-born share of the population was one-half percent higher.

4. The literature on immigrants in Los Angeles, although growing, remains underdeveloped, especially in comparison to the corpus available for New York City. The volume *Ethnic Los Angeles*, ed. Roger Waldinger and Mehdi Bozorgmehr (New York: Russell Sage Foundation, 1996), provides the most comprehensive overview, although it is largely, possibly excessively, based on information gleaned from U.S. population censuses through 1990. Much of the remaining section draws on this work, and also updates Roger Waldinger's "Not the promised city? Los Angeles and its immigrants," *Pacific Historical Review* 68, no. 2 (1999): 253–72. For another overview from a geographic perspective see James Allen and James Turner, *The ethnic quilt* (Los Angeles: California State University at Northridge, 1997). Thomas Muller and Thomas J. Espenshade's book, *The fourth wave: California's newest immigrants* (Washington, D.C.: Urban Institute Press, 1985), represents an early, now dated but still valuable, effort to assess Los Angeles's immigrant transformation. A number of recent collections contain additional valuable material on the region's history, with some attention to matters of immigration and ethnicity. Among the most notable are Allen J. Scott and Edward W. Soja, eds., *The city: Los Angeles and urban theory at the end of the twentieth century* (Berkeley and Los Angeles: University of California Press, 1996), and Michael J. Dear, H. Eric Schockman, and Greg Hise, eds. *Rethinking Los Angeles* (Thousand Oaks, Ca.: Sage Publications, 1996). The monographic literature and studies of individual ethnic groups remain in a state of bad repair, with a few exceptions. Koreans have received valuable treatment, especially by Ivan Light and Edna Bonacich in their *Immigrant entrepreneurs: Koreans in Los Angeles, 1965–1982* (Berkeley and Los Angeles: University of California Press, 1988); and Pyong Gap Min, *Caught in the middle: Korean communities in New York and Los Angeles* (Berkeley and Los Angeles: University of California Press, 1996). The Chinese settlement in Monterey Park, California, has also been the object of considerable work; John Horton's *The politics of diversity: immigration, resistance, and change in Monterey Park, California* (Philadelphia: Temple University Press, 1995) provides the best treatment. Amazingly, Mexicans have been relatively neglected, perhaps because the size of the group involved and the complexity of its experience makes study of the recent Mexican immigrant experience a daunting task. Valuable material can still be found in the Mueller and Espenshade book noted above. George Sanchez's *Becoming Mexican American: ethnicity, culture, and identity in Chicano Los Angeles, 1900–1945* (New York: Oxford University Press, 1993) is essential, but is limited to an earlier period. A key reference for the current period is Vilma Ortiz, "The Mexican-origin population: permanent working class or emerging middle class?" in *Ethnic Los Angeles*, ed. Waldinger and Bozorgmehr, pp. 247–78.

5. Leo Grebler, Jeffrey Lionel Berlant, Joan Moore, Ralph Guzman, *The Mexican-American people: the nation's second largest minority* (New York: Free Press, 1970).

6. Lucie Cheng and Philip Yang, "Asians: the 'model minority' deconstructed," in *Ethnic Los Angeles*, ed. Waldinger and Bozorgmehr, pp. 305–44; Mehdi Bozorgmehr, Georges Sabagh, and Claudia Der-Martirosian, "Middle Easterners: a new kind of immigrant," *ibid.*, pp. 345–78.

7. David Lopez, Eric Popkin, and Edward Telles, "Central Americans: at the bottom, struggling to get ahead," *ibid.*, pp. 279–304.

8. Allen J. Scott, *Technopolis: high-technology industry and regional development in Southern California* (Berkeley and Los Angeles: University of California Press, 1993), pp. 13–14.

9. Allen J. Scott, "The manufacturing economy: ethnic and gender divisions of labor," in *Ethnic Los Angeles*, ed. Waldinger and Bozorgmehr, pp. 215–44.

10. Roger Waldinger, "Ethnicity and opportunity in the plural city," *ibid.*, p. 457.

11. On the ethnic economy of the Chinese "ethnoburb" in the San Gabriel Valley, see Yu Zhou, "Beyond ethnic enclaves: location strategies of Chinese producer service firms in Los Angeles," *Economic Geography* 74, no. 3 (1998): 228–51; see also Yu Zhou, "How do places matter? a comparative study of Chinese ethnic economies in Los Angeles and New York City," *Urban Geography* 19, no. 6 (1998): 531–53.

12. Bureau of Labor Statistics, *Current population surveys*, for March 1988–98. Data were extracted for two-digit industries; no data were available for "Eating and drinking places before 1993."

13. Note, however, that shifts were taking place within health services, away from hospitals and toward smaller clinics. This was a result of the practices of insurers and HMOs, which demanded shorter hospital stays and more outpatient services. Unfortunately, this shift is hidden by the level of aggregation of the data used for this table.

14. In furniture, the production worker, regardless of skill, is almost always a man.

Index

affirmative action, 93–94
African-American employers, 142–43, 269n5
African-American workers: with "American attitude," 176–77; attitudes of, 171–75, 216–17; criminal records of, 138, 269n6; dual in-/out-group status of, 153, 180, 227; economic discrimination against, 141, 168; formal hiring's impact on, 93–94, 137–38; in higher-skilled jobs, 177–79, 209–10; in hospital industry, 211–12, 245, 246 table; in hotel industry, 248, 248 table; immigrants' competition with, 17, 18–20, 190–94, 205, 256n30, 273nn2,9; industry concentrations of, 206, 207 table, 208 table, 206, 209; and language issues, 78, 79; and less-skilled jobs, 213–15; migration of, to Los Angeles, 33, 236, 258n6; mismatch hypotheses on, 6–7, 253n5; and 1992 disturbances, 239–40; preferences/ aversions of, 182; in printing industry, 248, 249 table; in public sector jobs, 14, 19, 206, 207 table; racialized views on, 170–71; skill deficiencies of, 173–74; traditional stereotyping of, 168–69, 171–72; underclass stereotyping of, 169–70, 272n11; white workers' conflict with, 197–99
Allport, Gordon W., 271n18
Americanization of immigrants, 164–65, 227–29

Antelope Valley, 26, 27 fig.
appearance of applicant, 134–35
applications, job, 134
Aron, Betsy, 260n32
Asian immigrants: in hospital industry, 245, 246 table; skill level of, 167, 237; stereotyping of, 166; work ethic of, 158, 159. *See also* Pakistani immigrants; Tagalog; Taiwanese immigrants
assimilation, 164–65, 227–29
attitudes: of black workers, 171–75; detection of, during job interviews, 135–37; as hiring criteria, 15–16, 45, 45 table, 57–60, 145–46, 224–25, 256n23; of immigrant workers versus those of black workers, 175–76, 216–17; of interactive-service workers, 39, 49–50, 51–52, 54–55, 224, 262nn7,8, 269nn9,10; of native-born workers, 176–77; as political traits, 61, 263n13

Bailey, Thomas, 101
Becker, Gary, 141, 274n5
Bell, Daniel, 33
bilingualism: of assimilated Latinos, 165; blacks' lack of, 79; generational context of, 65–66; in hospital industry, 77, 79; of management, 70, 73–74; as market strategy, 67–68, 72–73, 264n14; of pressmen, 72

Text:	10/13 Sabon
Display:	Sabon
Index:	Patricia Deminna
Compositor:	Binghamton Valley Composition, LLC
Printer:	Maple-Vail Manufacturing Group